HIDDEN MAN

Popular Music History

Series Editor: Alyn Shipton, Royal Academy of Music, London.

This series publishes books that extend the field of popular music studies, examine the lives and careers of key musicians, interrogate histories of genres, focus on previously neglected forms, or engage in the formative history of popular music styles.

Published

An Unholy Row: Jazz in Britain and its Audience, 1945–1960
Dave Gelly

Being Prez: The Life and Music of Lester Young
Dave Gelly

Bill Russell and the New Orleans Jazz Revival
Ray Smith and Mike Pointon

Chasin' the Bird: The Life and Legacy of Charlie Parker
Brian Priestley

Eberhard Weber: A German Jazz Story
Eberhard Weber, translated by Heidi Kirk

Handful of Keys: Conversations with Thirty Jazz Pianists
Alyn Shipton

Hear My Train A Comin': The Songs of Jimi Hendrix
Kevin Le Gendre

Jazz Me Blues: The Autobiography of Chris Barber
Chris Barber with Alyn Shipton

Jazz Visions: Lennie Tristano and His Legacy
Peter Ind

Keith Jarrett: A Biography
Wolfgang Sandner, translated by Chris Jarrett

Komeda: A Private Life in Jazz
Magdalena Grzebalkowska, translated by Halina Boniszwska

Lee Morgan: His Life, Music and Culture
Tom Perchard

Lionel Richie: Hello
Sharon Davis

Mosaics: The Life and Works of Graham Collier
Duncan Heining

Mr P.C.: The Life and Music of Paul Chambers
Rob Palmer

Out of the Long Dark: The Life of Ian Carr
Alyn Shipton

Rufus Wainwright
Katherine Williams

Scouse Pop
Paul Skillen

Soul Unsung: Reflections on the Band in Black Popular Music
Kevin Le Gendre

The Godfather of British Jazz: The Life and Music of Stan Tracey
Clark Tracey

The History of European Jazz: The Music, Musicians and Audience in Context
Edited by Francesco Martinelli

The Last Miles: The Music of Miles Davis, 1980–1991
George Cole

The Long Shadow of the Little Giant (second edition): The Life, Work and Legacy of Tubby Hayes
Simon Spillett

The Ultimate Guide to Great Reggae: The Complete Story of Reggae Told through its Greatest Songs, Famous and Forgotten
Michael Garnice

This is Bop: Jon Hendricks and the Art of Vocal Jazz
Peter Jones

This is Hip: The Life of Mark Murphy
Peter Jones

Trad Dads, Dirty Boppers and Free Fusioneers: A History of British Jazz, 1960–1975
Duncan Heining

Two Bold Singermen and the English Folk Revival: The Lives, Song Traditions and Legacies of Sam Larner and Harry Cox
Bruce Lindsay

Vinyl Ventures: My Fifty Years at Rounder Records
Bill Nowlin

Hidden Man

My Many Musical Lives

John Altman

SHEFFIELD UK   BRISTOL CT

Published by Equinox Publishing Ltd

UK: Office 415, The Workstation, 15 Paternoster Row, Sheffield, South Yorkshire, S1 2BX
USA: ISD, 70 Enterprise Drive, Bristol, CT 06010

www.equinoxpub.com

First published 2022

© John Altman 2022

All rights reserved. No part of this publication may be reproduced or transmitted in any form or by any means, electronic or mechanical, including photocopying, recording or any information storage or retrieval system, without prior permission in writing from the publishers.

British Library Cataloguing-in-Publication Data

A catalogue record for this book is available from the British Library.

ISBN-13 978 1 80050 154 6   (hardback)
         978 1 80050 155 3   (paperback)
         978 1 80050 156 0   (ePDF)
         978 1 80050 169 0   (ePub)

Library of Congress Cataloging-in-Publication Data
Names: Altman, John, 1949- author.
Title: Hidden man : my many musical lives / John Altman.
Description: Bristol, CT : Equinox Publishing Ltd, 2022. | Series: Popular music history | Includes index. | Summary: "Everybody knows John Altman's music, but not so many people know his name. Yet he is one of the most prolific composers, conductors and arrangers in history and his saxophone playing has been heard live and on record with many great names. In this vivid account of over fifty years in the world of popular music, Altman explains why he is the 'Hidden Man'"-- Provided by publisher.
Identifiers: LCCN 2021043703 (print) | LCCN 2021043704 (ebook) | ISBN 9781800501546 (hardback) | ISBN 9781800501553 (paperback) | ISBN 9781800501560 (pdf) | ISBN 9781800501690 (epub)
Subjects: LCSH: Altman, John, 1949- | Composers--Biography. | Film composers--Biography. | Jazz musicians--Biography. | Saxophonists--Biography. | LCGFT: Autobiographies.
Classification: LCC ML410.A466 A3 2022 (print) | LCC ML410.A466 (ebook) | DDC 780.92 [B]--dc23
LC record available at https://lccn.loc.gov/2021043703
LC ebook record available at https://lccn.loc.gov/2021043704

Typeset by S.J.I. Services, New Delhi, India

Contents

	Acknowledgements	vii
	Testimonials	ix
	Introduction	1
1	All in the Family	3
2	School Days	11
3	We're Jamming	23
4	Legends (1) (Peter Green, Nick Drake, John Martyn, Harry Nilsson, Tim Hardin, Tim Buckley, Muddy Waters, Jimi Hendrix… and Robert Duvall)	33
5	The London Beat	45
6	Forty-eight Years (and counting) of Python	55
7	Whispering Wheels, You Sexy Thing, Muhammad Ali, and Freddie Mercury and the sausages	64
8	BBC, early Commercials, Bowie, Dietrich, Jule Styne and early Van	76
9	Sir Van the Man	83
10	More Legends (2) (Paul Kossoff, Bob Marley, Peter Cook, Dudley Moore, John Ogdon, Spike Milligan, Mick Jagger, George Harrison)	91

11	An Intrusion and an Explanation	99
12	Records	102
13	Television	120
14	Movies (1)	130
15	More Legends (3) (Classic movie and jazz stars including Orson Welles, Ava Gardner, Fred Astaire, Chet Baker)	144
16	Movies (2)	158
17	Commercials	176
18	Going Live	189
19	LA Life	211
20	Amy	229
21	More Legends (4) (Michael Jackson, Quincy Jones, Prince, Mark Ronson, Sacha Baron Cohen, Mike Stoller)	233
22	What Was That All About?	240
23	Shanghai, Honeymoons and Chat Shows, Paris and Vladivostok	245
24	Awards and Recognition	255
25	The Ones That Got Away	263
26	Today and Beyond	268
	Index	272

Acknowledgements

"You have some great stories – you should write a book!"

A mantra I have been hearing for the last thirty years or more. However, it took a worldwide pandemic to spur me into action and come up with this tome. Having just completed my work on *No Time to Die* for Hans Zimmer I had no musical commitments to fulfil at the start of lockdown – therefore I rolled up my sleeves and began writing. I have a lot of people to give thanks to along the way. Firstly, to Richard Williams (one of my favourite authors and people) for steering me in the direction of Equinox Publishing. Then to Alyn Shipton who agreed that my story was worth telling and took time out of his own busy writing career to edit my musings and offer many suggestions for improvement. Thanks to the team at Equinox – Val Hall and Sarah Lee and my copy-editor Sarah Norman for putting up with my naivety, to Carlina for introducing me to Lyndy Cooke, and to Jenny for her persistence in obtaining awards and Grammy certificates so easily after years of my complaining I had no way of ever seeing them. A vote of gratitude to Martin Lewis who jogged my memory when necessary.

Everyone in their career in "show business" really needs a mentor who will guide them and steer them into projects that quite often they feel are way beyond their capabilities. I probably wouldn't have got as far as I did in the musical universe without the belief in my abilities shown by Academy Award winning lyricist Don Black. When I was still in my mid-twenties he would regularly recommend me as an equal to industry giants I idolized – and it really was a case of "sink or swim". Luckily, we are still friends!

Thanks to the wonderful all-round talent Sanjeev Bhaskar whose advice along the way improved my writing efforts, and of course to all my heroes who so graciously and willingly wrote such amazing words about me and my career for the testimonials. I stand in awe of all your achievements. Thanks also to all the brilliant photographers who have contributed (and to Alyn for cutting my 1,500 photos down to 70-odd for the illustrations! Also to Garrett Gilchrist for performing miracles with some of my own faded photographs.) Apologies to those photographers we were unable to trace, despite our best efforts.

Special thanks to the great Terry Gilliam for his drawing of me as "the hidden man" which gave me the inspiration for the title of this book. And, of course, to my family for their constant support over the years.

To hear a playlist of John Altman's compositions, arrangements and saxophone and woodwind playing, please go to: https://open.spotify.com/playlist/7lOzXZOSd2FAQ8LBcJWFdL?si=0707ffc3005f4186

Testimonials

Big-time love and props to my long-time brother, John Altman, on the release of *Hidden Man*. From meeting him through our dear friend, Benny Carter, to having him write on the Michael Caine Albert Hall show, to transcribing my score for the *Italian Job* live performance, I can confirm that he is a rare find! Keep on keepin' on my brother and thank you for all you've done for me and the music community as a whole! – *Quincy Jones*

This is what I have to say about John Altman:
Think about it:
Without exaggeration, it can be assumed that half the music of the 20th century wouldn't exist without John's contribution. The other half is rubbish – *Hans Zimmer*

I've known John for over 25 years – a terrific musician and good guy. Always a pleasure to see him and play music with him. Love his stories – *Jeff Goldblum*

John Altman is such a wonderful musician and human being!! We've shared the stage many times and he always brings such a high level of mastery. It's always an honor to work together – *Jon Batiste* (Golden Globe, BAFTA and Oscar winning composer/bandleader)

Why does John Altman choose to be the Hidden Man? What is he ashamed of? I always thought he was tremendously talented. A great musician and an all-round nice guy. Perhaps I was wrong – *Terry Gilliam* (director, animator and Python)

I admit it, I like John Altman. Apart from being very good company, he is one of the few musicians, composers and arrangers prepared to work with people on crosses.

I've rung all the police stations in London, but no-one has a bad word for him – *Sir Michael Palin* (author, world traveller and Python)

John has always shined ever so brightly whenever our paths have crossed, it's hard not to notice his kind soul – *Joss Stone*

I feel that I've known John Altman forever. Our paths have crossed in sweaty marquees at cricket matches, at fancy film events and, of course, in jazz clubs. But I couldn't pin down where we had first met.

It was at a gig at the PizzaExpress in Dean Street, John was playing, I was talking, that I found out that we have in fact known each other forever.

Almost.

In the happy, hippy days of 1968 the Brighton Combination set up an alternative arts venue/café/theatre gig space in an old schoolhouse just off the Brighton seafront. I dropped out of Uni to join the Combination and as part of our artistic offering to the local community we ran all-night raves (although I'm not sure we called them that at the time). John reminded me that he would blow his sax all night and on into the dawn at these bacchanalian events. It's a wonder either of us survived.

John also wrote the soundtrack to a film that I was in with Jean Claude van Damme called *Legionnaire*.

But I prefer not to talk about that – *Jim Carter* (star of *Downton Abbey*)

What I know for sure is that *Hear My Song* without John Altman would be unthinkable. You gave this film such a gift, John. As you did on *Funny Bones* and *Shall We Dance*. You are unique. Your version of 'Beyond the Sea' randomly played on my iTunes this morning and I think I played it six times more! The power in that arrangement! There's no-one like you, John – *Peter Chelsom* (director)

Drawing by Terry Gilliam

Introduction

I was asked on to a network BBC Radio broadcast a few years ago and given an hour to summarize my life and career. My remit was to answer the questions the interviewer would kindly feed me – within minutes the tweets were flying: "who is this name dropper?" I must admit it – I made a rod for my own back. I made a conscious choice early on in my career to be the Hidden Man – eschewing the limelight so that I could live a quiet life and just get on with doing the work. It helped to have a supportive wife, four talented kids who have all made their mark in show business, either directly or indirectly, and thus far five grandchildren. I have to admit it always raises a smile when I'm standing behind someone and they start singing 'Always Look on the Bright Side of Life' (passport control in Barbados) or whistling the commercial for Sheilas' Wheels (local post office). I never tap them on the shoulder and say. "I'm responsible for that." I've probably saved myself a few black eyes! Of course, when I want to step into the glare of publicity and choose to discuss where I've been and what I've done along the way, there will be those who roll their eyes and accuse me of name-dropping. I guess it is, but it's different saying I saw x in a shop, or got y's autograph, to saying I arranged x's biggest hit record or worked on y's biggest ever movie.

And therein lies the paradox. To even summarize my many lives in music I must drop names furiously. When we lost Prince, David Bowie and George Michael in the same year I surmised that I was probably the only person in music who had played with, written for (or both) all three of these superstars. When people talk about James Bond or *Titanic* or *Monty Python* I know I'm the only person who has been heavily involved with all three modern classics. I connect those legendary figures Nick Drake, Bob Marley, Muddy Waters and Amy Winehouse, having played with all of them and many more along the way. I have written and conducted the musical arrangements for iconic records that are still selling after 30 or more years, written over 50 movie scores, and composed, arranged or produced the music for over 4,000 commercials worldwide. It now feels like the right time to get all these stories down on paper and that's what this book is about – my journey and the amazing people I have met, worked with and befriended along the way.

1 All in the Family

They made a handsome couple at their wedding ceremony. My father Harold was in his Army uniform. Although the war had been over for five months, he hadn't yet been de-mobbed. In fact he'd only arrived back in England a couple of days earlier from Cairo, where he'd remained in military intelligence after his stint as a Desert Rat. You can spot him everywhere in surviving footage and photos of the North African campaign in the Second World War. In *The World at War*, the multi-award-winning 1970s TV series, he's easily identifiable, standing up inside a tank, powering through Libya in hot pursuit of Rommel and the Afrika Corps. In the photo history of the Eighth Army, he's there at the gates of Tobruk when the Allies retook the city – second from the right. And so on.

Somehow this gentle man who devoted his life to public service – the youngest ever Deputy Mayor of a London Borough and a leading light of the Labour League of Youth in his twenties, then a distinguished social worker for the rest of his life — this quiet, unassuming fellow had been a not insignificant cog in the finest fighting machine the British Army ever produced. ("Your father was the best of us," said his Labour Party colleague and at the time Cabinet Minister Lord Greenwood when I introduced myself to him.)

And there he was in Cairo, riding a motorbike (all 1000cc of it) for the first *and* last time in his life, lying doggo while his pal in the next sleeping bag shot a scorpion off his chest and into oblivion, and running into my youngest uncle, aged twenty-two and already the number one jazz trombonist in Europe. Uncle Woolf Phillips would later conduct for many of the giants of twentieth-century show business: Sinatra, Judy Garland, Dean Martin, the Marx Brothers, Bob Hope, Jack Benny, Danny Kaye, Nat King Cole, Duke Ellington, Benny Goodman, Carmen Miranda, Betty Hutton (with whom I made my first stage appearance aged three) and many more, but for the moment in Cairo he led the Royal Army Medical Corps Band.

Figure 1: Harold Altman (father) – Military Intelligence Cairo. Author's collection.

My mother's four brothers were already household names. Uncle Sid Phillips was Britain's top clarinetist and dance band arranger – whilst in New York by invitation of Jimmy and Tommy Dorsey in 1937, he turned down a gig writing for Paul Whiteman which would pay him $1,000 a week, as the Americans didn't play cricket! He also rejected Frank Sinatra on that visit when Ol' Blue Eyes auditioned for him – saying the singer was too inexperienced! Thirteen years later when Sinatra was at the London Palladium, with Woolf conducting, he insisted they visit Sid at Le Suivi nightclub. Frank walked up to the bandstand and said, "Have I got enough experience for you yet?" At the age of seventeen Sid had led a band with two of his brothers around the Continent – the first British jazz band to tour Europe. They recorded in Italy as the Riviera Five and Sid had befriended, via an introduction by Toscanini, the great composer Puccini then in his seventies and ailing – they hung out and Sid taught Puccini all about jazz in return for valuable lessons in orchestration. He then attended Puccini's funeral and treasured an autographed framed manuscript that Puccini had given him. (Sadly, Sid's enormous dog Cromwell destroyed it some years later.)

In Zurich they fell foul of a gang of local toughs who waited for them outside the gig. Although Sid was quite a short man, he also happened to be the Junior Amateur Boxing Association Welterweight Champion, his brother Harry was pretty useful with his fists, and brother Ralph had represented Great Britain as a diver. The three made short shrift of the thugs – all were hauled up next morning before the magistrate who refused to believe that this all too well-known gang of ten had been trounced by three diminutive jazz musicians. The case was thrown out – taking no chances, the band fled Switzerland as quickly as possible!

Figure 2: The Riviera Five 1924. Sid Phillips (soprano saxophone), Harry Phillips (trumpet), Ralph Phillips (banjo). Author's collection.

Upon their return to London, the Melodians, as they were now known, secured a residency at the prestigious Café de Paris in the heart of Piccadilly. Apart from playing for dancing, one of their main functions was to accompany the world Charleston champion, George Raft (later to become a Hollywood icon in gangster movies!). In the early 1930s Sid, who had given up playing professionally, was lured back from his job as head of the arranging division for the music publisher Lawrence Wright by the top UK dance band leader Bert Ambrose as baritone saxophonist, clarinetist, and musical director/composer and arranger in chief. So, when my father first met my mother in 1935, he knew exactly who she was. As the next time he met her was on their wedding day in 1945, I need to backtrack slightly.

My mother Rose had to grow up quickly when her mother died in 1933 – as the eldest daughter in a family of eight children, the youngest of whom was only fourteen (but already working as an arranger, having learnt his craft by peering over brother Sid's shoulder as he wrote), she had to take charge of running the family. This included making meals at all hours of the night for whomever might drop in on their way home from gigs. Dame Vera Lynn, in her venerable old age, still talked fondly of my mother's 4am cook-ups.

She hung out with jazz and popular music luminaries such as Fats Waller, Coleman Hawkins, Connee Boswell, Al Bowlly and many others, but she and her eldest sister would escape every so often to Scheveningen in Holland, where they were the toast of the town. She was in a public house with Fats near the BBC when one of the party spotted an open piano and urged Fats to head over. He set off but was stopped in his tracks by the landlord yelling, "Don't touch that, professionals have to play it!"

Figure 3: Rose Altman (mother) – early 1930s. Author's collection.

Woolf had become assistant to his brother Sid at the age of fourteen in the arranging department of a leading music publisher. He used to sketch musical outlines which Sid would convert into full scores (all with no formal training). One day he had sketched an outline of 'Isn't This a Lovely Day' for the top British band led by Bert Ambrose. When Sid returned to the office he said "change this and this, then write the full arrangement" which Woolf proceeded to do as an exercise, little expecting what would happen next. Sid took the chart to the studio where the band recorded it, unaware that it was written by a 14-year-old! The record is in my collection and sounds terrific. By the age of sixteen Woolf had joined his brother Sid in the Ambrose Band on the recommendation of his trombone teacher. Sid asked Ambrose how he liked Woolf's playing and Ammie replied, "either he fits in perfectly or he wasn't playing!" He arrived for his first day with the band with a fresh haircut and Ambrose went mad. "You look about twelve," he wailed. After a stint with Jack Hylton, he joined the RAMC band, eventually becoming its conductor (although its youngest member and an "enlisted man"). Back in London in 1944 Woolf became close friends with Major Glenn Miller, in the UK with the AAF Band. The two of them would socialize regularly, with the proviso that Woolf changed into a suit as mixing between officers and enlisted men was forbidden. In later years Woolf spoke fondly of the Miller and Sam Donahue Navy Band who visited London during the war – he wrote arrangements for both bands while they were in Great Britain and maintained contact with many of the musicians over the subsequent years.

Figure 4: Woolf Phillips aged 18 with the Jack Hylton Band. Author's collection.

One day soon after the war, Woolf, by now the world famous conductor at the London Palladium, was in Belgium when someone pointed out a stooped figure in the corner. "That's Fud Candrix." He was the leading bandleader in Belgium and Holland before the war. During the war he had supposedly played jazz and recorded for the Nazi propaganda machine – swing hits with horrendous racist lyrics. He was tried as a war criminal but his defence that he was forced to do so was accepted. He also recorded with Django Reinhardt … which was a dicey one for a bandleader in Brussels in 1942. Woolf went over and said, "I'm Sid Phillips' brother." Candrix looked up and said, "How's Rose?"

Rose caught the eye of two handsome young Dutch friends – Harry and Dave – who both vied for her affection. She chose Harry, and by 1935 they were soon engaged. At about the same time she met my father at a wedding in London – they chatted, danced, and parted to carry on with their lives. Rose and Harry planned to be married some time in the future, but she had already decided that her first priority was to her father and family back in London. A problem soon arose – Woolf (then aged nineteen) was the star trombone soloist with the Jack Hylton Band, and they'd been invited to Germany to perform for Goebbels (Hylton led his favourite dance band) and Hitler. Of course they would have to give the Nazi salute – my mother, as Woolf's legal guardian, forbade the trip and he had to stay behind. Someone recently sent me the programme for the Berlin show and Woolf is named as the trombone soloist. They've printed his name as Wolfgang, no doubt to appease the Nazis. But the storm clouds were gathering and immediately after war broke out, all communication lines were cut to Europe. My mother had no idea what had happened to her fiancé until a telegram arrived in early 1940 stating that he was missing, presumed dead. This was days after her younger sister's fiancé had been killed in action, but in those terrible times life had to go on.

Meanwhile Woolf arrived in Cairo with the RAMC band and ran into my father.

"How's your sister Rose?"

"Well, her fiancé just died in Holland."

"I'm sorry to hear that – do you think she'd mind if I wrote to her?"

Four years and many letters later, these two "strangers" were about to marry – a marriage that would last forty-five years until they both passed away within five months of each other.

What of Harry and Dave in Holland? They had both joined the Dutch Resistance, been separated when the Nazis invaded, and when Harry's disappearance was reported, Dave had fled into the Dutch countryside. The Resistance movement assigned him to the care of an unmarried Dutch farmer in her early thirties named Beartje. Her job was to hide Dave from the Germans – a task made more difficult by the fact that the farmhouse had four German officers billeted there! Dave was concealed in the space *between* the attic and the ceiling above her bedroom – not high enough to stand upright, and certainly no opportunity to move around while anyone else was in the house. So, he lay flat on his back for nearly six years – the slightest creak, cough, sneeze, or random sound could have been enough to seal his fate. When the Germans left the house, he would be released into the attic where he could eat, exercise, and stand until the complex series of signals from the villagers (any one of whom could have literally blown the whistle at any time) alerted the house to the return of the Germans. Then it was back into the tiny hole, and thus life continued. Dave was lucky – he was never discovered – and when the war ended he married Beartje and helped run the farm.

Figure 5: In my cot with an Elvis quiff, anticipating Presley by five years! Notice the prominent drum – music was never far away! Author's collection.

I came along in 1949 – unusual for those days with both parents in their forties. My mother had nine miscarriages before and after my successful arrival, so she had to spend eighteen months in hospital – the entire pregnancy plus the first nine months of my existence.

I had a very happy, very musical childhood – we would vacation in Kent, Essex, the Isle of Wight and occasionally head off somewhere exotic like Belgium by boat! We even attended the Brussels World's Fair in 1958, visiting the Atomium and the Royal Canadian Mounties. Little did the eight-year-old me know that one day I would be a Mountie in the classic Monty Python Lumberjack sketch, or that many of my jazz heroes like Sidney Bechet, Benny Goodman, and Sarah Vaughan were performing at Expo 58 while I was sightseeing! So, in 1960 when I heard we were off to Holland to visit some of my mother's old friends from before the war, it was all quite exciting to me, yet at the same time pretty meaningless – as a normal ten-year-old I had no conception of who these people might be and how they related to my parents. We were driven in a taxi into the countryside to a farmhouse where we met a couple – a very jolly, plumpish lady and a fairly quiet, thin fellow. I remember that to a ten-year-old the contrast seemed quite amusing – like one of those seaside postcards of fat ladies with skinny men that Donald McGill drew so brilliantly. I don't remember too much of what happened but one incident stuck in my very young mind. Dave arose from the table at one point during lunch to answer a knock on the door. He returned and said gently to my mother – "I have a surprise for you." In walked her "late" fiancé Harry: someone who had supposedly died twenty years previously and whom she hadn't seen or heard of for twenty-one years.

Harry quietly explained that he had gone underground with the Resistance and been given a new identity – a false trail had been deliberately laid, and to all intents and purposes he had died in 1940. When the war ended he had begun trying to contact my mother, discovered that she had married and decided to fade away into his new identity, running a very successful chocolate manufacturers (the large packet of chocolate pastilles was far more exciting to me than these long-winded adult tales that were being told). Not unexpectedly, he had never married.

As we drove back to our hotel, both my parents were (unusually) very silent and reflective. I don't think they ever had any further contact with Harry, but I do recall, some sixteen years later when Dave passed away, my father telling me the whole story. By then I had followed my uncles into the music world and was playing in the number one pop band in the UK – Hot Chocolate. I had also started writing for, and performing with, a rather talented collective that went under the name of Monty Python's Flying Circus.

2 School Days

For as long as I can remember music was all around me. I was immersed in it from the earliest days – whether it was watching my uncle Sid Phillips on television with his band and realizing that the guy who put up my bedroom shelves had many more talents; meeting huge stars of the time such as the Andrews Sisters, Nat Cole, Sophie Tucker (who sang to my parents at their wedding anniversary dinner), Peter Sellers or Danny Kaye in the company of my uncle Woolf Phillips; or messing about with our vast collection of 78rpm records and playing them from the age of three rather than throwing them across the room as if they were primitive frisbees. At my primary school it was even suggested that we bring in our old 78s and make flowerpots out of them! All music spoke to me as if we shared a common secret. I greedily lapped up the music of Duke Ellington, Count Basie and Louis Armstrong. I think this is how I learnt to improvise and arrange and write music, as I only had formal music lessons from the age of seven to eleven. It was all one to me – I assumed solos and arrangements were part of the song. In addition I could hear that, for example, a bassoon might be doubling the celli for eight bars, or a flute was doubling a clarinet an octave higher. I could also hear the inner parts of an arrangement, little realizing that some twenty years later, I would be earning a part of my living transcribing from records.

Although the bulk of our records were jazz, I also fell in love with the classics and the contemporary sounds of early rock and roll. Unwittingly, this natural eclecticism would stand me in good stead when music became my career and life calling.

Uncle Woolf Phillips led the band at the London Palladium and then the Pigalle during the heyday of variety. He even conducted for Duke Ellington, who thereafter referred to him as "my bandleader". But he was much more: a master of ceremonies, a comedy stooge for the likes of Danny Kaye, Frank Sinatra and Jack Benny and a mentor for Judy Garland. His many duties meant he had to turn down playing trombone in the Benny Goodman Sextet. My mother was convinced I ran from the wings at the age of three to interrupt Judy's act when I saw my uncle onstage, calling out, "It's OK uncle, you have a rest and I'll conduct the band!" The problem with that story is the dates don't add up and the orchestra was in the pit. However I do have a photo of Betty Hutton onstage with the band where the dates make sense, so I suspect my stage debut was with her, rather than Judy Garland.

One matinee, my father was standing in the wings watching the Andrews Sisters, leaning on a jangle piano which suddenly sprang into action mid act! He frantically pushed every visible button and lever to no avail as it kept playing away. Mortified that he had ruined their show, he was relieved to discover later that it was operated remotely by the pianist in the orchestra pit! One late night Woolf brought Danny Kaye back to the apartment and they were pretty noisy till about 4am apparently. A downstairs neighbour rang at the door later that morning and demanded what all the noise was.

"I'm really sorry, Woolf brought Danny Kaye back here after the show and they were playing records till late."

"Danny Kaye was here, and you didn't call us?"

The great comedian Jack Benny was an occasional visitor to our flat. He used to use black boot polish on his head to hide his bald spot and my mother would remove the antimacassars that usually lived on the sofas of the 1940s and 50s as the polish would permanently stain them. The glamour of show business!

The tradition at the London Palladium was that the incoming artist was thrown a party on the Saturday night, by whoever had just finished their run. Thus, movie star and crooner Tony Martin was hosted by Judy Garland, and through the evening he was besieged by guests repeating the same thing: "Oh I'm so looking forward to hearing you this week, especially your Tenement Symphony!"

A puzzled Tony Martin wandered over to Woolf and asked, "What the hell is Tenement Symphony?"

Woolf replied, "It's the song you sang in the 1941 Marx Brothers movie *The Big Store*."

"That piece of s...! I took a suspension rather than have to sing it and only did it when they threatened a breach of contract lawsuit. I've never sung it or thought of it since!"

"Well, Tony, I'm afraid the film is still hugely popular here and it's the song you are best known by in the UK – the audience will riot if you don't sing it."

"But I don't have an arrangement and I don't know the words either!" So, Monday morning they hired the movie *The Big Store* and a screening room in central London and played the clip of the song over and over again – Tony jotting down the lyrics and Woolf the melody and chords. That afternoon Woolf went off and wrote an arrangement while Tony scrawled the lyric on idiot boards. Come that evening, the idiot cards were stuck to the floor and Tony read them walking across the stage. The song got a standing ovation and he had to repeat it three or four times. Later that week they went into EMI Abbey Road and recorded it – the record sold a million copies! Well into his nineties it was the centrepiece of his live act and he gleefully repeated the story to me when I dined with him and his wife Cyd Charisse at the wonderful Mancini Institute Gala.

One astonishing and unique fact about Woolf's career is that he appeared on the first day of BBC Television in the 1930s as a member of the Jack Hylton Band, and on the first day of Independent Television in 1955, conducting for Vera Lynn. Incidentally I recall him coming round after a Pigalle opening night and telling us, "I've just worked with the finest act I've ever seen in the business – Sammy Davis Junior. Remember the name!" He became great pals with Woolf and all the many stars he worked with remembered my uncle fondly – and bizarrely, many years later, I got to work with quite a few of them. Woolf had an open invitation to visit Sinatra when he moved to Los Angeles and one day in the early 2000s, when he and I were in the famous Nate N' Al's delicatessen in Beverly Hills, I persuaded Woolf to say hi to Frank Junior who told us, "My dad said you were the best conductor he ever had, and I should take lessons from you!" Woolf was so delighted. Junior invited me to his Royal Albert Hall tribute to his father. It began in darkness with the disembodied voice of the elder Sinatra singing 'All or Nothing at All' with the Harry James Band in the late 1930s, and a spotlight shone on a photograph of the young Frank with Harry James. Then the lights came up and to the astonishment of the audience it was Frank Junior singing in a voice eerily identical to his dad. Junior was a fine musician; however as he once said to me "I'm sixty years old, never had a hit record and wherever I perform people will be saying 'he's not as good as his old man'. I can't win – if I change my name they'll say 'oh yes that's Frank's lad', if I don't I am cashing in on his fame!"

In the years after the war, my uncle Sid had established himself as the leader of Britain's most instantly identifiable Dixieland band, with his brilliantly inventive arrangements and superb clarinet playing. A favourite of the royal family, he was chosen by Louis Armstrong to be one of the British All-Stars to accompany Louis at a London Gala performance. He even attempted, unsuccessfully, to teach his early 1950s next-door neighbour, Rex Harrison, jazz clarinet! I eventually inherited his clarinet which, being designed in a very unusual system, baffled not only me but also most of the world's major jazz and classical clarinettists when I thrust it in their hands! It's a covered hole saxophone fingering clarinet – four were given to the Ambrose saxophone section as a gimmick and Sid stuck with it as his main instrument, stripping out all the trill keys. How he got round it is a mystery to me – I remember attending one of his band's BBC recording sessions where the three saxophonists, all of whom played the standard Boehm system clarinet, challenged him to do certain technical exercises, all of which he accomplished with consummate ease. That was a memorable day not only for the music – as we drove to the BBC Studios, we both simultaneously spotted what we were sure was a UFO – and there were also dozens of other sightings around the vicinity that afternoon. Nearly sixty years later the top octave of the instrument remains a total mystery to me – standard fingering does not work.

Figure 6: Sid Phillips – clarinet with the Louis Armstrong All-Stars in 1956. Jack Parnell (drums), George Chisholm (trombone), Dill Jones (piano) and Lennie Bush (double bass). Author's collection.

My father ran a children's charity from the late 1940s until the 1980s. (He was always proud that when he ran a youth club in Hackney immediately after the war, he had convinced Mr Pinter to allow his son Harold to follow his dream and become a writer – Harold Pinter remained in contact with my dad thereafter.)

There was a shortage of "houseparents" so we moved into one of the children's homes when I was two years old, for a few years. It was a large house in Chiswick, since demolished, next door to the comedian Tommy Cooper. In 1955 we relocated to our own house in Edgware, Middlesex and I started at Edgware Primary School. I recall an occasion when I was seven years old – the teacher asked us all to bring in our favourite records. Amid the welter of Elvis, 'Sparky's Magic Piano' and novelty songs heard on *Children's Hour* I took in Count Basie's 'Texas Shuffle'. What a class full of seven-year-old kids made of this in 1957 is anyone's guess!

Some other momentous events occurred when I was seven – I started piano lessons and began composing small pieces almost simultaneously. And I discovered the game of cricket. I took to the piano pretty quickly. My mother played stride piano which she'd learnt by looking over her brother Sid's shoulder – exactly the way Woolf had learnt the piano and how to arrange. It must be a family gene to pick up music this way because Sid's son, my first cousin Simon Phillips, formerly of Toto, is rated one of the finest drummers in the world. He's had an amazing career as an in-demand drummer with the likes of The Who, Mick Jagger, Jeff Beck and latterly with the Japanese virtuoso pianist Hiromi and his own Grammy nominated band Protocol. Oddly enough, many years later I was able to use a piece I'd written at the age of seven for a commercial where the brief was "write something that sounds like it was composed by a seven-year-old!"

Figure 7: Peter Sellers and Terry-Thomas at my first cricket match. John Slater and Bonar Colleano, also in the photo, played cricket with the seven-year-old me that day. Author's collection.

Both Sid and Woolf, in addition to being terrific musicians, were fine, county standard, cricketers. Sid played for Middlesex and Northants 2nd XI and Woolf was offered a contract by Lancashire County Cricket team. He was advised against it by an England player, Eddie Paynter, who told him, "You make more money in a week playing the trombone with Jack Hylton than you would in a season of cricket!" Both uncles played a lot of showbiz charity cricket (something I would do for thirty-odd years in Eric Clapton's team that became the Bunburys, led by the indefatigable David English). And so it was that Woolf showed up at my house one day in 1957 to take me to a charity match in Surrey. In the back seat of the car were his next-door neighbour Peter Sellers and Terry-Thomas. I was hooked! Terry, or Tom as he liked to be known, didn't have any cricket gear, so Woolf lent him his cap, whites and pads. Years later he gave them to me – I have a photo of Terry-Thomas wearing the cap on that day and me wearing the same cap a quarter of a century later in the company of the greatest cricket all-rounder ever, Sir Garfield Sobers (who coincidentally also played in the 1957 charity game).

I became friendly with Peter Sellers' son Michael as we were practically the same age and I attended several of his birthday parties. Peter filmed them and I have a video somewhere of one of those parties. I particularly remember one party where we adjourned to Peter's attic cinema (a luxury he'd copied from Woolf) and watched the as-yet-unreleased *Tom Thumb* with a running commentary from Peter in the voice of the character he played in the movie. Flash forward to the early 1970s and I was involved with a British Film Institute retrospective of Peter's films. By now he was a major Hollywood star, and I was reasonably friendly with his long-time colleague Spike Milligan. I told Spike I was going to be in Peter's company and said, "Shall I remind him of those birthday parties?"

"I wouldn't if I were you!" replied Spike, shaking his head. "You'll only be disappointed."

I was a happy kid at primary school, advancing by leaps and bounds in my piano studies. Somehow I finished my 11 plus with the highest grade in the county of Middlesex and won a full scholarship to the prestigious City of London School. Around the same time my piano teacher selfishly decided to get married, so I enrolled for lessons with the school assistant music master. Big mistake! He dismissed everything about my playing – technique, hand position, posture, interpretation – and said, "We'd better go back to the very beginning." As I was already up to Grade 5 piano, I wasn't having that and thus ended my formal musical education at the age of eleven. So, I can't even boast a music "O level" – let alone a music college education.

Was I perhaps being too hasty? After all, my piano technique was fairly unorthodox – my previous teacher had possibly overindulged me? A few weeks later the same music master took my class for a scheduled music lesson. In quick succession, he played us some Mozart and then Frank Sinatra's classic version of 'I've Got You Under My Skin'. He then proceeded to compare the two pieces, rubbishing the Cole Porter song, words and music, Nelson Riddle's great arrangement, the orchestral playing and Sinatra's performance. I was dumbstruck, and that cemented my decision to have nothing to do with formal school music lessons.

I soon discovered that the school had a jazz society, so I turned up at registration, an 11-year-old in short trousers, much to the disgust of the 18-year-olds who made up 99 per cent of the membership. Noses were put further out of joint when it became apparent that my knowledge and appreciation of jazz seemed to outstrip theirs by a distance. In celebration of my academic achievements my parents bought me a Dansette record player, a must-have for the baby boomer generation in the 1960s. My first three purchases as an 11-year-old were Tchaikovsky's Piano Concerto, Bix Beiderbecke and His Gang, and Charlie Parker's *Dial Masters*. Eventually I wound up running the jazz society, along with the golf society (don't ask me why!). School was great fun, once I adjusted to the fact that the other twenty-nine lads in my form were also scholarship boys and most of them were endowed with some sort of genius. I settled comfortably into the middle of the pack and started to "enjoy" the delights of classical Greek and Latin. And the compulsory Army Cadet Force. When I joined the august ranks, it was 1964. I was already playing in local pop and blues bands, and the short back and sides discipline grated somewhat. Luckily I wasn't alone in my suffering – a bunch of like-minded individuals and I joined the Honourable Artillery Company, which meant we had one hour at their HQ in Moorgate on Monday afternoons and then were free to dash onto Moorgate station, change our clothes and toddle off home while the poor saps left at school had a whole afternoon plus of drilling, being yelled at and vainly trying to establish signal contact with a radio situated several hundred yards away. When our stint at the HAC ended, we all joined the Cadet Corps Band. (Behind me with a euphonium stood Adrian Levine, later the concert master of the Royal Philharmonic and a welcome presence on many of my recording sessions.) One of our four snare-drummers was Howard Pearce, who later was to become Governor-General of the Falkland Islands. I'm sure his percussive skills stood him in good stead for that appointment! The problem with our crew was that only two of us actually played instruments.

Figure 8: CCF Band 1966. Me on tenor saxophone, behind is Adrian Levine, later the leader of the Royal Philharmonic and top session violinist. The drummer on the extreme left later became Governor of the Falkland Islands. Author's collection.

The other four were assigned tubas – for some reason the storeroom was full of them. I had to play my tenor saxophone standing in front of the four tubas as they made a hideous racket, occasionally hitting a correct note. One friend who played the guitar pretty well decided to sing his part into the mouthpiece – this was quite acceptable until the enthusiastic bandmaster yelled, "Come on tubas – sing up!" At which point I collapsed in hysterics – to this day there are certain Sousa marches that automatically provoke gales of laughter – it wasn't by accident that Monty Python chose 'Liberty Bell' as their theme tune!

For a few weeks in 1966 my parents once again assumed the duties of houseparents, this time in Finsbury Park, North London. It so happened that the Brazilian football team, Pele *et al.*, were housed in a hotel opposite the park, before the World Cup competition got under way. That's how I found myself in an informal game of soccer in the park with a bunch of youngsters along with the great Brazilian team of 1966 – a wonderful memory.

By now I was a *bona fide* saxophonist. I'd always loved the sound of the saxophone and on the eve of my thirteenth birthday my Uncle Woolf brought round a tenor sax, showed me the basics and off I went. As I already played recorder, I had an idea of how to finger the instrument. What I can't believe to this day is that having got the sax on a Friday evening I played a gig on it the following night! I was already playing harmonica and maracas in a local blues band and I must have added the sax for maybe one song – I can't imagine my bandmates and audience tolerating much more of it.

I got bitten by the blues bug at the same time as many of my contemporaries. I guess I was around twelve years old when the blues first spoke to me, just before the blues boom exploded in the UK in 1962–63. When I started playing the tenor sax it was obvious that I would join a band of like-minded youngsters (including a pre-Free Paul Kossoff) in trying, in a North London middle-class way, to emulate our heroes – Buddy Guy, B.B. King, Lowell Fulson and especially Muddy Waters. If someone had told me then that barely eight years later, our schoolboy band, re-united at my twenty-first birthday party, would play the same set we'd put together in 1962, but this time with a different vocalist, one Muddy Waters, I'd have called for the nearest psychiatrist. (I tell the full story of that amazing night in Chapter 4.) Or that all the figures from my list would become at least colleagues and, in some cases, good friends – how insane! One of our crowd was a young student at Brondesbury and Kilburn High School for Girls, who had a crush on our rhythm guitarist. He ran a mile whenever she approached him, and even stood her up on a date. When she left school and became Twiggy, I would imagine he came to regret his callousness.

As I worked my way through local bands, I came into contact with many musicians of my age who went on to great celebrity in supergroups or as writers, engineers, producers or sound mixers. One band included Clive Franks and Stuart Epps, both later very much associated with Elton John and Jimmy

Page. Another band featured Kimberly Rew, who later penned 'Walking On Sunshine'. My drumming bandmate Martyn formed a band called Syn with Chris Squire. The band was later to morph into the supergroup Yes. Martyn was already a fine photographer and gave up his drum chair to concentrate on his photography, taking the photos on Yes's first album. After a Syn gig at the Marquee, he drove Chris and me home in his mini, drum kit piled on top of us. Chris was a six-footer plus and I wasn't far behind! We laughed about that for years after, whenever I'd meet up with Yes. After Martyn became an in-demand photographer he took an assignment for a magazine in Africa. They called him the day before he was due to travel to ask if he'd had his booster injections as required? "Booster? I haven't even had the first batch!" So he received the lot that day – every tropical ailment all at once. The trouble was he was driving me back from a gig in the West End. I sat in the front seat of his mini as sweat poured off him, he mumbled unintelligibly, twitching, shaking his head and laughing hysterically, and swerved all over the road. And no seat belts, mind you. Almost as hair raising as the later experience of Van Morrison tearing down the M40 on sheet ice at 70mph, with me as a passenger, and taking his hands off the wheel to gesticulate and emphasize a certain point. At least if my time was up that evening, I was going with a *bona fide* rock star – I had the same sentiment years later, on a six-seater plane being flown from LA to the Mojave Desert with Ridley Scott.

We did the rounds of all the London youth clubs, with various degrees of success and indifference. One evening I was delighted to notice two young lads standing by the side of the stage, studying my saxophone playing with intense concentration. "Budding musicians," I thought to myself as I pointedly directed all my solos in their direction for their approval and praise. When we came off stage, one of them tentatively approached me.

"Have you finished?" he asked.

"Yes, that was our last set," I responded.

"Good, you're using our table tennis table as part of your stage and we want to have a game!"

So much for my fan club!

A very young George Michael used to sit on the steps outside one schoolboy band rehearsal room (his father owned the restaurant next door) and he told me years later, when we collaborated on 'Kissing A Fool' for the album *Faith*, that we inspired him to take up music. This was quite a band for a bunch of schoolkids – Chas Jankel later wrote 'Ai No Corrida' for Quincy Jones and co-wrote all Ian Dury's songs. Ric Parnell was the drummer in the great movie *Spinal Tap*, music publisher/writer Jon Rose was the bass player, and Pete van Hooke, now managing Paul Carrack, was the drummer with Mike and the Mechanics and Van Morrison (which is how I came into Van's orbit a few years later).

I still pursued my love of cricket, but this came to a head one day when I made the school 2nd team. Being in the middle of the city of London we didn't have our own playing fields and so had to travel to Grove Park in South London for cricket and rugby (soccer was definitely off the menu!) This trip was fraught with danger as a bunch of public-school boys in garish summer uniforms and straw boaters were bound to invite the attention of the local yobs – and so it was that many one-sided fights occurred en route to and from the ground. On this particular day in 1967, our band had secured a gig that night, at the eighteenth birthday party of the daughter of a famous architect in the very upmarket commuter town of Virginia Water. This gig would pay each band member £80 – this was when the average weekly wage was around £10! As I stood in the gloomy drizzle of the outfield watching the other team's batsmen post a very hefty score, I vowed that this would be my first and last game of cricket for the school. I wasn't to hold a bat or play another game of competitive cricket for twenty-two years, when I played a benefit game and went in to bat and face possibly the finest fast bowler in history – one D.K. Lillee. A baptism of fire!

Figure 9: The band that inspired George Michael, 1968; left side Chaz Jankel (Blockheads and composer of 'Ai No Corrida' for Quincy Jones), me, a visiting Mitch Dalton; right side (?), Pete van Hooke (Van Morrison, Mike and the Mechanics), Ric Parnell (Mick Shrimpton in Spinal Tap). Author's collection.

I played rugby once and decided it wasn't for me. I got a medical note from a sympathetic doctor and this meant my Wednesday afternoons were free. I would take myself off to Dobell's Jazz Record Shop in the Charing Cross Road and increase my record collection. Occasionally I would meet up with the great American saxophonist Bud Freeman, who told me wonderful stories about playing with Bix Beiderbecke and Louis Armstrong, and we became friendly in later years – attending movies, theatres and concerts together. The elegant and fastidious Bud Freeman, born in Chicago in the early years of the twentieth century, always fancied himself as an upper-class Brit. He didn't like to be reminded of his age in the mid-1970s, so some friends set up a prank on a gig. During the interval he was approached by a beautiful young woman who asked:

"Are you Bud Freeman?"

Drawing himself up to his full height and with a devilish smile he assented, "Yes, indeed I am!"

"My grandmother said to say hello!"

One day a few years later, Bud and I parted company on Charing Cross Road. I walked about twenty paces and bumped into the great jazz pianist Horace Silver. "That's odd – I've just left Bud Freeman!" I exclaimed.

"I've always wanted to meet Bud Freeman," said Horace. But sadly, he never did.

My schooldays at City of London were generally very happy. All my schoolfriends went on to great things in medicine, education, politics, business, literature, journalism and music. Academically I found my métier in the study of English Literature, particularly the novels of the great Victorian writers – Dickens, Thackeray, Trollope and George Eliot. I had decided by the sixth form that my future lay in studying and writing about the English, American and European novel. I had also developed a lifelong obsession with classic cinema that led me to run the school (and subsequently the university) film society, little envisaging that I would eventually become an active participant in the worldwide film industry.

My friend Michael's father was a home movie enthusiast. He always owned the newest Bell and Howell camera and would fully and eagerly document his family's life and times. One summer in the early 1960s, his North London crew took off for a vacation driving round the USA, filming as they went. Travelling through Monument Valley they came across John Ford, cast and crew filming *Cheyenne Autumn.* Michael's father asked if he could take some footage and, intrigued by the state-of-the-art camera, Ford summoned cinematographer William Clothier and allowed Michael's dad to sit on the main camera rostrum and film the confrontation between the Cheyenne and US Army. When they broke for lunch Ford invited the family to stay and join them and then the tannoy put out a call for Carroll Baker, Richard Widmark etc. With Clothier filming the scene on the Bell and Howell, John Ford and principal cast members stood in a line with the family, waving at the camera and grinning inanely. I saw this surreal film at the time, which began with Michael and his brother washing their car outside their suburban London home and suddenly jumped to the extraordinary scenes in Utah. I would love to know two things – where that footage is now, and what was the reaction at the time of the lab technician developing the film!

Life at and after school became a round of playing and attending gigs. Not only did I see and hear Duke Ellington, Ella Fitzgerald, Count Basie, Wes Montgomery, Bill Evans (often in the company of the fine actor John Le Mesurier, father of one of my great pals – Rod Stewart's long-time guitarist Robin), Coleman Hawkins, Ben Webster, Miles Davis and many other jazz giants in their prime, I also went with my bandmates to Led Zeppelin's first ever gig and attended the debuts of Fleetwood Mac, the Jeff Beck Group, and Cream as well as being a regular at shows featuring the likes of John Mayall's Bluesbreakers, the Jimi Hendrix Experience, Junior Walker All Stars, The Who, Otis Redding, James Brown and many, many more. I also attended the only two shows that featured the Beatles *and* the Rolling Stones on the same bill – not that I could hear a note they played above the screaming! In addition I'd started playing at some of the venues around London and with some of the people mentioned above.

3 We're Jamming

I wasn't only playing in bands and attending gigs in the 1960s – I also became an active participant in jam sessions.

How did this all start? I'd been playing for a few years and had made the acquaintance of a jazz double bass player named John Hart. John was a member of a wealthy family and had a very large house in Hampstead, one of the most upmarket areas of London, then and now. The great American jazz drummer Philly Joe Jones came to London to live in his place – mainly because he could legally register as an addict – and although he wasn't allowed to work, he soon began holding informal jam sessions. At the age of sixteen, having been playing for about three years, I took my place among a group of Britain's finest jazz players and anxiously awaited my turn. We were playing a 12-bar blues and the other horn players were effortlessly reeling off chorus after chorus of practiced "licks" in an effort to impress. I couldn't play like that – moreover I didn't want to play like that – so when my turn to solo arrived I played one note, repeated it, added another, and formed "a story" with a beginning, middle and ending. As I played, I thought to myself, "this is how you do it." I played maybe four choruses and sat down. At the end of the tune Joe came over to me and said, "You play like Joe Henderson!"

There and then I formulated my approach to soloing – tell a story and communicate with your listeners. I found most organized jam sessions very dispiriting as the competitive mentality seemed to encourage the musicians to show off what they could do, rather than listen to the other players and interact. I took the same approach to my writing – and I believe it all stemmed from that "Eureka" moment at John Hart's house. Thirty years later and newly arrived in Los Angeles, I showed up at a jam session organized by legendary drummer and Wrecking Crew stalwart Earl Palmer. After I played my solo, brief and concise in the context of the other sax players, Earl ran after me and said, "you can play with us any time you like – no need to queue up!" (We became fast friends, and I was able to bring his dear colleague Maria Muldaur to surprise him at his 80th birthday party).

A few years after the Philly Joe experience the great tenor player Hank Mobley came to stay with John and I got a call: "Can you lend Hank your tenor, he's come to England without one." I was dubious and asked John, "What mouthpiece and reeds does he have?"

"Oh, he wants the lot – he brought nothing!"

I demurred and Ronnie Scott lent him the necessary. Many years later the wonderful tenor player and composer Jimmy Heath, told me, "Good job you didn't. You'd never have seen that again!"

Tragically John was killed in a car crash in France a few years later, but through meeting him, my appetite had been whetted for jamming and I flung myself wholeheartedly into the scene.

One of the most interesting weekly events was the all-nighter at Les Cousins, a nondescript Soho cellar. Saturday night was given over to the all-night gig. Paul Simon had a long-time residency there, but by the time I arrived on the scene there was a whole new generation of performers queueing up to have their name on the list. As a pretty competent flautist by now, having added the flute and clarinet to my armoury, I was keenly sought after to "enhance" some of the performances and often I'd play an entire set with an artist performing songs I'd never heard before! Patrons paid 5 shillings entrance fee (about 25p or 30 cents in today's money) and descended into a room where the stage faced two or three long benches, usually occupied by comatose, often snoring, bodies. The bulk of the audience was off either to the left or right side of the room and it was very disconcerting to perform directly at the sleepers. Particularly as they never realized just what or whom they were missing.

For example, there is one night there I'll never forget. I went down to play with Bridget St. John and John Martyn, both of whom I had played with on many occasions at John's flat in Hampstead. John's friend Nick Drake was there. I'd met him in John's front room, and we had tried out some new songs that found their way onto his new album, *Bryter Later*, but he didn't like performing to people who wouldn't listen to his songs and the sleepers definitely sealed his lack of interest! (I'll discuss more about Nick, now a major cult figure in musical history, in the next chapter.) A gangly American I'd never seen before took the stage. His name? James Taylor! He sounded pretty good too and told me he was living in London. Next up was Mimi Farina, Joan Baez's very talented sister, passing through London. She'd heard about the club and headed down to sing a few numbers. Then came Cat Stevens, already a pop star but here revealing an acoustic side no one knew about. John Martyn went on solo, brought up Bridget and then me. Then he left the stage to just Bridget and me. Nick Drake hovered around trying to shush the chatter of the patrons, while we tried to engage with the one occupant of the benches who had stirred himself to listen but fell asleep again in the middle of the second song. We finished our set and then I set off for home – probably around 3am. I've often wondered who else may have been there that night – possibly the legendary Jackson C. Frank who had returned to the UK but was in the throes of depression. He hung out a lot with Al Stewart, and Al was often there. It's tempting to imagine Nick Drake and Jackson over in the corner listening to us play – in these days of camera phones and instant uploads all these legendary performances would be up on YouTube and Facebook before the gig was over – but can you imagine James Taylor, John Martyn, Bridget St. John, Mimi Farina, Cat Stevens and Nick Drake all in the same gig for 30 cents! And part of the audience sleeping through it all!

In 1968 I went off to the University of Sussex to study English and American Literature. I'd used my time off school productively, working as an editorial assistant for one of Fleet Street's leading industrial book and magazine publishers – the *Timber Trades Directory*, *Electrical Trade Journal* and *Wood Monthly* were three of the exciting titles I was attached to ("my timber isn't staining, what should I do?"). I headed to Italy one summer, playing with a band there (running into the incipient Mott The Hoople), jamming with the legendary blues guitarist/vocalist Bobby ('Watch Your Step') Parker, who was a big influence on The Beatles and Led Zeppelin, and then spending the following summer in Majorca playing flute and organ with a Spanish soul band. We played two sets a night, each consisting of one song for 45 minutes! First set 'Knock on Wood', second set 'Hold on I'm Coming'. I can honestly say I never want to hear either song again as long as I live!

Figure 10: Poster advertising a gig I played in 1967 in Riccione on the Adriatic. Author's collection.

All through my years of studying I had what, in retrospect, stood me in good stead for my subsequent career. Not, as you might imagine, my academic training – though that did prove useful in interpreting the unmusical wishes of movie and advertising clients. Rather it was the freedom I had on a full grant to eschew touring the provinces backing a visiting chart sensation or taking a summer season at a dreadful seaside holiday camp. Instead, I was able to flex my musical muscles with a mind-boggling assortment of fellow musicians and performers, many of whom were later to achieve legendary status. This was aside from meeting some wonderful lifelong friends and heroes at the University of Sussex, including the major novelist Sir Ian McEwan, the star of *Downton Abbey* Jim Carter, the late Nik Powell (co-founder of Virgin with Richard Branson and later to produce several movies I was involved with), and Alan Melina, my roommate, who became social secretary. Alan later became a major figure in worldwide music publishing and was eventually based in Los Angeles. His company represented me for a while, along with Barry White, Richard Pryor and more recently Lady Gaga.

The amazing thing about having a roommate who was social secretary was that I was able to convince him to book all the acts with whom I'd established a playing relationship in London, so I would always be certain of being invited onstage to participate! I also organized my All-Stars, who appeared on several festivals, to collective groans of "not him again!" from the audiences. I even put on my own festival and persuaded various performers to play at the College of Education opposite the University. One person I convinced to come was a pre-*Tubular Bells* Mike Oldfield. We charged three shillings (15p) admission and one patron demanded his money back stating he'd never heard of anyone on the bill! Of course, my All-Star band (a moveable feast) was featured, which no doubt incurred his displeasure. On one festival we were even billed above Genesis. By this time, I'd established onstage relationships with an array of talented artists who shaped the sound of the 1960s and 70s.

My lodgings for the first year of university, along with some forty other young lads, were in a run-down (now a refurbished five-star) seafront hotel in Brighton. My room was located on the fifth floor, complete with a balcony, looking out at the exit to the Top Rank Suite. The Top Rank was a dance hall which exhibited a sign outside with two cartoon figures displayed. Underneath the one with a neat suit and haircut was the word YES; below the caricatured long-haired, kaftaned hippie was NO. This immediately alienated the long-haired kaftaned hippies who made up our numbers – my contribution to our "revenge" was lying on my balcony at 4am, clarinet at the ready for the be-suited drunks who would often be ejected from the Top Rank Suite for starting fights etc. I would then play the Laurel and Hardy theme in time with their hesitant walks, stopping for their bewildered pauses and resuming as they staggered on. Because of the peculiarities of sound travelling on the seafront they could never work out from where the ghostly music was emanating. This was slightly gentler and less dangerous to my own safety than my roommate's tactic. He would shout "Oi" and as the Top Rank patrons looked up, empty a jug of water on their heads. Another favourite pastime was placing two speakers by an open window, then playing the album of choice at full volume while we sat on the beach by the sea. The music was loud and clear by the water but for some reason inaudible to those walking on the street opposite the hotel. At least that's what our resident scientist told us!

I'm afraid my studies were severely impacted by all my musical activities. I was still an avaricious reader and used to disappear into the fields behind the university (now all covered with college buildings) with my novel of choice – in those days I didn't suffer from violent hay fever. By the time I left Sussex I had read all of Dickens, all of Thackeray, most of Trollope and many minor Victorian novelists. I found that while Dickens' universes were complete in themselves and all had their own individual structures, Thackeray's narrative stance meant many of his characters could, and would, recur. Over fifty years after reading *The Newcomes* I still recall my amazement at the reintroduction of Becky Sharp, the heroine of *Vanity Fair*, with one sentence perfectly summing up her character. On more than one occasion my tutors had to enlist other lecturers to assist in marking my essays as they hadn't read the books I wrote about! All this intense study gave me a far deeper insight into how certain authors thought than just reading and writing about one selected novel and I naïvely felt that I was breaking new ground in my analysis of the great novelists.

Another useful thing about studying at Sussex University was its proximity to London – only 55 minutes by train. Occasionally I would catch the much-missed Brighton Belle train to and from Victoria and breakfast on kippers with Brighton residents Sir Laurence Olivier or Dame Flora Robson – a special treat. It was very handy for maintaining my London music contacts and putting in appearances at various clubs around town. I also became the chairman of the Music Federation and therefore sat on the University Council. Our Vice Chancellor at the time was Lord Richard Attenborough and I recall him suggesting I get a chauffeur to save money on parking the car in the West End. I didn't even own a car then! The soundtrack of my university years was the album *Forever Changes* by the West Coast group Love. Little did I know then that half a century later I'd be guesting on a live performance of this seminal album by the latest incarnation of the band, led by original member Johnny Echols. (I seem to have made a habit of guesting on performances of classic albums as I joined Denny Laine for his recreation of *Band on the Run* in Los Angeles a few years ago.)

I'd also begun playing on records as a reed player. The first album I recorded on was *I Wish You Would* by the Brunning Sunflower Blues Band with members of Fleetwood Mac and other British blues stars – an album in a day for a budget label, recorded at a studio located in Sigmund Freud's old house in Swiss Cottage. (I'm sure there's some symbolism there!) We made up the whole album (words and music) on the spot, were paid a flat fee and the record was sold for 10 shillings (50 cents) on railway stations and in newsagents. I'm told these records are highly sought after now by collectors.

The studio engineer told us that the day before our session he had been recording the winners of a marching band competition. The bandmaster glanced at the row of seats neatly set out and said, "What's all this then?"

"It's how we are set up to record you."

"Listen lad, we're a marching band. We rehearse marching – there's no way the band will be able to play sitting down!"

The engineer hastily rigged up a boom mic and the tape operator stood in the middle of the room following the band around as they marched and played in their stockinged feet (see Chapter 15 for Ennio Morricone's clever use of this idea!). At the end of the day's recording the producer of the record asked the bandmaster to fill out a form for payment for the thirty-odd musicians.

"The session fee is £21," said the producer.

"Give it to me and I'll split it between the band members," said the bandleader, obviously not realizing that the £21 was for each musician!

I also recorded on tenor sax with our university band Jellybread for the legendary Blue Horizon label – a cover of the classic *Rockin' Pneumonia and the Boogie Woogie Flu*. When I examined the comprehensive sleeve notes for the Complete Blue Horizon box set a few years ago I was delighted to see my label credit – unknown tenor saxophone! At least I was correctly credited for playing flute and clarinet on Dave Kelly's solo album, although I wish a recording of our studio jam with Peter Green would surface one day. I also appeared with Dave on the popular Mike Raven Blues Show on the BBC, and with Bridget St. John on John Peel's Radio 1 show.

I've already mentioned the all-night sessions at Les Cousins, but this was just one exciting venue where I was welcome to "ply my wares." Apart from informal jams at people's flats and houses where I first met Leo Sayer (then known as Gerry the harmonica player!), Bridget St. John, Kevin Ayers and Nick Drake, as well as the Martyns, there were venues like Studio 51 (where the Stones rehearsed and had a residency in their early days), the Roundhouse (home of so much innovation in British alternative music), the Speakeasy (where superstars would frequently crash the stage in varying degrees of sobriety), Bunjies folk cellar, the 100 Club and the Marquee (where many bands made their debut and where, on certain nights, organized jam sessions were held). In addition, one could turn up at almost any gig and find one's way onstage. Even knowing a friend of a friend was enough to get you up there – after that it was up to you. In this way I created relationships with the likes of Peter Green, Kevin Ayers, John Martyn and many more whom I first encountered in jamming sessions. Studio 51 and the 100 Club were primarily devoted to the blues and traditional jazz so I would jam with the likes of Jo-Ann and Dave Kelly, Andy Fernbach and members of bands like Fleetwood Mac and Savoy Brown. Sometimes I'd even get to play with the great American bluesmen such as Champion Jack Dupree, Son House and

Mississippi Fred McDowell. I loved playing with Jack – he was wonderful when he stood in front of the band and let Pete Wingfield play the piano, but he had a far more cavalier attitude to conventional blues form when he played piano. He would change chord whenever he felt like it – it could be after one bar, seven bars or whatever took his fancy. The trick was always to watch his left hand – when that moved you moved with it.

I was very excited when Son House was rediscovered – the man who taught Robert Johnson to play. When he appeared at the Folk Blues Festival in 1967 the curtains opened to him sat on a chair in the middle of the stage, apparently semi-comatose. Someone brought his guitar out for him then suddenly he began playing and singing with immense power and presence. I wondered how a man of his age could manage to perform at such a level of intensity – at the time of writing I'm seven years older than he was then! Ron Watts brought him to the UK three years later and he sat in with us at the 100 Club. He particularly enjoyed playing with Jo-Ann and Dave Kelly and my friend Will asked him to autograph a harmonica case. He managed laboriously to scratch something resembling a signature as we realized that, like Django Reinhardt, he'd never really learnt to write.

I became very friendly with Fred McDowell after scaring him half to death on Tottenham Court Road station. I was on the platform with a terrific performer, Andy Fernbach, when Andy pointed along the platform and said, "That looks like Fred McDowell." We knew he had just arrived to do a tour and we ran over to where he stood and Andy asked, "are you Mississippi Fred McDowell?" The poor man looked terrified at being recognized and even more amazed that anyone knew who he was. Subsequently I played and hung out with him frequently at various venues around the UK. One evening we were in Hove near Brighton and Fred was visited by Paul Oliver, author of the classic history, *Story of the Blues*. Paul presented him with an inscribed copy of his excellent book and Fred brought it straight over to me.

"What does it say?"

"To Fred McDowell in admiration. Paul Oliver."

"Is he famous?"

"He's probably the world's leading authority on the history of the Blues."

"Good, I'll get a lot of money back home when I sell it!"

One memorable 100 Club experience was a show with Peter Green, Duster Bennett and others (more about that night later). The club loomed large in my performing and listening life from the late 1960s right through to recent times. On one session I was less than delighted to be introduced by the MC as Joe Orton. Apart from being a controversial playwright, he had recently been murdered by his lover!

Bunjies was more of an acoustic night, so my flute playing was welcomed. I managed to play there with most performers on the folk and folk-blues scenes including Dave and Jo-Ann Kelly, Bridget St. John and John Martyn. Bunjies and Les Cousins were a hotbed of creativity at the time – all these venues were within walking distance of each other, so club-hopping was very straightforward.

The Roundhouse in Chalk Farm, North London was the hub of progressive contemporary, quite often psychedelic, music, so I got to perform with artists and bands like Kevin Ayers and the Whole World, which included a 17-year-old Mike Oldfield, Gong, Gary Farr, the MC5 and many more. I would show up at Jeff Dexter's Implosion events, sax in hand, every Sunday afternoon and inveigle my way into as many sets as possible. At one Roundhouse session with the band Gong, I decided to wear a three-piece suit onstage for effect. A member of the audience dressed in a pixie hat and long cloak came up to me and said, "Why are you dressed so weirdly?" Onstage one Sunday with the anarchic Kevin Ayers and the Whole World I started to play a saxophone solo. Kevin waved his arm which I took to be a request to end my contribution. His main saxophonist Lol Coxhill edged up to me and asked, "Why have you stopped?" I indicated Kevin the bandleader and Lol immediately responded, 'Don't take any notice of him, you play!"

One afternoon I was eavesdropping on a conversation between Nico, the enigmatic German model/performer, who was a favourite of Andy Warhol and fronted the Velvet Underground, and a bearded, ponytailed roadie – T-shirt barely covering his stomach.

Nico (in a thick German accent – w's pronounced v): "I want to sound like the wind, whistling over the empty waters of eternal nothingness!"

Roadie (scratching his head): "You want more treble?"

A 14-year-old pupil of mine (see Chapter 5 for more on my post-Sussex career), Ian Tyson, was a regular Roundhouse attendee with his cousin of a similar age, Alan Rickman. Quite frequently I would come across students of mine from local schools (as I later point out I was doing the rounds as a supply teacher while I worked on my eternally unfinished doctorate). I think I was more embarrassed to see them than they were to see me ("Aren't you our English teacher?"). I was always very careful to keep my saxophone case in my hands the whole time I was at the Roundhouse and not actually performing as things had a habit of "walking." I would also never drink or eat anything other than sealed bottled water as I suspected (with some justification) that a lot of the comestibles and squeezed fruit juices were spiked. Occasionally I would help the duty doctor tend to the tripping audience, as backstage often resembled a Crimean War battlefield.

The Marquee featured Al Stewart's band on a Monday night and a jam session during the evening so I would generally play saxophone. The jam would feature many superstars from the rock world. It wasn't unusual to find members of Iron Maiden, Led Zeppelin, Deep Purple, the Rolling Stones, Free and others onstage with you. I recall Al lurking at the side of the stage while we jammed. I gestured to the great King Crimson drummer Ian Wallace (later to become an even closer friend when we both found ourselves based in Los Angeles after he left Bob Dylan's band) that Al was itching to start his second set. Ian replied dismissively, 'Don't take any notice of him, we're having fun up here!"

The Speakeasy was home from home for many years. I had started playing there as a 17-year-old and somehow no one seemed to bat an eyelid when I would show up on nights when I wasn't playing and was waved in with no charge and no membership card. I jammed there briefly with Jimi Hendrix – he played bass while Peter Green played guitar. I learnt to solo on saxophone with my eyes open as Keith Moon would pull the horn from my mouth if he spotted my eyes closed. I hung out with (and away from when they got too out of order) Harry Nilsson, Viv Stanshall, Moon and Ringo – I generally had a great night out. In the '70s I took the Doobie Brothers to the club in my car, narrowly avoiding decimating them in a close encounter with a taxi as I forgot there was a roundabout at Marble Arch. And I invited the Wailers for dinner at Hendrix's favourite table (it made their week, they told me!). Heady days for a young musician on the fringes of the music scene.

On my first visit to Los Angeles in 1972, I managed to play all over town – with the likes of Danny Dugmore who later became a key sideman for Linda Ronstadt and James Taylor (a regular attendee at our gigs was legendary record producer Randy Wood), and Randy California from Spirit. And Milton Berle, for whom my uncle Woolf had become musical director and who knew the verse to every standard song – you couldn't catch him out!

Woolf told me an amazing story about his time on the road with Milton Berle. Like so many of his generation, Berle was "friendly" with some disturbing people, obviously heavily involved in organized crime. Riding in a limo in Chicago with Uncle Miltie and several of these dubious characters, Woolf kept his mouth shut. The main man turned to Woolf and said, "I like you, Englishman. Take my card and if you ever need ANYTHING show it to whomever!"

Woolf didn't recognize the name on the card and put it in his pocket. A few months later he was due back in Los Angeles to conduct a television show for Anthony Newley but was stranded at a snowed-in Midwest airport, having been told at check-in that there were no flights available to LA. He telephoned his wife to find out whom he should call – the show would need to collect the music for the special and hire another conductor. As he fished around in his pocket for something on which to write the producer's number, he pulled out this mysterious business card, which in truth he had forgotten about. A thought suddenly crossed his mind: 'Don't do anything yet!"

Returning to the check-in desk he was met by the same negative response. He showed the card to the desk clerk and said, "Would you give this to your superior?"

The clerk returned and escorted him immediately to a plane which returned him to LA. When he told me the story some years later, he still had no idea who this man with so much influence was! At one of Berle's parties I met choreographer Jack Cole who was literally responsible for all the moves Marilyn Monroe made on screen – not just the wonderful dance routines. He took great delight in imparting all the Hollywood scandal to a wide-eyed 22-year-old! I substituted on flute for one chaotic rehearsal with Frank Zappa where I didn't get to play one note – the music was impossible to play for every member of the 32-piece band, prompting the following exchange between one of the trombonists and Frank.

Figure 11: Milton Berle, one of the biggest stars of the 1950s. Author's collection.

Trombonist: "Hey Frank, how come we get all this difficult s*** and you get to solo on an endless D minor chord?"

Zappa: "Because it's MY band!"

I also spent a lot of time in the company of Billy Gussak, who drummed on the original recording of 'Rock Around the Clock', little realizing that thirty-something years later I would play with the surviving Comets from that session at the 50th anniversary of that iconic record.

4 Legends (1)

(Peter Green, Nick Drake, John Martyn, Harry Nilsson, Tim Hardin, Tim Buckley, Muddy Waters, Jimi Hendrix… and Robert Duvall)

There was always something extra special about the late Peter Green, something that set him apart from the other guitar heroes of the late 1960s – Hendrix, Clapton, Beck and Page. Something that hit a nerve in B.B. King, Carlos Santana and Barney Kessel and resonated with many fans who first came to his playing via John Mayall's Bluesbreakers and the early incarnation of Fleetwood Mac. It was very hard to define – something other-worldly, spiritual, an extra dimension maybe – but we all sensed and felt it. I had followed Peter since he was with John Mayall, replacing Eric Clapton, and then attended the Mac's debut gig in Windsor, having become casually friendly with the band. Around 1969 Fleetwood Mac, who had been another (albeit excellent) blues band on the London scene, suddenly "upped their game" and began evolving at a rapid pace. Tracks like 'Black Magic Woman', 'Albatross', 'Oh Well' and 'Green Manalishi' were quite unlike the output of any other band. Blues, psychedelia, jazz, new age – all were present, but in a radically different form. And the driving force appeared to be Peter Green.

We had heard rumours (if you'll pardon the pun) that all was not well within the Fleetwood Mac camp. Peter and Danny Kirwan weren't getting on. He was thinking of changing musical direction, and then he announced he was leaving the band in May 1970. So, when we invited him to Sussex University to jam and hang out at a benefit concert for Timothy Leary and the underground paper *Mole* and got the word back that he was definitely coming, we were cautiously optimistic that something memorable might happen. But we were totally unprepared for the magic that ensued. Peter arrived in mid-afternoon and enjoyed the whole atmosphere of the festival. Around 8pm he found himself in a small debating chamber in the University main building, where a bunch of people had been creating a complex rhythmic farrago of drums, bottles, cans and anything else that could make a noise, for the best part of an hour. The atmosphere was already intense as Peter plugged in a guitar, I assembled my various horns, bottleneck guitar virtuoso Sammy

Mitchell (later to play the famous bottleneck solo on 'Maggie May' by Rod Stewart) and Traffic's drummer Jim Capaldi materialized from nowhere, and the whole ensemble magically joined in with the intense percussion. Eight hours later we were *still* playing, borne on a wave of euphoria none of us, including Peter, had ever experienced before.

Looking back today, it is still impossible to put into words exactly what that music sounded like. There was no pre-planning, no discussion about what we were going to play, we just started, and the music evolved as we played. Our connection was instant and magical. Peter was enthused enough to want to do it again and we did three more gigs at various venues around London including the night when we broke the record for attendance at the 100 Club, and a chaotic benefit at the Roundhouse where a young Gary Moore showed up late to join in. I was removed from the stage, saxophone in hand, by the Hell's Angels (I didn't think it wise to argue) and listened to one of the most bizarre people I ever met, Harvey Matusow (Google his incredible life story), who told me in 1970 that one day everyone will have a computer in their pocket from which they will be able to make telephone calls and play music. Peter and I also participated in numerous jamming sessions in recording studios (one with me playing harpsichord!) and front rooms, before an emergency call had Peter returning to Fleetwood Mac to fill in for Jeremy Spencer who had suddenly disappeared with a cult. Then we started to hear disturbing tales about Peter's mental state – the stories became more frequent and more bizarre, and tragically he never fully recovered. But we still had the memories of those wonderful gigs that everyone who attended remembers vividly to this day, and in recent years quite a few photos of our 100 Club benefit gig have surfaced, especially one of Peter, the much-missed Duster Bennett and myself locked in mutual concentration.

In the late 1970s when I was Van Morrison's musical director, his keyboard player was Peter Bardens who had led a band in the mid-1960s which featured Peter, Mick Fleetwood and Rod Stewart. Peter knew I'd been close to Peter Green and told me he was visiting "Greeny" the next day. "Can I come with you?" I asked eagerly.

"Because you're our friend I'm going to say no – it will be too upsetting for you."

The official word on Peter has long been that he attended a party in Germany while with Fleetwood Mac and took drugs that sent him into a downward spiral. Having been a close musical and personal associate of his for seven or eight months after that night, I would dispute that account. For one thing, he seemed completely on the ball – more so than many I came across during that period. For another, his account of his musical revelation that evening in Germany ties in with my experience of the music we played during that time period. I wish we had some recordings of those sessions.

Figure 12: Peter Green, Duster Bennett and me – 100 Club, London, 25 August 1970. Photographer unknown

In 2015 my 18-piece big band was performing in Southend with the wonderful vocalist James (son of Mel) Torme. I'd heard that Peter was living nearby and suggested to his nephew Joe that he might enjoy the show if he came along. To my amazement he showed up and stayed for the whole show, and we had a joyous reunion forty-five years later. He was very impressed by Mitch Dalton's guitar playing and sound and I was delighted to pass on that compliment. Peter and I looked at photos taken at some of our shows that have come into my possession years later and he recognized old friends like Duster Bennett. I was very torn that night on stage – I really wanted to acknowledge his presence (and importance to me) to the audience but was very aware that it might make him feel uncomfortable. In a way this was borne out when he showed no interest in attending a tribute concert arranged by Mick Fleetwood at the London Palladium a few months before his passing as he didn't relish the attention. He was truly a legend and someone very special.

During my musical career I've been very lucky and privileged to share a stage or recording studio with some of the most influential artistes of the last half century or more. The list is daunting and inspiring – from Jule Styne and Elmer Bernstein to Little Richard and The Damned through to Bob Marley,

Eric Clapton, Sting, Hendrix, Chet Baker and Amy Winehouse. I want to talk about some more extraordinary people I got to know in the late 1960s and early '70s. First up are Harry Nilsson and Nick Drake – sadly I never got to play with Harry, and with Nick only in the front room of another extraordinary musician in front of an audience of several more extraordinary musicians.

I first heard and met Nick Drake at an anti-Vietnam war gig at the Roundhouse in London in 1968 at which my jazz group also appeared. Our drummer had dual nationality – British and American – and had just been rejected for the draft. He still had his draft card though and sadly refused to burn it onstage, a gesture that would have immediately endeared us to the audience. Nick was not a fan of public appearances where he felt the audiences weren't listening; however, he was happy to play his new songs and jam with other musicians in the comfort of John and Beverly Martyn's front room in Hampstead. John and Beverly attracted a wide circle of talented songwriters including Bridget St. John, Kevin Ayers and Andy Fernbach – they were immensely talented too, and some of the music made in front of five or six people would amaze people today in the age of YouTube and instant videos on people's phones. As it was, I wish someone had brought a camera or a tape machine but who was to know that within a few years Nick would become a legend?

I remember trying out some of Nick's new songs that found their way onto *Bryter Later* where Ray Warleigh, later a member of my big band, was the saxophonist and flautist. There was no set arrangement or protocol to these sessions – if I felt like joining in, I would just grab an instrument and play – no one ever stopped me. I also recall playing flute at John Martyn's flat with Bridget St. John and then appearing with them in clubs and, as I mentioned in the last chapter, on John Peel's radio show – but Nick never showed much interest in playing gigs or clubs. His own gigs were usually disastrous – I attended one at Westfield College London in June 1970 where the audience talked throughout and he sat and stared at the floor. John Martyn and I, with occasional help from Billy Connolly and Gerry Rafferty – also on the bill together – then talked with him for an hour trying to convince him not to give up playing live gigs. My diary entry for that evening documents the conversation. We all missed the headliner, a fan of Nick's named Elton John! Our pep talk didn't have much effect as a week later he walked offstage during a show supporting Ralph McTell and that was that. A postscript to this story is that the next night after the Westfield gig I was playing harpsichord with Peter Green in Phillips Studio in Stanhope Place and the night after that jamming with Son House at the 100 Club – three legends in three days! Oh for a time machine.

A few months later I was putting together a band for a festival in Brighton and John suggested I call Nick. I did and his response was "I don't do that anymore." John and Bridget performed in my All Stars at that festival.

Figure 13: Poster for the benefit festival at Sussex University for which I tried unsuccessfully to recruit Nick Drake for my All Stars. Author's collection.

Whenever I would play with John or Bridget or Cat Stevens or Mimi Farina at the all-nighters at Les Cousins, Nick would only occasionally perform although he might often show up in the audience. I can't claim to have known Nick well, but it seems that hardly anyone did. Even his great friend John Martyn once told me he wished he could get closer to Nick.

John Martyn was a mess of contradictions – a sensitive, caring, gentle man and a hard drinking and drugging Glaswegian. I have heard terrible stories about his behaviour to his family and friends, and yet to me he was always respectful, friendly and personable. If I asked him to perform at a benefit festival as a favour, he would always show up and suggest others whom he might call to join us. I went to various jazz gigs with him – he loved Dudu Pukwana and the Brotherhood of Breath (and I'm pretty certain it was while I was depping in the band, when we both attended the Country Club in North London, that I found myself sharing a piano stool with Chick Corea!). I also played with him at innumerable venues around the country. He seemed to have a love/hate relationship with Nick and was equally in awe of and exasperated by him. The last time I saw John was bizarrely at the Oxford Street Virgin Megastore where he was signing copies of his new album. I stood in line and when he saw me a guilty look spread over his face and he gestured to his new wife, "It was her – she made me do it!" Our paths diverged for many years and I never ran into him again, although one of his band brought up my name once in passing and he responded, "Oh yes, he's a monster!" I take that as a compliment – I hope!

Another who would turn up at gigs around this time was Harry Nilsson, then resident in London. Like Nick, he hated performing live – unlike Nick, who would accept gigs from time to time, Harry would *not* appear on stage, until many years later. Harry wanted to have a good time – all the time! I have to say my heart would sink if he showed up at one of my gigs – even more so if he was accompanied by Keith Moon or Viv Stanshall of the Bonzo Dog Band. I recall countless evenings at the Speakeasy Club or at Tramp where I literally had to bolt for the door rather than get caught up in some disastrous shenanigans. The great Derek Taylor (publicist of Beatles fame, and later an influential producer) was Harry's champion (as well as mine!) and called me one day to come into CTS Studios in Wembley to hear something very special. That's how I got to be a fly on the wall at the recording of the classic *A Little Touch of Schmilsson in the Night* with the magnificent Gordon Jenkins and the London Symphony Orchestra. Derek later gave me a cassette of the arrangements without Harry's vocals. If you want to check out Nilsson's extraordinary ability, the two shows produced and directed by his greatest fan and friend, my pal Stanley Dorfman, are on YouTube – the music of Harry Nilsson and a studio performance of the album with the LSO. Harry had it all – looks, talent, voice, great compositional flair and a truly engaging personality – along with an incredible propensity to self-destruct. One unique experience we shared was appearing at different times as Mounties in the Monty Python 'Lumberjack Song'. Harry's appearance ended more spectacularly than mine – exiting forwards instead of stepping back, as the safety curtain came down, he fell into the orchestra pit and broke his arm! The last time I saw him, he yelled across a busy London street, "I've recorded your song!" ('Always Look on the Bright Side of Life').

And yet Harry, Nick and John have endured – their music lives on and goes from strength to strength with a new generation of fans. I'm very proud to have known them, and to have been able to find a copy of *The Point*, with Harry's brilliant songs, for George Harrison, during his last illness. I just wish I'd had the opportunity to make some music with Harry instead of dodging his pub crawls, and the chance to write for and play more with Nick and with John.

Then there were the two Tims – Hardin and Buckley. Two genuine artists who shared more than a common first name: a remarkable talent and a propensity to shoot themselves in the foot. I won't dwell too much on their sickness here. It's well documented in all the writings about their respective careers. What I would like to do is share some of my memories of sitting in late-night coffee bars in London with Tim Hardin talking music, and some quiet time shared with Tim Buckley, after he opened the first Knebworth Festival – which also featured the Doobie Brothers (several of whom, as I've already indicated, I nearly wrote off in my car on the Marble Arch roundabout!), the Mahavishnu Orchestra, the Sensational Alex Harvey Band, the Allman Brothers and Van Morrison (whose band I was to join shortly thereafter). Sadly, I never got to play in public with either Tim (I guess late-night coffee bar jam sessions with Tim Hardin don't really count as public performances!), but I'm glad I saw and heard them – and they both sounded good!

Tim Hardin arrived in London around 1973 – after an abortive ignominious "tour" in 1968 where he either fell over on stage or just didn't bother to show up. He recorded an album with Jimmy Horowitz and seemingly took root in London for the next few years, showing up around town, particularly at our late-night "hang" – the coffee bar Tricky Dick's on the Finchley Road in North London (just down the road from the "squat" he was living in at the time). My old friend Chaz Jankel (later to write all Ian Dury's hits, and 'Ai No Corrida' for Quincy Jones) had started to play gigs with Tim and write with him, and he soon became a welcome addition to our informal "round tables" where discussion might cover everything from bossa nova to Louis Armstrong through to Bob Dylan, and where jam sessions would spontaneously "erupt". (I always had my baritone sax stashed away in the trunk of the car.) Tricky Dick's became the favourite haunt of many in the mid-1970s – it is where I first met a young Lenny Henry and where two young lads named Rusty Egan and Steve Strange, later to spearhead the New Romantic movement in London, would listen in awe to the music sessions.

I do remember making some cassettes for Tim of the hugely underrated jazz singer Lee Wiley, one of his favourites, and going with him to Ronnie Scott's to hear the Ruby Braff/George Barnes quartet. Tim's addiction was manageable in the UK, as he was registered and I never saw him out of control. One particular evening I remember a long discussion about Robert Johnson, King of the Delta Bluesmen, and how Tim tried to achieve the same intensity in his writing and singing. He was particularly impressed with the fact that I had met and played with Johnson's mentor, the legendary Son House, and that I had also had Muddy Waters perform at my 21st birthday party (see below). The best of Tim Hardin lives on in his fantastic catalogue of songs ('Misty Roses', 'The Lady Came from Baltimore', 'If I Were a Carpenter' etc.) and the respect accorded by all who followed him. My friend who owned Tricky Dick's once asked him if he had his time over, would he change anything? (He'd sold his entire catalogue of great songs for a pittance to buy drugs.) Tim answered, "I wouldn't change a thing."

People are surprised when I tell them how far Tim Hardin was into jazz and how knowledgeable he was about it. They're perhaps less surprised by Tim Buckley's love for jazz. Tim Buckley was a revelation to me from the day I heard 'Goodbye and Hello' and then 'Happy Sad' while a student at Sussex University. When I visited California in 1972 and found myself jamming with Randy California of Spirit, I remember trying to track down Tim Buckley, only to be warned that he wasn't in a fit state to be around! So it was with a mixture of delight and trepidation that I heard he was to open the first Knebworth Festival. Through my friends Pete Wingfield, Jerome Rimson and Pete van Hooke – who had been recruited at Montreux by Van Morrison and found themselves to be his working band – I was the social organizer and designated driver for the visiting musicians – notably The Doobies, the more fun-loving members of the Mahavishnu Orchestra and Tim Buckley's band. I ferried them to the Speakeasy, Biba's and various other "dens of iniquity" and drove up early to Knebworth in time for Tim's opening set. I was blown away by his (to me) newfound jazzy approach – he was even scat singing – and after the set went up to him backstage to compliment him. To my surprise he was quite down about himself and the show – I think he was upset by the fact that he was the first act on and most of the audience was either en route or staking their claims to a patch of land they could occupy for the next twelve hours! We quickly moved on to talk about John McLaughlin and Van and Coltrane and I was struck by his love for jazz and improvisation – and we had a laugh about Van's wobbly caravan, balanced on logs, that tipped if you ran from end to end, and very unlike the personalized Winnebagos (and catering) of the Allman Brothers. Pete Wingfield, my university buddy (now playing with Van) and I queued at the catering truck for lunch. As we reached the end of the line with our plates heaving, one of the chefs asked, "Allman Brothers?"

"Van Morrison," replied Pete, and the chef snatched our trays back!

Figure 14: Van Morrison and band from the stage at the first Knebworth Festival. Photograph by the author. Author's collection.

I really looked forward to meeting Tim Buckley again and maybe playing with him, but within a year I was a member of Hot Chocolate and he was gone in mysterious circumstances leaving behind some amazing music and a son who was also too briefly to set the musical world ablaze. I'm so glad that, however fleetingly, my life intersected with these two masters of their art.

During my early days at Sussex University, I met pianist/producer Pete Wingfield and his then band Jellybread and began my usual "tipping up and sitting in" routine. We started jamming with most visitors to the Brighton and London blues clubs, including Champion Jack Dupree, Mississippi Fred McDowell, Son House and others, so when my 21st birthday approached I was already a known performer on the British blues circuit – having recorded and jammed with Fleetwood Mac and other British blues tyros. My university roommate Alan Melina, now one of the most respected publishers and managers in the American music industry, had booked Muddy Waters and his band to play at the university that night. He suggested I go to Brighton station to meet them off the train, take them to the gig, and invite them to my party to eat (and possibly jam?). That's how I found myself waiting on the platform at Brighton station with a bottle of brandy for Muddy in my hand (contractual obligation!) – and waiting, and waiting. No sign of anyone remotely resembling Muddy, no mobile phone to check up, and two hours until all my guests started arriving at my party. I finally decided to call it a night and headed back to college, where a message awaited from Alan. "Muddy and band arrived by car. Will bring them down after gig."

My guests began arriving. Ric Parnell, later to be Mick Shrimpton in Spinal Tap, arrived with drum kit. My original band showed up with guitars and basses. I had a piano in situ and several fine harmonica players – but no amps and no microphones! But we did have catering – and finding food in the UK after 9pm in 1970 was well-nigh impossible. So, when Muddy, resplendent in his pink suit, and the band showed up I directed them to the buffet. What I hadn't noticed was an exchange between two of the roadies and a girl at my party.

"Don't I know you? Didn't you look after us at Woodstock. We were with Canned Heat?"

Of course! My friend had been a volunteer at the festival in 1969 and had indeed taken care of Canned Heat. They greeted each other effusively, then one roadie said, "What's with the drums and things?"

"Oh, such a shame, no one brought any amps or mics down."

Next thing I knew, the back doors had swung open and in came a load of gear marked "Rolling Stones – Fragile", and "Keith Richards – this way up"! As soon as I realized what was happening and marshalled my friends onstage to play, Muddy emerged with his band from the other room and stood listening. As we finished the first song, he walked over to me (on crutches at the time). "Get off the stage," was the most polite thing I could imagine him saying. Instead, he said, 'Do you mind if we play a bit?"

I nodded in agreement and amazement, and as I left the stage, he said, "Where are you going? You play with us."

For the next seven hours we were in blues heaven as Muddy's band "mixed and matched" with my friends. Pinetop Perkins was knocked out by Pete Wingfield's piano playing, Carey Bell played a harmonica trio feature of 'Jook' with my friends Will Stallibrass and the late Chris Elvin, Muddy sang a whole set backed by my childhood friends, and danced on crutches with my girlfriend, while his band and Ric played some James Brown grooves. We finally got thrown out at 7am by the caretaker, but it was a night to remember. I had messages from Charlie Watts, who was living in Lewes – I had befriended him when he visited the University Jazz Club which I ran at the time – as well as Peter Green, just back from the USA, and the great British blues pioneer and good friend Alexis Korner. Muddy and the band were still talking about the great party a week later to all and sundry as they boarded the flight home. "Why wasn't I invited?" was the comment I frequently heard in the ensuing weeks from major rock stars I would never have dreamt of inviting to a student's 21st birthday bash. Stephen, the guitarist in my earliest band who was later to become an eminent circuit judge, to this day maintains Muddy's praise of his guitar playing was the high point of his life.

As for me, I only regret having no photos or tapes of the night – and that I later discovered that the tour promoter was a crook and Muddy never got paid for the European tour! But for everyone present on the night of 4 December 1970 it remains a wonderful lasting memory.

As I mentioned, I only played the once with Jimi Hendrix (at the Speakeasy along with Peter Green in a jam session for one tune) but I saw him both with his Experience and jamming with others around London. People don't realize that when he arrived in the UK he knew no one and so would regularly show up checking out other musicians. That's how he came to hear a 19-year-old John Etheridge and showed up at several gigs to cheer him on. John, whom I first met when I joined Abednego, told me he always regretted dissing Hendrix's guitar sound when Jimi asked him what he thought of *Electric Ladyland* (the folly of youth!). Jimi's first tour was twenty-one dates in clubs round London – testament to a now-vanished scene. We had several residencies in London venues over the years but it beggars belief that you could go to your local pub's back room and hear Hendrix in all his glory. I saw the first gig of the Experience at the Golders Green Refectory, the band at the Marquee and the Saville Theatre, various jam sessions at the Speakeasy and one memorable night sitting in with John Mayall at Klooks Kleek. Jimi was "showboating" – not really playing anything remarkable – when someone in the very knowledgeable audience shouted, "Play some blues!". Jimi threw his head back and roared with laughter, then launched into five choruses of blistering blues before returning the guitar (which he'd played upside down) to the stunned Mick Taylor and exiting into the North London night.

Figure 15: Poster for Muddy Waters gig the night of my 21st birthday. He and the band came to my party and we jammed till dawn. Author's collection.

Further to that story about John Etheridge, the great actor Robert Duvall became very friendly with him while John was playing with Stephane Grappelli's group. One time Duvall hired John to play some guitar at a party he was throwing with Donald Sutherland in London. Robert wandered over and asked him softly, "Are you improvising?" When John nodded his assent, Robert bellowed, "Shut the f*** up, this man is improvising!!" It rather dampened the party spirit! Another time Robert rang John to get together as he was in London. "Sorry, Bob, but I'm playing in the Nice Jazz Festival this weekend."

"Jazz festival – is that where all the jazz musicians get together to work out who's the best?"

"Err not really – I mean I wouldn't say who's the best, you or Brando."

"That's easy," replied Duvall. "Me of course!"

5 The London Beat

My three years at Sussex University completed and already established as a recording musician, with many possible openings for a full-blown career, you'd be forgiven for thinking I would have plunged straight into the musical mainstream. But you'd be wrong: I returned to London to my parents' house in Edgware in order to undertake a PhD at Birkbeck College, London University specializing in concepts of time and chronology in the mid-Victorian novel, and saw my future either in academia, writing books about the movies or producing radio shows. In fact, I gave them all a go – working as a supply teacher in London schools and teaching a London University extra-mural literature course, helping the British Film Institute design seasons of classic and forgotten British movies for the National Film Theatre and being taken on by the fledgling Capital Radio to produce a weekly easy listening show to be hosted by Dirk Bogarde.

    I had become interested in different conceptions of time and chronology in the Victorian novel via my voracious reading and the sense that writers like Dickens and Thackeray were already aware of a sensibility usually attributed as a discovery to later writers like James Joyce and Virginia Woolf. I had first become conscious of this deft manipulation of time while reading *Bleak House* by Charles Dickens. The third-person, past tense narrative is given to the most flawed character, Esther Summerson, while the author's first-person narrative is set in the present tense. Therefore, the usual expectations of narrative structure are turned upside down – the usually omniscient narrator is watching things unfold with the reader while Esther is given the past tense although she misunderstands many of the events. The chronology of the novel also makes little sense until you substitute the timings of the sessions of the law courts, which underpin the whole structure of the novel. And all this is achieved without any fuss or egotistic "look at what I'm doing". On the other hand, Thackeray enjoys being the puppet master and will happily utter asides to his readers with a wink. My tutor at Birkbeck was the eminent literary critic Professor Barbara Hardy. I remember attending one cocktail party where she introduced me to the various distinguished guests as "the man who has read the complete works of Thackeray!" Birkbeck being a college for mature students, not only did I find that I was one of the youngest alumni but I was occasionally asked to take classes as a Doctoral student. Not only were most of the group much older than me, in one class one of the students looked very familiar. I realized that he had been my English master at the City of London School when I was about thirteen years of age and the last time I had seen him was when he gave me a detention for not wearing my school cap on Blackfriars station!

Among my students at various schools were Danny Clifford, the world-famous photographer (who has over subsequent years taken many photos of me, some of which appear in these pages), a top music manager (Colin Lester), a best-selling songwriter (Grant Black), a major Los Angeles furniture designer (Ian Tyson) and the eventual New York boss of one of the biggest record companies on the planet (David Novik). Somehow, I got away with being their form teacher – apparently, I went into the classroom and asked the students which music they particularly enjoyed. I'm not sure I had many more skills at my disposal. Moreover, they all credit me with being a major influence in their lives. Who knew!

As a supply teacher one was shunted around the borough to whichever school needed you to teach whatever subject. I wound up teaching geography at one school – a subject I had given up at the age of twelve in order to pursue the Classical education my school demanded of its "star pupils". Occasionally I would be asked to remain at a school where I made a good impression for a term or two – today I would never be allowed anywhere near any of those schools with no teaching qualifications. Bizarrely, because the council paid the equivalent of a teacher's annual salary, including holiday pay, I was earning more per week than my friends and colleagues touring with chart-topping bands. At one school I taught alongside my good friend guitarist Mitch Dalton, who had just left medical school and was soon to become a lifelong colleague in the session world. Also on staff was Jill Sinclair, the future Mrs Trevor Horn and very influential in my subsequent musical life.

At the same time as I was teaching and studying, my fascination with cinema led me to the British Film Institute. I had a great interest in film adaptations of classic novels and how condensing them into ninety-minute screenplays might affect key ideas. For instance, in David Lean's classic movie *Oliver Twist*, Oliver is shown successfully, if unwillingly, stealing. In the novel Oliver is on the side of the angels; he is never allowed to thieve even when it seems likely that he will. Working on Ronald Neame's last film, as musical director, I was able to quiz him extensively about this movie and *Great Expectations*, both of which he produced with David Lean. At the end of our "collaboration" he presented me with post-production scripts of *Oliver Twist* and *Great Expectations* – prized possessions. During my time researching at the BFI, I organized seasons of British film musicals of the 1930s and met such icons as Harold Lloyd, Peter Sellers (as mentioned), the pioneer film maker Allan Dwan, Mary Pickford's last husband Buddy Rogers, and Jessie Matthews with director Victor Saville at a gala event we put on. What I discovered much later to my horror was that Jessie Matthews, whose star had waned over the years, was so emotionally overcome by being feted that evening that she returned home and (unsuccessfully) attempted suicide.

One day, I had been viewing a particularly inept batch of 1930s British B movies and was looking forward to escaping into the summer evening when I noticed a lot of movement and excitement at the back of the room with several people appearing with drinks and sandwiches.

"What's happening later?" I asked.

"We can't tell you, but stick around, you won't regret it!"

What transpired was the highlight of my dreary, solitary days of research. Sitting in a tiny screening room was Charlie Chaplin and his family – plus friends such as Claire Bloom and Robert Vaughn – watching *Limelight* (which hadn't been seen for twenty years at the time) while Chaplin issued a running commentary. "Watch Buster!" he exhorted during his scenes with Keaton.

I lurked at the back of the screening room, hoping no one would ask, "Who's this interloper?" Oh, for a camera – I was too shy to ask for an autograph! Chaplin was wheelchair bound at the time – I shook his hand and my pal Geoff dared to get his signature. I hope he's treasured it to this day.

I spent most mornings, afternoons and sometimes evenings in that room watching wonderful (and not so wonderful) British movies of the 1930s, some of which haven't been seen since then, with good reason. A forgotten Noel Coward movie actually caught fire on the moviola while we were watching it; the projectionist said, "Oh this happens all the time!" as he contained the flames. I developed a particular interest in film adaptations of major novels, that tied in with my doctoral research into the Victorian novel. One afternoon I had been screening the Cavalcanti classic version of Charles Dickens' *Nicholas Nickleby* and was waiting for a ride home. A man came up to me and said, "What's in the cans?"

A film buff I thought, and answered, "*Nicholas Nickleby*."

He took a pace backwards and said, "Why are you hiding it under your coat?" Anyone who has ever handled nitrate film reels, especially half a dozen of them, will know that because of their size the last thing you can do is conceal them under your coat! He was also flashing a card at me, which I realized was his plain clothes police authorization. "I've just been screening this in the theatre upstairs!"

"Is there anyone who can back you up on this?"

"Yes, the projectionist is upstairs."

I led the suspicious policeman into the small rickety elevator, pressed the floor button and, as the door slammed, realized that he had a colleague who had vainly tried to stop the lift doors from closing. My newfound "friend" backed away into a corner, eyeing me warily, as the elevator slowly climbed to the screening-room floor where a baffled projectionist, who had said goodbye to me for the day ten minutes earlier, validated my story.

"I'll just fill out a report," said the policeman. "Date of birth?"

I resisted the urge to ask, "Report about what?" and gave him my 5 December birthdate. He wrote down and repeated 5 as the month, rather than 12. Once again, I said, "December."

He testily responded, "Yes 5!"

Then he realized his error and laughed. In the elevator on the way down he decided to try a different tack. "Family film, is it?"

"Yes, it is."

"So, when do we get to see it in our local cinema?"

"You'll have a long wait – it was made in 1947."

"Oh, it's an *old* film."

The elevator reached the ground floor, and his colleague was waiting, ready to pounce on the "mad axe murderer". My ride home had given up and cleared off. I dare say I still have a police record nearly fifty years later!

The lowlight of my time at the BFI was discovering a cache of supposedly lost films behind a sealed door at Dickens House, and then have the head of the BFI go on national television announcing his discovery! I was alerted to this broadcast by my incensed tutor at Birkbeck and friend Michael Slater who was coincidentally the chairman of Dickens House and the man I'd originally informed. When Dickens House co-operated with the film companies in their research for adaptations of Dickens' novels, as a mark of gratitude the House would be presented with copies of the finished movie. The films dated back to 1909 and supposedly included several movies then presumed lost. Not having any projection equipment, the curators of the museum just stacked the reels of film in a basement. Of course, being on nitrate stock these were very flammable, so it was imperative to get them out as quickly as possible. I contacted the BFI and they came to inspect the site. We decided it was too dangerous to use an oxy-acetylene blowtorch to prise the door open and we would break in with sledgehammers. The next thing I heard was the TV broadcast. To compound matters, all the film had perished except for one movie stored in the House itself. This was a version of the MGM *David Copperfield* starring W.C. Fields with some twenty minutes extra footage which had been subsequently deleted before release. Such a discovery merited a special screening at the National Film Theatre – of course I wasn't informed about it and only found out later. At that point I left the BFI, muttering to myself, "The only way I'll ever come back is if they give me an award!" I had no idea I'd even be involved in movies, but crazily they did give me an award some twenty years later for my score for the movie *Hear My Song* and I was able to thank the guilty party for my career, much to his bewilderment.

My short-lived tenure at Capital Radio ended before the station even went on air, as a new controller decided that the policy of the station was to be more contemporary pop oriented than MOR. I had initially been hired, I believe, as a favour to my father by his old friend, board member Lord Ted Willis, who had kindly extolled my many virtues to the then controller of the fledging station. When the new man arrived, I was never even asked about my musical tastes or abilities, just told I wasn't wanted on voyage. Many years later karma bit, as the same controller hired me and my orchestra to record an album under my name for late-night "needle time" – a concession that allowed them to have a licence to broadcast. Once again, I never let on that he had got rid of me some years earlier.

Speaking of radio, I still maintained my circle of friends in Brighton after I'd left the university, centred around the wonderful Annie Nightingale. I used to go down to Brighton with her and stay in her spare room. One late evening I was in the Radio 1 studio waiting for her after her show. Her late show aired from the basement of Broadcasting House, while the loos were several floors up. Annie put on an album track and charged out of the studio. I watched, with mounting trepidation, the stylus nearing the end of the song and no sign of Annie! To my horror I realized that I would have to fill in the airtime somehow. Of course, she reappeared just in time to voice the link – a true professional. Some years later I was back in Broadcasting House talking to various local radio stations around the country about my latest project. By now there were no engineers or producers anywhere in sight. A notice affixed to the mixing console explained how to dial yourself into each show, the idea being that to the listening audience it sounded as if you were in the room with the interviewer. This worked well for several hours until I was in a four-way discussion on a show for Radio Scotland. I heard a noise at the studio door and looked round to see the famous Labour politician Denis Healey, once Chancellor of the Exchequer, face pressed against the glass of the control room and contorting it in the way youngsters love to mess around with windows. Completely at a loss for words and with my chain of thought disrupted mid-sentence, I stuttered and stammered for what seemed like several minutes until the presenter, sensing that something had happened, stepped in with "I think what you're trying to say is…." Luckily this was my last interview after some five hours and as I stepped into the studio lobby, I met an apologetic Baron Healey.

"I'm so sorry if I startled you – I'm next on and was trying to find an engineer or producer but there doesn't seem to be anyone around."

I explained the new DIY BBC to him and fervently hoped that Scotland hadn't decided to boycott my movies and records thanks to my car crash performance.

I don't want to give the impression that I'd stopped playing music while I explored these other avenues for my future. There's no doubt I made a big academic mistake by returning to London and the heart of the music scene – my university life was definitely sidetracked by the musical opportunities that surfaced. If truth be told, I never had any ambition for my music other than having fun with it, although by now I was not only recording but playing with many "movers and shakers" on the current scene. I joined a new jazz/rock band called Abednego and we played all over the UK and toured the Netherlands – a foretaste of life on the road.

Figure 16: Abednego publicity photo: from right – John Etheridge, Jimmy Chambers (London Beat) behind John, and Dennis Cowan (Bonzo Dog Doo-Dah Band Band) next to me. Bandleader Hamish Stewart to my right. Author's collection.

The first two days of the tour indicated what was to follow. The van, driven by our roadie (a descendant of A.A. Milne), arrived at my house at 4am to take all of us to Dover. I don't recall there being any seats in the back, but I have blanked a lot of it out of my memory. We arrived to find that we had missed the ferry and had to take the next one to Ostend. There followed a long drive through Belgium to The Hague in Holland where we discovered that the first gig was a couple of hours across the Netherlands. Once there, several hours later, we had to unload all the equipment, play, reload the gear and drive back to Den Haag; moreover, someone knocked my saxophone off the stand before the show, rendering it useless for the tour so I wound up playing piano and faking a trumpet I had brought along for the ride! We arrived at our lodgings at about 5am to learn that all eight of us were sleeping in the same room. Not that there was much sleep involved as we were up at 8am to drive across the country again to unload, gig, and reload at a lunchtime show, head back to the hotel, then across the country in the other direction to repeat the process in the evening. No wonder I lay sprawled on a table backstage before the show, groaning. My abiding memory of the trip is sitting next to the roadie in the van at about 3am as we drove along foggy freeways, chattering inanely as I observed him dozing off at the wheel! In Delft we played in the town hall, where I experienced a clammy coldness in our dressing room and pointed this out to the organizer of the gig.

"Oh, this was SS headquarters during the war, and it was in this room that the Gestapo interrogated prisoners." No wonder my flesh crawled. I can't say the continuous sense of exhaustion appealed to me that much either. To cap it all, our van broke down outside Dover on the way home and we had to hitchhike back to London.

The band included John Etheridge on guitar, Jimmy Chambers of London Beat and later Lynton Naiff on keyboards, arranger of 'You to Me Are Everything' for the Real Thing. Our original bass player was Dennis Cowan, formerly with the Bonzo Dog Band. We had a showcase gig upstairs at Ronnie Scott's for potential bookers. Viv Stanshall of the Bonzos showed up with Keith Moon, legendary drummer of The Who, to offer "moral support", which consisted, unbeknown to us, of slipping Dennis a "Mickey Finn" in his drink. The result was Dennis slithering unconscious down his amp in the middle of the first song. Totally bewildered by this, we carried on playing with Dennis comatose propped up by his bass stack. Needless to say, we got no bookings from that evening.

We also did a residency at the original Cavern Club in Liverpool where you were drenched in condensation sweat before you'd played a note of music and the instruments all drifted totally out of tune. Occasionally we would share the bill with old friends like Fleetwood Mac or Kevin Ayers and the Whole World and that would be a bonus for me as I got to sit in on their sets. One chaotic night at the University of East Anglia I convinced our vocalist/conga player Jimmy Chambers to sit in with Kevin's band. One by one they passed out inebriated (which seems to be a common thread for my gigs in the early 1970s!) until Jimmy and I were the only ones left playing. I did get some funny looks from Jim but after the experience with Dennis I guess we were used to it. The audience didn't seem to mind anyway.

I also played around London with a very fine soul band where I met Al Anderson, later to become a lynchpin for Bob Marley and the Wailers, and jammed with Eddy Grant, who remains a lifelong pal.

At the same time, I started playing with, and writing for, the Spiteri brothers who led what was really the first genuine salsa band in the UK. This was a wonderful, moving feast of musicians – a large brass section, terrific South American percussionists and among the vocalists a dear friend, Joan Shenton, who also at the time presented the national 6 o'clock TV news. She is Chilean on her mother's side and speaks fluent Spanish, although one would never guess from seeing her on television. The double takes were something to behold as audiences watched this ball of energy dancing, playing the tambourine and singing in Spanish. "Isn't that… no it can't be!" The rhythm section "grooved" like no other I knew at the time. The only problem was their time keeping – punctuality as opposed to musical. We wound up telling them the gigs started three hours earlier than they did, to ensure they'd get there just before the start.

Figure 17: Spiteri with vocalist Joan Shenton. Author's collection. Photographer unknown.

I also began playing mainstream jazz every Sunday evening at a North London public house, on baritone sax and clarinet with a fine band led by a moonlighting Queen's Counsel and circuit judge, who would profess ignorance if anyone he had prosecuted showed up in the audience and recognized him. The packed receptive audience always included a coterie of hard drinking, very well-known actors – Ian Hendry, Ronnie Fraser, Peter Jeffrey, Joan Turner, Nyree Dawn Porter, James Villiers and Cherie Blair's father Tony Booth – all of whom I befriended and occasionally helped home! They all enthusiastically loved the music and were weekly fixtures at the table in front of the stage. James Villiers, the elegant, very tall, aristocratic veteran of many British movies would occasionally buttonhole me as I left the stage and, towering over me, would declaim "BIX BEI-DER-BECKE" in his best theatrical manner, poking me in the chest to emphasize each syllable. "BIX BEI-DER-BECKE BASS SAX."

"Adrian Rollini?" I would reply querulously.

"BIX BEI-DER-BECKE" would be the response, accompanied by more finger jabbing. A sympathetic Ian Hendry (at one time the highest paid British actor) would usually come to my rescue. When I met the actor and comedian Lenny Henry at the aforementioned Tricky Dick's just after his first audition in London, I invited him down and he too became a regular sober attendee.

Around this time, I became an active member of the Delius Society. I found his music irresistible and soon got to know Dr Eric Fenby, Delius' amanuensis and President of the society. He told me that as a young student he had lodged with the composer Norman O'Neill and his wife Addie, a celebrated concert pianist who later became Head of Music at St. Paul's Girls School. Apparently, Addie's piano teacher had been the great Clara Schumann; however, she was unavailable one day and sent a substitute – Brahms!

Occasionally I played at Ronnie Scott's Jazz Club, notably with Maria Muldaur. Ronnie used to tell me the same story every time he saw me:

> "Your uncle Woolf Phillips wrote the arrangements for the Ted Heath Band for the movie *London Town*. One chart required four clarinets. Only two people in the band played clarinet – me, who was dreadful, and Johnny Gray who was worse. So, they hired Reginald Kell and Jack Brymer, probably the two finest clarinet players in the world to round off the section – weirdest clarinet section ever!"

(I'm reminded of a commercial where we employed Britain's premiere jazz clarinetist. One of the accounts people from the advertising agency announced to the control room, "I studied clarinet for three months at school and he's playing it all wrong!")

Another evening at Ronnie's was spent waiting for the mesmerizing but utterly unpredictable Nina Simone. After a short delay Ronnie appeared onstage and announced apologetically that Ms Simone would not be appearing that evening due to a severe attack of influenza. A voice from the audience retorted, "Well, she looked OK to me when we left her in the restaurant fifteen minutes ago!"

When Cedar Walton's quartet appeared at Ronnie's one late night, a drunk suddenly rushed the stage. Ronnie was seated at the table next to the band, rugby-tackled the man, and they rolled around on the floor wrestling until the bouncers were able to eject the offender. As soon as the disturbance started, Cedar leapt from the piano stool and disappeared into the back room. Saxophonist George Coleman observed the fracas while standing in the well of the piano, with a wry smile on his face, while Sam Jones on bass and Billy Higgins on drums didn't miss a beat – they'd obviously seen it all before! On another occasion I visited the club in the afternoon to catch up with some old friends. The bandleaders, trumpeter Woody Shaw and saxophonist Junior Cook, had had a falling out that culminated in fisticuffs, and Woody, whose eyesight wasn't the greatest, had missed Junior with his punch and slammed his fist into the wall, breaking his right hand. He played the whole week left-handed and sounded amazing – but I think that was the end of their joint quintet!

I was still a fixture on the London club scene, jamming with all and sundry, and I'd also started to play rock and roll revival shows with the likes of Marty Wilde and Vince Eager, which is how I later came to play saxophone on Kim Wilde's debut recording. In the early 1970s I also met and recorded with a group of people who were to become very important in my life – the collective known to the world as *Monty Python's Flying Circus*.

6 Forty-eight Years (and counting) of Python

I'm often asked how my association with Monty Python came about. I'm ashamed to say it was all down to the ill-famed Gary Glitter. On Wednesday 3rd October 1973, after a very late Tempest (Jon Hiseman's band prior to the better-known Colosseum) gig at the Marquee the previous night, guitarist and good friend Ollie Halsall and I drove to the Workhouse Studio on the Old Kent Road (owned by Manfred Mann) to join Andy Roberts, Zoot Money, Neil Innes and all the Pythons, minus John Cleese, to record a Gary Glitter sendup for the album *Matching Tie and Handkerchief*. In those pre-home video days the only way to savour Python sketches, apart from viewing the programmes when originally broadcast, was to buy their albums which sold remarkably well. Ollie and Neil had casually asked me if I fancied doing a Python session. Would I! I'd idolized them since the first series burst onto our TV screens in 1969. It was decided that they didn't need saxophone on the track, so I wound up performing handclaps and backing vocals on a Gary Glitter spoof. And thus began a joyous association for me with one of the great comedy teams of all time (if not the greatest). I didn't hear the results for over forty-four years, until someone sent me the recording and my awful singing rang out loud and clear!

Somehow, I had managed to become a part of the Pythons' inner circle. Over the next few years, I collaborated with Neil Innes and Eric Idle on the Beatles' spoof – *The Rutles – All You Need Is Cash*, writing all the orchestral and brass arrangements and establishing a lasting friendship with George Harrison in the process. The show had originated as a one-off sketch on Eric and Neil's TV show, *Rutland Weekend Television*. The idea behind the series was that Rutland being the smallest county in England, their television station would run on a shoestring with cheap programming. The Rutles obviously parodied The Beatles and when Eric hosted the American show *Saturday Night* (the Live was added later) he showed the sequence as a one-off gag. The response was tremendous and the producer Lorne Michaels suggested making a full-length "rockumentary" (the first, in effect, predating *This Is Spinal*

Tap and *The Bad News Tour* among others). So, Neil wrote twenty new songs in a couple of weeks, Eric came up with a screenplay and I entered the scene as the "George Martin of the Rutles".

As we were making the programme only a few years after The Beatles had split up, I was able to book several of the musicians who had played on the original Beatles records. The cellists in particular were very helpful in demonstrating the vibratos and glissandi employed on the *Sgt. Pepper* album. When we did our take on 'Penny Lane' (Double Back Alley) I rang David Mason who had played the piccolo trumpet on that record, but he was busy and recommended Cliff Haines, who was brilliant. I was very wary of meeting George Martin after that as I had parodied his arrangements, but when Don Black eventually introduced us, George winked at me and said, "Oh, I *know* John!" Later he recommended me for arranging gigs he felt he couldn't handle due to his hearing loss – a great honour for me.

The Rutles movie still holds up today and was a landmark forerunner of the many "mockumentaries" that have followed. It had an extraordinary cast that matched *Saturday Night* stalwarts John Belushi, Dan Aykroyd, Bill Murray and Gilda Radner with Python greats like Eric and Michael Palin and hilarious guest appearances by the likes of Paul Simon, Mick Jagger, Bianca Jagger and Ronnie Wood and even an unrecognizable George Harrison playing a reporter. At the time it was way down the ratings (Eric says it was beaten by a documentary on bee keeping) but over the years the reputations of both the film and the music have grown immensely. The late great Neil Innes, with whom I worked for nearly fifty years, said there should be a verb "to Rutle" meaning "to make an affectionate parody". Certainly, no malice was ever intended or perceived.

Neil Innes was a joy to work with and his premature passing in 2019 was a shock to all. We had forty-six years of uninterrupted collaboration through TV series (which I will delve into in more depth in a later chapter), records, live shows and movies. Several of the live shows occurred during Python or Rutles celebrations in Los Angeles, when we got some valuable socializing time with all the Pythons, which strengthened our camaraderie. For the 25th anniversary celebration of *Monty Python* the two Terrys (Jones and Gilliam), Carol Cleveland, Neil and I hooked up with Eric Idle for a week of events, both official and social. At a party at the British consulate I met my heroes Sid Caesar and Richard Pryor (by then, both sadly wheelchair-bound), hung out with Steve Martin and Robin Williams and felt honoured to be part of the Pythons' inner circle. Mention of the great Robin Williams reminds me of a time when he visited my band backstage and in the dressing room did a hilarious forty-minute non-stop routine for five people. It was at the same time magnificent and disturbing – for me a strange brew of emotions.

At another party on the same anniversary junket, hosted by famous record producer Bob Ezrin, Neil and Eric played an acoustic set in front of another star-studded roster of guests including my old friend and colleague Ray Cooper.

We also performed the first ever live gig of the Rutles at the Troubadour, in front of an audience that sang along with every lyric and included Jeff Lynne, Julian Lennon and several members of Spinal Tap. Another evening with Neil and Eric Idle was spent in the company of Simpsons' creator Matt Groening, who turned out to be a huge fan of Neil's from his student days in the 1960s when he slavishly followed the Bonzo Dog Doo-Dah Band shows around London.

In 1978 we started work on *Life of Brian* (it was a given that I was going to collaborate on any songs that might appear in the body of the film – the score was to be composed by Geoffrey Burgon with some library music, which had worked well in *The Holy Grail*, thrown in at appropriate moments), and there I was in script meetings throwing in gag ideas (one of my suggestions actually made the final film – the ex-leper! At least I think it was one of my suggestions, thinking of the ex-parrot). Neil Innes and I had already started working on the *Innes Book of Records*, so he was only able to fly out to Tunisia for one day of filming – which is why he only makes a cameo appearance in the film. They had no ending for the movie, so Eric wrote a little ditty and sent me a cassette of his guitar and voice. The rest of the team grudgingly agreed to try it out and I rang Terry Jones to find out how much of the song was needed for playback. "Oh about 20 seconds," was his reply. (Terry always maintained that he disliked the song, the others certainly weren't over-enthusiastic.) Eric's response to this was more expletive laden, but we went ahead anyway and recorded the whole song, with my suggestion, based on Eric's cheerful lyrics, that it should be treated as a 1930s Hollywood extravaganza. (I've always believed that a serious arrangement of a comedy song works far better to point up the humour than nudging the listener in the ribs with deliberately comical music.) I still possess my original notes from a script meeting on Python headed notepaper indicating how we should record – a cherished memento. The original idea, according to my notes, was to start with just the rhythm section, overdub brass and strings and then have all the Pythons singing the whole song. However, it was soon decided that it would be a feature for Eric (although the tone of the vocal wasn't arrived at until they were all on location) and we would do the complete backing track live. We recorded the song at Chappell's in New Bond Street with the brilliant Steve James (son of Sid) engineering, as he did for most of Neil's output too, including the Rutles and the *Innes Book of Records*. It was the morning after the passing of Keith Moon (a great friend of Graham Chapman) who was intended to have several parts in the movie. I conducted my arrangement and joined in the whistling with the Fred Tomlinson singers. Eric apparently later recorded the lead vocal as we know it in a Tunisian hotel room.

Believe it or not, I did another session that afternoon (if only I'd known what the future held!). We all know what happened in the years that followed. Here's a brief history of the phenomenon. It proved to be a perfect ending for the film – in fact the song 'Always Look on the Bright Side of Life' played out beyond the fade ending that was supposed to be mixed in on the dub and disintegrates on the movie soundtrack. The Busby Berkeley Hollywood touches are a perfect corollary to the moment although Terry Jones did point out to me the incongruous sight of an electrician in modern-day garb walking through one of the shots behind the crosses! It took him thirty years to spot it. The song's first lease of life came when the crews of HMS *Sheffield* and HMS *Coventry* sang the song as they were rescued from the sinking ships during the Falklands War. Then it was taken up by football crowds, both in the UK and abroad. (Michael Palin once rang me to ask if I was watching a football final between Germany and Denmark where the whole crowd was singing it.) On the back of this interest it was re-released as a single and made the top three. I went on *Top of the Pops* and got to squirt Eric with a Selzer bottle as he was about to sing the "s" word. It's now the most popular music for funerals in the UK and Eric sang it at the Olympic Games closing ceremony in 2012 – it has even been shoehorned into *Spamalot* as a singalong highlight for the audience and cast. On UK TV *Life of Brian* has been voted the funniest movie ever made and the song the most classic moment in cinema history. (Eric took me to one side at the 40th anniversary extravaganza at the Royal Albert Hall and very generously said, "I owe it all to you!")

During my *Innes Book of Records* days, I directed the music for the first *Secret Policeman's Ball* in 1979 where, with John Cleese, I was privileged to be a two-man audience for Peter Cook's debut of his classic sketch portraying the judge summing up in the Jeremy Thorpe case. (Thorpe was the leader of the Liberal Party and accused of plotting to murder a former homosexual lover.) Peter arrived in the theatre the afternoon after our endless opening night (which started at midnight and went on till daylight) brandishing a review which bemoaned the absence of satire in the show. "So I wrote this, this morning. Is it any good?" he asked us. John and I were busy cutting sketches but this was too good to omit. The brilliant classic sketch can be found on YouTube.

I even had a scene with John Cleese, where the whole cast was enacting Henry Vth's pep talk to the troops at Agincourt. My trumpets kept interrupting him until he blew up in a Basil Fawlty rage directed at me in full fifteenth-century costume. Sadly, the whole sketch was cut before opening night as we were already overrunning by hours.

The show was a huge critical success and we planned a follow-up to be called *The Secret Policeman's Other Ball*. The 9th September 1981 was an unusually hot day in London and I arrived at the Theatre Royal at 9.30 am. Rehearsals went on all day and in those laxer times for parking restrictions I left my car on a meter, put in two hours' worth of coins and forgot about it. I emerged from the theatre at 5.30 pm trying to decide whether to return home or remain in London until the show started at midnight. The car was gone – a frantic call to the police to report it stolen revealed that it had been towed to the pound. The producers of the show reimbursed me for the taxi to retrieve the vehicle and for the parking fine – moreover the car pound was over halfway home, avoiding all the congestion of rush-hour central London – my decision was made for me! I am sure I am the only person who ever entered the facility smiling and whistling – it certainly gave the woman collecting the fines behind the grille a shock and a pleasant change from the usual procession of irate motorists.

It was Bob my eldest son's first birthday and having returned to the theatre for our midnight start, by 2am I was ready to drop with exhaustion. Little did I, or anyone else for that matter, know that within a few minutes I, with the help of those assembled with me onstage at the Drury Lane theatre, was literally about to affect the course of world history! In front of the curtain stood the comedian Billy Connolly, now drastically overrunning his allotted timeslot. From my unusual vantage point (behind a raised keyboard, rather than in the middle of the rather large horn section) I was able to scan the stage. As musical director my biggest worry was that some band members might not be "all systems go" as soon as the curtains opened. A sweep to my left took in the assembled backing singers and guitar section, a 180-degree turn made sure that bass and drums were in place, and a swivel to the right ensured that horns were in their correct places and the offstage piano had someone seated at the keyboard, ready to play. I knew the lead vocalist was in place as he stood directly in front of me, making some last-minute adjustments to his guitar.

So, what exactly were my eyes focusing on and why was it such an important event? Well to my left, Eric Clapton was audibly exhorting Billy Connolly to get on with it or "get the hook" (the way to remove a performer who had outstayed his welcome). This elicited much mirth from Jeff Beck, standing next to Eric. Meanwhile a glance down the line picked out Phil Collins juggling silently with a tambourine, Bob Geldof and Midge Ure whispering to each other, three more guitarists standing poised, bass and drums all ready to go, my childhood pal Chaz Jankel waving from the piano, Mark Isham and his section mates looking over the horn parts, and Sting ready to lead the way as our motley crew, dubbed the Secret Police, were about to make musical and social history.

Finally, Billy left the stage, the curtains opened, and my cousin Simon Phillips, for over twenty years the powerhouse behind Toto, played the drum intro to 'I Shall Be Released', specially arranged for the Amnesty International show by Sting and myself. The audience were ecstatic – no one had seen a gathering of so many stellar names on one stage since the Concert for Bangladesh or the Last Waltz. And what we did was to plant a seed in Bob Geldof and Midge Ure's mind that led directly to Live Aid and the many concerts for Amnesty International that have followed. How did this all happen? Well, largely thanks to Martin Lewis, the producer, with my collusion.

The first *Secret Policeman's Ball* had included some music – acoustic sets by Pete Townshend, Neil Innes, guitarist John Williams, Donovan, Victoria Wood and Dame Edna Everage! Pete was extremely nervous as it was his first solo performance, both playing and singing, and we decided he would perform a duet with guitarist John Williams on 'Pinball Wizard'. The inevitable happened – Pete missed out a huge chunk of the song while the classical virtuoso John Williams diligently followed the music that had been written out for him. Somehow it got back on track after a few minutes of atonal chaos. The big surprise was revealing my big band for one number with Neil Innes. Martin and I decided for the next show that the music content should be raised to equal the comedy. And my input was that the big names we hoped to secure should be backed up by a solid bunch of highly respected backroom musicians who would be the glue to hold the ensemble together. The breakthrough came when we landed Simon and Mo Foster on drums and bass. Martin rang Eric Clapton's management hoping that he would join us, and he asked if he could bring a friend. The "friend" was Jeff Beck. This, incredibly, was their first onstage encounter. When Martin was able to involve Sting, we knew we were all set. We then added my old colleague John Etheridge, the session guitarist, who Sting once said he aspired to be when he first attempted a musical career. Asking Ray Russell, another guitar hero, was my idea, and I got Chaz Jankel (who wrote 'Ai No Corrida' for Quincy Jones) and Mark Isham, now one of the world's leading movie composers, to pitch in too. Whitesnake's Neil Murray filled in on bass when Mo wasn't available, Neil Innes was there as well, along with Sheena Easton and Donovan, plus an all-star horn section. And the band rocked! Eric Clapton was excited to play with Sting, who was excited to play with Jeff. Phil Collins begged us to be included – I'm sure we could have stretched the ensemble even more had we had more time. Getting the musicians on and off stage was quite a logistical nightmare. We decided to have an offstage piano for Eric and Jeff's set which I would play, as the comedy sketches were interspersed with musical interludes. Thus, I became probably the most incompetent pianist ever to record with Clapton and Beck! My concentration wasn't helped by people tapping me on the shoulder while performing and demanding "Have you seen John Cleese anywhere?" or "Where's the stage door?" On the YouTube video of the duo performing 'Further on Down the Road' you can hear my ghostly piano for a couple of choruses before it stops abruptly – obviously I was pointing someone in the direction of something.

One idea that was too complicated to be realized in the time we had was Johnny Rotten with a string quartet performing 'Anarchy in the UK' – that could have been a lot of fun! (A few years earlier I was conducting a string quartet arrangement I had written for a songwriter's album recording at the Marquee Studios which backed on to the club. Every take was interrupted by the intense volume of the band onstage in the Marquee Club – the Sex Pistols. We had to wait until each "song" finished and hurriedly record the quartet before the next number began. However, I swear that you can hear the Pistols on the track as the echo dies away at the end of the album cut.)

Figure 18: Rehearsals – Jeff Beck, John Cleese, Eric Clapton and me. Author's collection (Amnesty International publicity).

Eric Clapton said to me during rehearsals, "You're the bandleader. What do you want us to do?" The keys to the success of the Secret Police lay in that sentence – no one tried to outdo or outshine the others. Everyone listened to everyone else, showing musical consideration to each other and respect for the song performed. It was a true lesson in musical democracy and humility, and marked a momentous turning point for musicians with social consciences. And I'm proud to have been in the thick of it. Possibly my most lasting contribution to the legacy of The Police was fixing Sting's saxophone at rehearsals!

Figure 19: Sting and the Secret Police. Me marshalling the band on keyboards behind Sting. Author's collection (Amnesty International publicity).

There followed Terry Jones's movie *Erik the Viking* and TV show *Fairy Tales*, where I orchestrated and conducted Neil's music, and later gigs included appearing in various Monty Python performances over the years and being a Mountie in the 'Lumberjack Song' along with Neil, André Jacquemin (composer of the opening title songs for *Life of Brian* and *The Meaning of Life*), Sanjeev Bhaskar and the two Terrys as Michael reprised this long-term favourite with Carole Cleveland at the Python 40th anniversary celebrations at the Royal Albert Hall. Then there was the aforementioned *Top of the Pops* appearance when 'Bright Side of Life' hit the top of the charts in the early 1990s, and the estimable Sir Michael Palin being my guest for my one-on-one chat show in London. I visited Terry Jones often during his final tragic illness and I was so happy he came to the London Film Festival Gala screening of the restored silent movie *Shooting Stars* for which I composed and conducted a new score, and that he attended my chat with comedian Rob Brydon, another huge fan of Terry's work. I miss him and my other frequent collaborator Neil Innes a great deal.

Figure 20: 'Lumberjack Song' at the Albert Hall for the Python 40th anniversary – (l to r) me, Terry Gilliam, Neil Innes, Sanjeev Bhaskar, Terry Jones, Carole Cleveland, Michael Palin. Author's collection.

I also have many random memories gathered over the years – at the premiere of *Life of Brian*, John Cleese asked me what I thought of the previous night's *Fawlty Towers* (I assured him that the episode with the rat was brilliant). I was asked to play the piano at Graham Chapman's notorious memorial service (the scene of one of John Cleese's funniest speeches). We gathered before the memorial service in a pub near Smithfield market – I'll never forget the look on the faces of two American tourists as they rounded a corner on a quiet Sunday afternoon to walk into all the remaining Pythons and their entourages. At the party that night to celebrate twenty years of Python (Graham's timing was impeccable) I realized that this could be the last time they were all together and got them all to personalize and sign a T-shirt which hangs framed in my library.

Then we went about reuniting the Rutles in Los Angeles.

"How can you reunite a band that has never been together in the first place?" asked Eric.

I sat next to Michael Palin at the premiere of the 70mm print of *Life of Brian* – he nudged me and said, "*Our* film has held up well!". Terry Gilliam sketched me as "the Hidden Man" as I was always lurking in the shadows – I prize that drawing. I also participated in birthday videos for all the team as a double act with Sanjeev Bhaskar. (Michael once said to me, "You should have been a comedian, you always make me laugh!" – hopefully he wasn't referring to my saxophone playing.) And lately our friend Ann has organized several Python Zoom reunions online. Not a bad association for a redundant radio producer!

7 Whispering Wheels, You Sexy Thing, Muhammad Ali, and Freddie Mercury and the sausages

I turned twenty-five in 1974, a momentous year for me. I was still sporadically playing on records, and I had started arranging in earnest. This came about in a very roundabout way. My great friend Pete van Hooke had recommended me to Eric Burdon as a percussionist. I guess he thought he was doing me a favour, although my percussion skills wouldn't give Ray Cooper sleepless nights. I showed up at Studio 51 (Gt. Newport St) in central London for rehearsals and was directed to a huge percussion rig. I honestly had no clue what to bang or shake and I asked if I could play saxophone or keyboards as well. There was no microphone for a sax and there were already two amplified keyboards in the band so I was directed to the Studio 51 out-of-tune piano, again with no amplification. I struggled along for a couple of days, occasionally hitting something in a vain attempt to demonstrate my percussive credentials. By the second day it was pretty obvious that my services would no longer be required and I was gently let go. (There were no hard feelings, in fact years later Eric and I jammed together with Donovan and Moby Grape at the 40th anniversary of the concert film *Monterey Pop* in California. And this time I was *not* playing percussion!)

As it was the middle of an extremely hot summer and Studio 51 had no air conditioning, we all took our break on the scorching but slightly more bearable street. A producer I had done some sessions for on saxophone walked past on his way to his office. We nodded at each other. He rounded the corner and then headed back towards me. "You write arrangements, don't you?" he asked, more in hope than conviction. Of course I said yes, although my arranging skills thus far ran to writing horn lines for friends' demos and a Dixieland chart of 'Someone's Rocking My Dreamboat' for Murray Head that actually made it to *Top of the Pops*.

"My arranger has gone off to the States in the middle of recording an album with the Sandpipers (of 'Guantanamera' fame) and we have six tracks left to record." My new freedom meant I could almost immediately visit his office, meet the band and *voilà*, I was officially an arranger.

The first track we worked on was a disco version of the McCoys' hit 'Hang on Sloopy'. Would you believe it, it made the charts! Suddenly I had credibility as an arranger. How, you may wonder, did I gather the skills to write and orchestrate with only the most basic musical education? It may sound trite to say it, but I just knew what to do. A lot was trial and error, plus the wonderful session musicians were always willing to straighten me out if I wrote something impossible. One thing was certain: once they'd put me right, I'd never do it again!

I cut my teeth as an arranger with this particular producer, and for one session we hired a pre-fame Elaine Paige as a backing vocalist. She brought this rather diminutive fellow to the session and he promptly fell asleep on the couch at the back of the control room. "Get him out of here," hissed the producer to the engineer.

"But that's Dustin Hoffman," my colleague replied.

"I don't care who he is, no one sleeps on my sessions!" I think he stayed, as I don't recall a *contretemps*. The producer was – and is – a lovely man but always seemed slightly out of touch with everything that went on in the world of showbusiness, including music terminology I'm afraid. On another session the producer was exhorting the guitarist to be inspired: "Play something."

"Give me a clue what you're after?"

"Something... over there!" he said, enigmatically.

Early on, working with this producer, who also owned a record label, I traded any notion I may have had of receiving regular paychecks for the chance to experiment with orchestrations and establish myself as a familiar figure on the session scene. Many of the musicians we hired had worked with, or were even fans of, my uncles, while many of the younger players saw me as a friend and contemporary whom they were only too happy to help along the way. It was a great training ground and hopefully I was a fast learner.

One early gig for an independent label was to arrange both sides of a single for the controversial soccer manager Brian Clough – so controversial he later had a movie made about him starring Michael Sheen, *The Damned United*. I told the band and backing singers that we had to take the whole enterprise very seriously. If it seemed as if we were sending the whole thing up it wouldn't work. It obviously succeeded, as the record made a few compilations as one of the worst singles ever! Cloughy showed up drunk (apparently not unusual for him) but was very pleasant and professional as he spoke the dialogue written for him by the Canadian composer (who incidentally had no idea as to the rules of soccer) which was placed between the lyrics sung by the backing singers. He then regaled me with tales of his idol Frank Sinatra and told me he was such a huge fan of The Inkspots that he queued outside their dressing room at a club date in the north of England for an hour to tell them how much their music had meant to him. I didn't have the heart to tell this man who was an icon of his sport that probably none of that incarnation of the group had even been born during the heyday of the band's popularity. Our single, 'It's Only a Game/You Can't Win 'Em All' has, of course, surfaced online in recent years.

I was still teaching in schools and for London University, but musical adventures kept cropping up. A well-known music manager, Tony Hall, hired me to transcribe "top lines" (take down the melodies and chords for publishers) for a chart-topping songwriting team. I found myself playing clarinet on a Kevin Ayers record with Elton John at the piano, hooking up with Van Morrison through his new drummer, Pete van Hooke who wisely suggested I play saxophone rather than percussion; taking my saxophone to the first Knebworth festival with Van and co (where I was surplus to performing requirements but wound up as the only person onstage taking photos); watching vintage comedy shows and heading out for late-night meals with Van who had taken up residence at Pete's house, and getting reacquainted with Al Anderson, who rang me on the day of my 25th birthday bash asking if anything was going on that night. And that's how the Wailers came to jam at my party. Al had auditioned the day before and was now a member of that soon-to-be classic band. A few months later I became their London guide, taking them to the Speakeasy to sit at Jimi Hendrix's favourite table, to Dingwalls to hear Ian Dury with Kilburn and the High Roads, and to a string session I was conducting at Trident Studios (they'd never been to a string session before). And from there we went to the Lyceum theatre in Central London where Bob Marley and the Wailers made musical history!

The reggae singer Susan Cadogan had hit the Top 10 with 'Hurts So Good', produced by the legendary eccentric Lee "Scratch" Perry, and was being brought over from Jamaica to tour. She needed a band and I got the call, along with my good friends Mitch Dalton, Chaz Jankel, Pete van Hooke, Noel Norris and Kuma Harada. We went for an outfit fitting as we were due to play the notorious Baileys club circuit. The Baileys clubs were known as the "chicken in a basket" circuit and at the time hosted a bizarre mixture of fading showbiz stars, up and coming soon-to-be famous young acts and current chart sensations in cabaret. They were part of a club culture in the 1960s and 70s that hosted superstars like Sinatra, Louis Armstrong and Ella Fitzgerald. Our gear looked like it had been abandoned by the Chi-Lites, puce-coloured satin shirts split to the waist and skin-tight, low-cut, white flared trousers. Not the best look for three North London Jewish guys, a bearded middle-aged trumpeter and a Japanese bassist! Thankfully the outfits bit the dust and we went for something more sensible. Our first warm-up gig was at the Whispering Wheels roller-skating rink in Wolverhampton for Jamaican Independence Day. I sensed trouble as a bottle hit Mitch before we'd played a note and there followed a steady barrage of bottles and cans. Susan, bless her, waded into the audience threatening to punch anyone else who dared throw anything. Two numbers later we fled the stage, Peter Waterman (later of Stock, Aitken and Waterman fame) whispering, "I've got the money, let's meet at the next motorway services!" Not the most auspicious start to a tour (although the reggae band Steel Pulse who followed us got the same treatment as we did, so I guess it was nothing personal). The Baileys shows fared much better and we became quite popular on their circuit although on one show in Leicester we waited for the revolving stage to begin, revealing us minus our keyboard player Chaz Jankel. As the stage began turning, he breathlessly leapt into position and explained afterwards that he had come from a show with Tim Hardin in Glasgow and realized part of the way down that he had left his gig bag with all his connectors, plugs and pedals at the Glasgow club and had to turn back to collect it. On another occasion the revolving stage got stuck as it rotated, demolishing the drumkit!

Another foray into bandleading at the time met with mixed success. I assembled an 18-piece big band for Muhammad Ali's birthday gala party at the Grosvenor House hotel. We were due to accompany a vocalist whose claim to fame was that he sounded like Nat King Cole, Ali's favourite singer. The evening got off to an odd start as the whole band arrived, complaining they had been harassed by Ali's bodyguards, including a pre-*A Team* Mr. T. All that is except for guitarist Ollie Halsall who had somehow found his way in through the main entrance carrying his guitar nonchalantly over his shoulder.

Events took an even more bizarre turn as Ali rose to respond to a toast delivered by an imposing black schoolmaster with a cut-glass upper-class English accent. This so fascinated the birthday boy that he proceeded to get up and speak ... and speak ... and speak – for two hours non-stop.

During this sadly rambling discourse (hopefully not an early sign of his eventual tragic illness) various elderly people on the top table actually dozed off in their soup plates, while our vocalist fortified himself backstage by drinking an entire bottle of brandy, and we stood and waited, and waited, and waited.

The result, when we finally got to perform, was total chaos. Our vocalist proceeded to end some songs halfway through, while he managed still to be singing on some after the band had finished. Each song became more surreal than the last until a voice from the crowd yelled "Sing 'Mona Lisa'!" "OK boys, 'Mona Lisa', here we go," and off he went. Trouble was we had no rehearsal or, come to that, music for 'Mona Lisa', and we were already eight bars into the song, brass players and saxophonists madly scuffling through manuscripts in an effort to find a relevant page, when enter Ollie, who had been diligently attempting to follow the now completely useless sheet music throughout the gig, most of which bore no relevance to what our star was singing. Now he suddenly perked up – "Hang on, 'Mona Lisa', I know that." And he began accompanying, beautifully, what turned out to be the musical high point of the evening.

Five chaotic numbers later, it was all over. I swivelled round as the lights came up to see – nothing! No one except the gig promoter (who approached the stage in a daze, tripped and fell and broke his nose!). The entire Grosvenor House audience, including Ali and his entourage, had vanished – the room was empty, our cheque bounced, and I had to sit outside the vocalist's flat for half a day to get our money. A couple of weeks later, guitarist Mitch Dalton who was also lucky enough to be on the gig brought in a copy of *West Indian World*. There on the cover was a photo of our vocalist in mid-song, my back to the camera shrugging my shoulders, and Mitch with his guitar balanced on his lap, leaning backwards and laughing his head off.

At the end of all these forays into the weird and wacky world of showbusiness, I would always return to the comparative sanity of the schoolroom and the London University Extra-Mural Literature class I taught. One day in early 1975, I received a call from the wonderful saxophonist Chris Mercer from John Mayall's classic Bluesbreakers band. "I've been asked to put a horn section together for Hot Chocolate but I don't fancy it – would you like to take it on?"

Figure 21: My Hot Chocolate publicity photo. Photograph by Danny Clifford.

I agreed and was told by the band that they had no arrangements handy. "No problem," I replied. "I'll take them down from the records." I enlisted Noel Norris again on trumpet and Pat Kyle on tenor sax whilst I decided to play alto and baritone with a bit of flute and clarinet as needed. (A young lady said to me as I walked out onstage carrying saxes, flute and clarinet: "Are you anything to do with the band?") If they required a second keyboard player that would be my responsibility too. We attended the first rehearsal at the Richmond athletic ground, where the Rolling Stones had launched themselves and we immediately hit it off with the band. I later discovered that they had the music all the time but wanted to see how committed we were to get the gig – apparently another brass section showed up before we did and said, "Sorry we can't do anything without the music." So, we joined the band as an on-the-road addition, just as 'You Sexy Thing' was released.

Our first official gig was at Salford University. The tour manager had hired a bus for us, and it broke down in the car park after the show. It was like a scene from a Beatles movie as a crowd of screaming teenagers rocked the bus from side to side. An exasperated Errol Brown, the face of the band, banged his fist on a chair and said, "That's it! From now on we travel in our own cars to venues." That's how I came to be a regular passenger in Errol's green Cadillac and got the chance to spend many hours with him, hearing his fascinating life story.

He had been a clerk in the Treasury and had never been involved with music or bands, but his neighbour Tony was an aspiring guitarist and songwriter. Errol used to hang out with him and sing snatches of music. "What's that you're singing?" asked Tony. "Just something I made up," replied Errol. So they started writing together and assembled a demo tape. They needed an extra song so they recorded a spoof reggae version of 'Give Peace a Chance'. Their then-manager incorrectly advised them that they would need John Lennon's permission so they sent a tape to Apple. A secretary played it to Lennon who loved it, phoned them and asked if they were a band. When they said, "We could be," John asked them to play the song at the Lyceum, opening for the Plastic Ono Band that weekend. "I'll call you Hot Chocolate," he said.

So they played the concert, were signed as a one-off to Apple for the single release of that song, which crept into the top thirty, and were then let go. However, they carried on writing together and came up with a song they thought would be perfect for Herman's Hermits. They made an appointment to see Mickey Most but when they arrived at his office, he told them his reel-to-reel machine was broken. "Leave the tape with me and I'll get round to listening to it."

They politely declined and went on their way. A few months later the song was still on their minds, so they made another appointment with Mickey. He listened to the song and said "Don't like it – got anything else?" The next song on the tape was 'Love Is Life'. By the time it finished playing he'd signed them to a record deal, and they became the most successful singles band in the UK after The Beatles.

One day Errol told me, "We want to be a funk band like Kool and the Gang and the Ohio Players, but the horn charts are very jazzy and busy." So, I volunteered to rewrite the arrangements. They loved my revisions, and it was one more affirmation that I could pursue writing seriously.

I was also writing arrangements for Chappell's (the music publisher's) songwriters and arranged for two writers, with whom I was to work, to attend our Edinburgh show. We had never met but I had front-row VIP seats in the balcony reserved for them. They had sent me a tape of their songs recorded on a home cassette recorder in a living room. It was extremely lo-fi with dogs barking, kids yelling and cups of tea and biscuits materializing at regular intervals. They had recorded on one side of a C90 and I had put a Tower of Power album on the B side to listen to on my portable cassette player. At this particular gig there was a technical malfunction which delayed our show. I went up onstage to find out from our monitor engineer how long it would be before our set and he replied, "Quite a while, have you got any tapes on you? I've played all mine."

I gave him the cassette tape and said, "Whatever you do, don't play the B side as it's these songwriters at home." Of course, I should have said A side. Half an hour later I wandered back onstage and heard something vaguely familiar booming out into the Usher Hall. At that moment I heard a telephone ring and one of the wives shouting, "It's for you!"

"For heaven's sake, turn it off," I beseeched the sound guy.

"Sounds pretty good to me," was his response as I looked up to see four conspicuously empty seats in the balcony! I was convinced my entire career as an arranger was over there and then – luckily the songwriting pair had been delayed and took their seats a few minutes later, just before we went on. A huge sigh of relief – I have no idea what the audience made of the frequent pauses for tea and biscuits!

Our first trumpet player was my old friend Noel Norris, possessor of a very dry sense of humour and a favourite with the whole band. On one gig Errol and Noel finished a bottle of wine between them before the show. When they appeared onstage, Errol joined the horn section and Noel started singing 'You Sexy Thing' at the main microphone, much to the amusement of the group and bemusement of the audience. Another evening we were staying in the Mayfair hotel, Morecambe, a place that had seen better days, and run by an incarnation of Basil Fawlty. There was no food after 10 o'clock, no bar, none of the bathroom fittings seemed to work, and the manager frequently complained about everything possible. As we left the hotel early the next morning, Noel gazed back at the illuminated sign glowing in the mist for the hotel, missing the M and r from Mayfair and H from Hotel. He shook his head and opined, "All in all, not a patch on their London branch!"

One of our shows was in a seaside town in Kent. We were visited before the show by the local constabulary, who advised us that there would almost certainly be a major confrontation between two local gangs during the show and showed us where to take refuge under the stage should a riot kick off. Sure enough, mid-set, all hell broke loose, and we scurried to our designated hiding place. After about 30 minutes, a policeman appeared and said, "All under control. You can go back on now." We resumed to a delighted full house as if nothing had happened. I thought, "This must have been what it was like for a jazz musician in Chicago during Prohibition!"

HOT CHOCOLATE ITINERARY

			GetIn	Arrive	Doors	OnStage
22 October	Cardiff University	12pm	6.30	8pm	10.30	
23						
24	Salford Uni	12pm		8pm	10.30	
25						
26	Wolverhampton Civic	12pm		7pm	8.45	
27						
28	Pavilion Hemel Hempstead	12pm		7.30		
29	Chatham Central Hall			7pm		
30						
31	Corn Exchange Ipswich					
1 November	Swansea Brangwyn Hall	12pm		7pm		
2						
3						
4						
5	LeasCliff Hall Folkestone	12pm		7.30		
6	Victoria Halls Hanley	12pm		7pm	8.45	
7	Lancaster Uni	12pm		8pm	10pm	
8	Leeds Uni	12pm	5pm	7.30	9.30	
9	Theatre Royal Norwich	12pm		7.15	9.15	
10						
11	Newcastle City Hall	12pm		7pm		
12	Edinburgh Leith Hall	12pm		7pm		
13	Aberdeen Music Hall	12pm		7pm		
14						
15	York University	12pm		8pm	10pm	
16	Royal Court Theatre Liverpool	12pm		7pm		
17	Off					
18	Fairfield Halls Croydon	12pm		7.30		

Figure 22: Hot Chocolate tour itinerary. Author's collection.

In Manchester we would frequent the nightclub Slack Alice as guests of the great soccer star George Best, who co-owned the club. Twenty years later I sat with George, by now a hopeless alcoholic, at a charity lunch at Blenheim Palace, home of the Duke of Marlborough, where the cricket match we were due to play was rained off. At one point he indicated that he needed the bathroom and I helped him across the marquee. As we moved very slowly through the crowd, with me holding his arm to steady his gait, I couldn't help thinking, "This is possibly the greatest athlete I ever saw in action and here he can barely walk without assistance!" A sad, unnecessary decline and fall.

Our eagerly awaited London show at the New Victoria theatre was a chaotic sell out, so I was amazed to find my closest friend Pete van Hooke waiting in the wings for me as I came off stage. Even more so, as I could see Mickey Most, Hot Chocolate's guru and owner of their record label, at the stage door trying in vain to get past the bouncers to congratulate us. But then I shouldn't have been surprised – Pete had a knack of showing up anywhere and walking in as if he owned the place. He once wound up in an elevator at the Royal Albert Hall with Frank Sinatra! When we went to see George Benson at the same venue in the early 1970s, we sauntered in past the security at the artist's entrance and made our way down into the dressing-room area – all without tickets! If we were booked into a restaurant in Covent Garden, where no one could ever find parking, you can bet that Pete would roar up and park right outside, minutes before we were shown to our table. The drummers had a motor-racing team and Pete showed up at the track in T-shirt and jeans, much to the disgust of one of his colleagues. "You can't drive dressed like that, go and find some proper clothes!" So, Pete went into a dressing room, where someone was changing into everyday wear and asked, "Can I borrow your gear?"

"Sure," said the other guy, which is how Pete re-emerged wearing racing gear with "Ayrton Senna – world champion" emblazoned all over his top. To add insult to injury he then beat all the other drivers' times. An unforgettable moment was when we went to see a classic incarnation of Weather Report at the Hammersmith Odeon in Pete's Lotus. As we rounded the roundabout to park the car, I demonstrated that Wayne Shorter had a tic where his left arm would shoot up in the air. Unfortunately, my left arm thudded extremely hard into the roof stanchion of the car and throbbed and ached through the entire show. Of course, Wayne's arm remained perfectly still throughout the evening. Pete has had an amazing career as a drummer with Van Morrison, Al Jarreau, Mike and the Mechanics and many, many more and now manages one of the finest vocalists Britain has ever produced – Paul Carrack. And we're still friends!

I usually travelled to and from Hot Chocolate gigs with Errol, or with his bass player and co-writer Tony Wilson, with much anticipated stops at the legendary motorway service stations. The UK motorway (freeway) services were a meeting point for every other band criss-crossing the country

– usually between the hours of 1 and 5am! Their usefulness was only offset by their awfulness in the 1960s and 70s when I was "privileged" to be a frequent patron. The height of culinary delight was two fried eggs swimming in a plate full of grease – acceptable fare at 3am to the hungry muso and truck driver. There should be a book written about the dining adventures of touring musicians over the years. One of my favourite stories concerns an exchange between the great American singer Jack Jones and a waitress somewhere in the UK.

Jones (pointing at the menu): "What's the duck like?"

Waitress (after a moment's thought): "It's like a big chicken!"

By far the favourite stop-off was the legendary "Blue Boar" at the Watford Gap services, where, if you waited long enough, you were sure to run into everyone who ever played in a British band (and many unfortunate touring US artists too – I once found myself queueing behind the Four Tops).

This particular story concerns Salisbury Plain services (not actually a qualitative description – Salisbury Plain happens to be a major area for British Army manoeuvres). Hot Chocolate were booked by the agency that represented Queen and we found ourselves on this particular tour one day ahead of Freddie Mercury and company in our itinerary. Often this meant meeting them checking into hotels as we checked out. Occasionally it meant we got to hang out and go to each other's shows. (I recall the amazement of their lighting designer and chief roadie at discovering they'd both independently been at my 21st birthday jam session with Muddy Waters.) This particular night we arrived at Salisbury services heading back to London to find Queen heading down to where we'd just been. It was probably around 2am and the "restaurant" was deserted apart from a few long-distance lorry drivers, the bands and road crews, and the British Army on a training exercise – hence my standing in line in front of Freddie Mercury and, behind him, a guy in full army camouflage with actual tree branches growing out of his backpack!

"Yes?" snapped the charming young lady behind the counter.

"Eggs, chips and beans please," I said.

"Sausage, egg, chips and beans," replied my server.

"Well I don't want the sausage, thank you," I responded.

"You have to have it," she insisted, pointing at the uninspiring photograph above the serving area.

"Well, I don't want it – I'll pay for it but I don't want to have it on my plate."

"It says sausage, egg, chips and beans," she insisted.

"May I please see your supervisor."

Off she went and returned with an even grumpier lady.

"Yes?"

"Egg, chips and beans please."

"Sausage, egg, chips and beans."

Once again, stalemate. The supervisor threatened me with the police – "The sausage police?" I responded.

"Put it on another plate?" I offered.

"One plate per order," she insisted.

When I threatened to throw it straight in the trash, she threatened the police again. I said, "It's my sausage, I've bought it, I can wear it if I want!" Thoughts of a confrontation à la *Five Easy Pieces* crossed my mind, but when she threatened the police again I thought it wisest to acquiesce, took the sausage and theatrically announced, "Who wants a sausage?" before scooping it onto the plate of a grateful trucker. All this time the soldier with the tree in his backpack stood watching impassively, while Freddie Mercury, bless him, rolled about on the floor clutching his side, laughing helplessly. From that day on, we were a double act. If I saw Freddie anywhere, I'd sneak up behind him and say, "Eggs, chips and beans." Without looking round he'd say, "Sausage, eggs, chips and beans," and we'd do the entire altercation to the complete mystification of all around us.

The service stations now serve healthier food and the plates of eggs swimming in grease are long gone – but I still smile when I enter one, and just once again I'd like to order eggs, chips and beans!

A few months earlier I had been recording in SARM East in Whitechapel. Every time I emerged from the control room throughout the day, I heard the same few bars of a capella vocals over and over again. Finally, I knocked on the control-room door and asked one of the Garys, Lyons or Langan, what on earth they were up to. "Oh, we are combing through the vocal tracks for a song for the new Queen album trying to create some sort of order!"

"Good luck with that!" I muttered, shaking my head in disbelief. When I left the studio after a rewarding but exhausting 11-hour day I could still hear the quasi-operatic segment for about the 150th time. "No chance of that ever catching on," I smugly asserted to one of my colleagues, dismissing 'Bohemian Rhapsody' as yet another prog rock excess. Shows what I know!

About five years later I was recording in CTS Studio 2 in Wembley. On a break I headed for the staircase to the bar when from the control room of Studio 1, I heard another few bars of an a cappella vocal over and over again. As the main door was open, I stuck my head into the control room to find the harassed composer Howard Blake trying to craft a music cue around this one phrase of unaccompanied voices. Once again it was Queen – for the movie *Flash Gordon*. I should have realized by now.

I loved my time with Hot Chocolate (apart from having to sing "Sexy thing, you sexy thing" every night!) and was sorry to quit a year later. I had overheard the new trumpeter and saxophonist discussing what they were going to do when the tour finished, and summer seasons in British holiday camps seemed to be the main option. Not for me, thanks! I went back to academia – as a footnote I played keyboards on Errol's farewell gig when he left Hot Chocolate eleven years later. At the same charity gala (in aid of sickle cell anemia research) I was the pianist for singer/songwriter Labi Siffre. He had just written a new song about the incarcerated Nelson Mandela entitled

'Something Inside So Strong' and we debuted it at the event. As soon as I heard it at rehearsals, I told him, "That's a number one hit song you've written" and of course it was – an instant classic!

Errol was always so encouraging to me and proud of my later career. I miss him a lot. One result of my stay with Hot Chocolate was that I finally decided to abandon the doctorate and the teaching. Not before I made a trip from Leicester to London – to teach a class on the European novel – and then up to Newcastle (with a diversion to Leicester as I'd left my flute at the De Montfort Hall!). I think that's the trip that convinced me that my future lay in the world of music.

Incidentally, many years later I re-established contact with Chris Mercer and told him how much that phone call meant to me, and how it changed my life. He responded, "I'm delighted, but I honestly don't remember getting that call from Hot Chocolate or calling you to suggest you take the gig!"

A bizarre footnote about Queen's chief roadie who had been at my 21st. I lost touch with him and sadly he passed away quite a few years ago. About five years ago I had some correspondence with a friend's assistant who shared the same unusual surname. I asked if she was related and she replied, "it's my husband's surname, I'll ask him." She came back to me saying he had no knowledge of my friend and I left it at that. A year later I was at an event hosted by her boss, and she came over to tell me something. Her husband's father had passed away and on his deathbed he'd confessed that he had a family prior to marrying her mother in law. And it turned out that my old friend was her husband's secret half-brother!

8 BBC, early Commercials, Bowie, Dietrich, Jule Styne and early Van

Once I'd left Hot Chocolate in 1976, I discovered a new talent that I had no idea I had. The BBC and various record labels started employing me to do "takedowns". In those pre-computer days, overseas performers would be booked on television variety shows and usually arrive in the UK from Los Angeles, Nashville, New York or Paris – never carrying music or scores for their latest single. I would therefore be sent a cassette tape of the record and I had not only to transcribe the musical arrangement but also adapt it to the orchestral make-up of *The Two Ronnies*, *Top of the Pops*, *Parkinson* or *Russell Harty*. The head of music at the BBC at the time, Ronnie Hazelhurst, and most of the arrangers he hired were, like him, veterans of the golden age of the dance band. In fact, Ronnie had been in my uncle Woolf Phillips' orchestra at the Pigalle. I'm not sure how I came to his attention, but I started to get all the cast-offs that other arrangers didn't want to touch – country records, soul tracks, reggae, funk, as well as out and out pop songs. Even UK-based acts like the Nolan Sisters required this service, which I could never quite work out – surely, they had access to their own arrangements? Be that as it may, I had fun transcribing songs by acts like The Stylistics, Don Williams and Telly Savalas. Telly was probably the best-known actor in the world at the time thanks to Kojak and he had already had a number one hit record in the UK with his version of David Gates's 'If'.

Accordingly, I'd gone to the BBC TV studios, in my capacity as his musical director, to do the Michael Parkinson show with him. He had just been at a big horse-racing event and had phoned his mother in the States to tell her all about his European adventures – judging international film festivals, appearing on chat shows, being feted worldwide as a superstar and attending the races as a guest of honour. Her only comment was "I hope you wore your sweater!" His comment to me was "It doesn't matter how old, wealthy, successful or famous you are, you can trust your mother to make a helpless kid out of you!" At the studio Telly took me to one side and said, "*I* know I can't sing. *You* know I can't sing. Why should *they* know?" And promptly bailed. (Incidentally, I'm now great friends with his daughter Ariana who *can* sing – a wonderful performer in her own right and a mainstay of my friend Scott Bradlee's Postmodern Jukebox.)

However, the producers suggested I might conduct a performance of 'As Time Goes By', freeing the show's resident bandleader Harry Stoneham to play piano. I agreed, and while waiting backstage amid the discarded coffee cups and cigarette butts (the glamour of TV studios!), felt two hands on my shoulders. I looked round and it was the iconic Ingrid Bergman. She said, "Do you mind if I sit with you, it's really lonely on my own in the dressing room?"

I grabbed a chair for her and we chatted away happily. I told her I'd be conducting 'As Time Goes By' and she said, "Oh how wonderful! I get really nervous on chat shows so when I come on, I'll give you a big smile and I'll be fine!" I was then called onstage by the floor manager to be asked if I would fill the piano chair while Harry conducted Ingrid's play-on – then we'd switch places during her interview. As she walked on, I realized she wouldn't be able to see me, and turning to face her would have implied that I wasn't actually playing the piano, so I did a futile, clumsy half-twist forward to catch her eye.

I was very nervous about conducting the orchestra in front of millions of television viewers for the first time – this was very different from the recording studio. I stood with my arms aloft, ready for my cue after Ingrid's interview, and waited and waited. My headphones had failed – apparently the producer of the show was screaming blue murder at me to start the song while I remained poised in blissful ignorance. I was rudely awakened by the aforementioned floor manager tearing the headphones from my ears and handing me a replacement pair. At last, they resumed the taping and off we went. For some reason the new headphones I'd been given had the producer's feed to Parkinson and the camera and floor crew rather than the band but by now I was so flustered I ploughed on. After about ten seconds of the song, a disembodied voice rang out, "Band sounds dreadful today!" And so it went on in the same vein throughout the entire song – I think the most encouraging remark amidst all the "camera three, move yourself for heaven's sakes" was "I've a good mind to sack the whole lot of them and get a new orchestra – they're speeding up again!"

Suitably chastened, I finished the song and waited until the finale where we performed again – I didn't have the heart or the courage to stop the show or complain about the headphones. I walked dejectedly off the set to be greeted by a beaming producer: "Sounded wonderful tonight – thank you so much." Welcome to the world of network television!

After the show in the green room, Ingrid Bergman came over to me and said, "Oh my, I gave you a big smile and this stranger just ignored me! It really threw me, but I spotted you at the piano and gave you a nice big smile, although you wouldn't have seen me." Telly and I spent an hour chatting with her. He was as much in awe as I was, dropping to his knees and kissing her hand when I made the unnecessary formal introduction. Amazingly, Ingrid seemed in awe of Telly – definitely a mutual admiration society! Years later I found a videotape of the show and was able to freeze frame the exact moment of recognition so at last I could see Ingrid Bergman's smile!

Telly told me some incredible stories about his career and life: he'd been a drama lecturer at an American university and one of his students had sent his headshot to the producers of *The Birdman of Alcatraz*, the rest is history! While filming the *Dirty Dozen*, one nameless actor, forced onto the movie by the studio, had been giving the director Robert Aldrich attitude, and was exhibiting diva behaviour on the first few days of filming. As they wrapped the shoot at the end of one particularly fraught day, Aldrich turned to the scriptwriter and his assistant and hissed, "Kill him tomorrow!" Perhaps the most intriguing story was that Telly had worked for the Central Intelligence Agency debriefing Russian defectors. Coincidentally, around the same time, I arranged and conducted an album for the songwriter Tom Springfield of his favourite songs, both originals and covers. It was never destined for release but was a lot of fun. During the recordings he told me that he had worked for the Secret Service decoding Russian naval intelligence! What a dull life I'd led by comparison. Years later I was approached to arrange an album of classic standards for his sister Dusty – sadly by then she was too sick to take the project any further. She was definitely one that got away (see Chapter 26 for some more about that!).

One thing that amused me during all my time working for the BBC was that they paid by the bar of music. On a slow ballad each beat would be written as a whole bar – no repeats as you weren't paid for them! The drummer for The Stylistics' appearance had to have eight music stands arranged in a semi-circle to accommodate the pages and pages of manuscript. In addition it was very difficult to read, as the way it was written was totally unnatural. BBC fees were never even vaguely in a ballpark of fairness – what we were told to do was add "consultation fees" with the director. It's amazing how many hours after midnight I spent consulting with the directors about my music. At least the right boxes were ticked and no one ever queried my invoices!

Round about this time I began writing for advertising. The late Jill Sinclair, later to marry the terrific producer Trevor Horn with whom I worked a lot in later years, recommended me to Jeff Wayne Music as a potential composer/arranger. My first ever commercial assignment was to arrange a brass band for a Walkers Crisps advertisement for one of Jeff's composers. "Have you ever scored for brass band?" I was asked.

"Oh yes," I lied and rushed to the library to get a book on writing for that very specialized ensemble. I must have done OK as I went on the live shoot and the leader of the brass band asked if I had any more pieces they could play.

I continued to arrange various pieces in a variety of styles for commercials until the fateful day when a Dutch advertising agency couldn't license a piece of music for a baby food commercial and asked me if I could compose something for them instead. *Et voilà*, I was a commercials composer! Thus began a career of writing, arranging and producing over 4,000 spots worldwide and I owe it all to Olvarit.

I found that my background in English literature and fascination with movies helped me immeasurably when dealing with non-musicians. Someone once said when you enter a roomful of people for a meeting on a commercial which may include clients, agency people, directors and their producers, editors and others, they will all know who you are, but you may well struggle to remember who they are. A tip I was given in my early days of composing for the media was "find out whose voice is the most important and carries the most weight on a project." It sounds pretty cynical, but on quite a few occasions that knowledge would have saved a lot of wasted time and effort. If someone said, "Can you make it more green?" or "What's that instrument they use when people are really sick?" it's not too much of a stretch to be able to answer rather than throw whole notes and time signatures at people who haven't a clue what you're talking about. One unfortunate by-product for me of this use of psychology was I inherited a number of "difficult" clients who liked working with me as other composers refused to go near them!

Something I learned very early in my career was to be very wary of genre suggestions. "I like jazz" could mean Louis Armstrong or Ornette Coleman. "I don't like jazz but I do like Ella Fitzgerald/Frank Sinatra etc." "Classical music" can mean Bach or Stravinsky. "Country" could refer to Dolly Parton or hoedowns. So, I would always push further to find out what people actually meant. In addition, one had to take on board and respect cultural differences across the globe. George Fenton told me that when he, Richard Attenborough and Ravi Shankar were discussing how to score a frightening scene for *Ghandi*, Ravi suggested using "that scary instrument that instantly suggests terror." After coming up with many suggestions for what he might mean, George admitted defeat. "I remember," exclaimed Ravi, "a xylophone!"

I also began working on movies and theatre arrangements – both assignments came about in totally random ways. My knowledge of 1920s dance bands had landed me the gig as chief arranger for the Pasadena Roof Orchestra, which specialized in early jazz and dance music. They were asked to contribute period pieces to the score of a movie – *Just a Gigolo* – starring the unlikely combination of David Bowie and Marlene Dietrich, directed by David Hemmings and set in early 1930s Berlin. The first sequence we were to record was to accompany a spectacular Busby Berkeley dance sequence interrupted by the arrival of the Nazi stormtroopers. I asked to see the sequence and was told there was a problem with the film stock and was given a metronome marking with a proviso that the track should disintegrate around three minutes when the Nazis broke up the screening. The problem turned out to be that German customs had impounded the movie as bills hadn't been paid! That set the tone for the whole project – Bowie refused to leave Berlin to shoot his scenes with Dietrich, who refused to leave Paris. Therefore, the scenes where they were supposedly together were intercut to give the impression they were in the same room. When I finally saw the finished movie the dance scene had gone and the music was used for a party sequence. Of course, the music disintegrated at the agreed moment but the party carried on! The other tracks I had written and recorded were now repeated throughout the film and had in effect become the score. I went to the premiere of the film where somehow the editor's copy had been sent with several takes of various scenes. Welcome to the world of international movies!

Bowie's saxophone teacher was Ronnie Ross, who was a mainstay of my big band and sessions. It is he who plays the baritone solo on 'Walk on the Wild Side' by Lou Reed which David produced dressed as Ziggy Stardust. David had asked for Ronnie who didn't remember him and certainly didn't recognize him "in character". Whenever Ronnie was later interviewed by Bowie biographers, he would tell them what they wanted to hear as he had no idea how many lessons he'd given the young David. I later arranged a track for Goldie on which David Bowie performed, and David and I fondly reminisced about the one time we sat together at Ronnie Scott's club listening to the Charlie Watts Quintet. Occasionally Ronnie Ross would be booked on a recording session and be asked to play "like the saxophone soloist on 'Walk on the Wild Side'". To which he would respond, "I *am* the saxophone soloist on 'Walk on the Wild Side'!"

My introduction to the theatre was equally random. I noticed in the newspaper that the great songwriter Jule Styne (*Gypsy*, *Funny Girl*) was coming to London to score a musical version of *Bar Mitzvah Boy* with lyricist Don Black. Don had been my mentor from the early days, and continued for many years to suggest me for gigs that I thought were way beyond my capacity. I really wanted to meet Jule, so I phoned Don and we had a good chat, but even when he mentioned he was working with Jule I couldn't seize the moment to ask if I could possibly meet him sometime. The next evening, I was at home when the phone rang – it was Don. "You know I'm working with Jule Styne? There's a song we've written and I think you should arrange it. Can you be at Arthur Schwartz's house in Knightsbridge tomorrow morning at 9?"

Arthur was another great writer of the classic American songbook ('That's Entertainment' etc.) and I'd got to know him while he lived in London. So, I thought, "Here goes nothing" and made my way to Walton Street. There to greet me were Don, Jule, the great arranger Irwin Kostal (*West Side Story*, *The Sound of Music* etc.), producer Martin Charnin (lyricist of *Annie*) and choreographer Peter Gennaro. One of the first songs that I'd absorbed on the family radiogram was an obscure tune, 'I Don't Want Anybody At All', written by Jule Styne and Herb Magidson, and recorded by the Charlie Barnet band. I'd always harboured this fantasy that I would meet Jule one day, tell him about this song and we'd instantly bond. So I blurted out this story and his eyes lit up. "You know that song? I wrote it for Roy Rogers and his horse!" He ran over to the piano and started singing and playing it. When he got to the middle eight, he paused and muttered, "I can't remember the bridge section."

I edged onto the piano stool, and we finished the song four-handed. He then hugged me and said, "We're going to get along great!" And we did – he told me many wonderful stories about his early career as a pianist in Chicago mixing with all the jazz giants of the mid- and late 1920s. He was astonished that I could recite the full personnel of the 1927 Ben Pollack band and told me with delight about bundling his bandmate Glenn Miller into a car and driving a hundred miles to hear Bix Beiderbecke, whom Miller had never heard in person. I once asked him what his favourite recording of all his songs was – Frank Sinatra's version of 'Guess I'll Hang My Tears Out to Dry'. As soon as I heard Jule's song I knew why I'd got the call – it was a rock song, way out of Irwin's comfort zone. However, the first couple of bars had four chord changes – not any sort of rock music I'd ever heard. So, I simplified the chord sequence, changed the beat and hired a great rock vocalist to perform it. Jule was charging round the recording studio control room chuckling, "I've written a rock song!" Reading his biography a good few years later, I discovered he'd punched a Broadway arranger who dared to change one of his chords. I got off pretty lightly!

Unfortunately, the song I arranged never made it past the previews and the show was a flop, but it was quite a baptism of fire. Welcome to the world of musical theatre!

The only long-running stage production I was involved was when I subbed on baritone sax for the Ghanaian saxophonist George Larnyoh in the West End show *The Black Mikado* when he had to return home for a month. George had adapted *The Mikado* to showcase an all-black cast. I'm sure the show wouldn't have played in the modern politically correct era, but this was a different time. The band were onstage wearing loincloths – as the only white musician I felt rather self-conscious to say the least. The cast was amazingly talented – it included Floella (later Lady) Benjamin, Patti Boulaye, Derek Griffiths (who did his best to make the band laugh every night), Norman Beaton and Michael Denison. I soon realized that I didn't really have the appetite to play in a long-running show and I marvelled at friends who spent fourteen years in the band for musicals such as *Miss Saigon*. Years later, when I wrote some music for Terence Frisby's musical adaptation of his memoir *Kisses on a Postcard*, I went to see a performance of it in Barnstaple in Devon (where he'd been evacuated during the war) and seeing the pleasure the audience gained from a night at the theatre, especially since they left whistling my "showstopping" song (thanks, *Daily Telegraph*!) rekindled my love of live stage musicals – sadly, despite great reviews it never got a West End showcase. (Although it is being kept alive by Terence's family so you never know!)

Meanwhile my friendship with Van Morrison had intensified to the point where I was included in any musical plans he was making. For the TV show *So It Goes*, the brainchild of Factory Records' Tony Wilson, Van was booked with Dr. John on keyboards, Mick Ronson of David Bowie fame on guitar, Mo Foster on bass, and Pete van Hooke on drums. This band performed the first half of the evening at Maunkberry's Jermyn Street nightclub in front of an invited audience. The second half of the show was a jam session where this line-up was joined by organist Brian Auger, guitarists Bobby Tench and Ray Russell, vocalist Roger Chapman and me on baritone sax. The music came alive and the session is still fondly remembered by all the participants. Needless to say, it still languishes un-broadcast somewhere in the Granada TV archives. But our onstage charisma sparked something in Van as we began collaborating on re-arranging and adapting his whole back catalogue – a task that ultimately led me into his band as musical director.

Figure 23: Van Morrison, me, Dr. John and Mick Ronson (from the back) after our showcase/TV special at Maunkberrys in London, 1977. Author's collection.

9 Sir Van the Man

In 1978 trumpeter Digby Fairweather and I drove down to Richard Branson's studio, the Manor in Oxfordshire, to contribute some horns to Van Morrison's album *Wavelength*. We arrived at around 10am to find Van had gone into town for a massage. So, we sat and waited. By 6pm it was pretty obvious that we wouldn't be recording that day, so we drove back to London. We never did get to work on that record, but Van then asked me to join the band touring on the back of the album's release and to rework more of his classic arrangements. This time around, he was staying with his friend the songwriter and producer Kenny Young in Oxford and Pete van Hooke drove me down to the house. The idea was that he would record with Kenny, and Van and I would commence writing in earnest.

As we got closer to Kenny's place, the snow started coming down in droves and by the time we got there, about 10am, it was drifting quite considerably. Pete went into the studio, while I sat in the kitchen nursing a cup of hot chocolate and waiting for Van. And I waited and waited. At about 7pm Van materialized and said, "This weather is ghastly. Shall we head back to London?" I agreed and we took off in Van's hire car, average speed around 70mph, on sheet ice! After a while I stopped gripping the dashboard and relaxed and we reached central London in about 40 minutes. I caught a taxi home and by the time I got there I found myself snowed in – for a week. I called Van at his hotel to let him know I wasn't going to come in, only to be told, "Oh, he checked out this morning. No forwarding address!"

I rang Kenny to see if he'd had second thoughts and headed back to Oxford – negative. And there the trail ended for about a week with the concert tour looming. No phone call, no anything. Finally, I was unburdening my growing anxiety to Pete, who said, "Oh, Van's at the Royal Garden hotel with Phil Lynott, front man of the band Thin Lizzy. I just spoke to him." I rang the hotel, got put through to a blithely unconcerned Van Morrison, who said, "Yeah, come on over." A couple of hours later I was ensconced in his suite with Phil Lynott, a room service meal and sheafs of music score paper.

The Royal Garden hotel in those days was quite a musician's social hub, probably because of its proximity to the Royal Albert Hall. Van, Phil and I gatecrashed a record company reception for Marie Osmond at which Chalkie Davies took a famous photo of Van desperately trying to avoid Marie's hug! One evening Van and I coincided with Billy Joel and his band and spent the whole night swapping stories. Another legendary evening saw George Harrison take a suite of rooms so he could buy a drink at the bar (for Clapton and Van) as a hotel guest after being refused late-night service while waiting for Bob Dylan to emerge from his room. (Bob never showed up!)

I have to say that writing for Van was one of the easiest and most pleasant jobs I've ever had. He left everything up to me. I already had the rhythm charts locked in from his previous tour but added horns and violin and modified some of the rhythm parts accordingly. If I had said, "'Brown Eyed Girl' is now reggae," he would reply, "OK, just show me where to come in."

Incidentally, I did write an arrangement of 'Brown Eyed Girl', and we did perform it, contrary to the received information that for years he never played that song live. With the tragic recent passing of Chick Corea, guitarist Larry Carlton posted an all-star video of Van Morrison performing in 1990 with Larry, Freddie Hubbard, Herbie Hancock and Chick. I was astonished and deeply affected to hear my arrangement of 'Moondance' performed, eleven years after I wrote it.

The music came together in no time, once I got into the groove of writing. Rehearsals went well, and off went the band and roadies to Ireland for shows in Cork, Belfast and Dublin, with a movie crew in tow including two debutants: the future BAFTA-winning director Michael Radford and the Oscar-winning cameraman Sir Roger Deakins. Our trip to Belfast was at the height of the Troubles. We were told by the management that if we wanted to back out, we could, but no one did. Van was the first homegrown artist to return to Belfast to perform since the bombings had begun, and we were all treated like conquering heroes. Still, it was surreal to see tanks on the streets, army snipers on the roofs, bombed-out bars and storefronts and barbed wire all round our hotel. Not only did we have to enter single file and be thoroughly searched but the machine gunners on top of the hotel didn't exactly calm our nerves. The shows were wonderful and can be found on YouTube – the band was roaring, and Van was on top form. Apparently, tickets for the Belfast show were exchanging on the black market for hundreds of pounds. When we arrived at the venue, I noticed two guys looking forlornly at the stage door. I discovered they were huge fans who had been unable to obtain tickets and had come to catch a glimpse of Van before or after the show. I fished out two complimentary tickets from my pocket and they were in! I completely forgot about this, but some twenty-five years later I'd been given the phone number of the organizer of the Belfast Jazz Festival to see if it was possible to get my big band booked. During our conversation he said, "You won't remember me, but I was one of the guys to whom you gave passes in Belfast for Van Morrison!" I'm afraid that act of kindness still didn't get me a jazz festival booking! I'm told that the young, then unknown, members of U2 were hanging around Dublin waiting for a word from their hero Van, but I honestly have no recollection of that.

Our London shows at what was then the Hammersmith Odeon were interesting. Van was never particularly fond of playing in London and quite often we would come offstage into the afterparty to find all the food and drink being consumed by a throng of people none of us knew! One night I went onstage with a splitting headache and motioned for the tour manager to find some ibuprofen. During a ballad feature for Katie Kissoon, I was able to leave the stage and quickly take the pills. Van was also backstage and asked me what I was doing. I showed him the pills and he said, "I've got a splitting headache, I'll take some too."

Figure 24: Van and Eric Clapton in a Portsmouth hotel, 1979. Author's collection.

What we hadn't realized was that Katie's song merited a moody spotlight which illuminated our ten-foot shadows on the backdrop behind Katie, so the audience got to see us happily popping pills backstage. One afternoon before the gig, I was in the newsagent adjacent to a London hotel, when I fell into conversation with a cinematic hero of mine, the wonderful actor Tony Franciosa. He was shooting *The World Is Full of Married Men* in London and cheekily I asked if he fancied a couple of tickets to the Van Morrison gig that night. Not only did he come along, but he sent me a charming note thanking me for a great evening out.

The tour around the UK continued successfully through the early months of 1979 and we found ourselves in Edinburgh. In the hotel bar I played the piano while Van sang standards. An American businessman went up to Van and said, "You sound good – have you ever thought of doing this for a living?" Van and his fellow Northern Irish singer and guitarist Herbie Armstrong had played music together since their teens and, sitting in Henderson's wine bar at lunchtime after our gig the previous night, they started telling hilarious stories about their early days in Irish showbands. Soon everyone in the restaurant had gathered round and the laughter and bonhomie rang out. Several of the patrons were aware we were to play Glasgow that night and said, "We're all going to come along – it should be quite a night!"

We got to the Glasgow Apollo and sound-checked without Van. All was in order. When it came to gig time, we all took our places for 'Moondance', our tour manager announced Van and off we went. As musical director it was my job to watch Van to see when I needed to cut off the band at the end of the song, so I looked round to gauge the moment – and there was no one there! The voice was booming out over the sound system but there was no sign of Van the Man. Apparently, he had come out onstage, saw the huge drop from the stage to the stalls and bolted behind the bass amplifier from where he was singing. Amid cries of, "We can't see you!" from the notoriously tricky Glasgow audience and with only me in plain view at the front of the stage, we anticipated a riot. We got through the gig (twenty minutes and no encores) and fled backstage to find our boss incandescent with rage. "No one told me about that drop – it's not safe and someone could get killed!" (A bit extreme, we all thought, until our lighting man later went on to Kate Bush's tour and fell to a tragic demise down an open trap door in a Bristol theatre.) I headed to the stage door where the Edinburgh contingent were waiting, looking like the audience for "Springtime for Hitler" in *The Producers*.

The rest of the tour passed without incident except the snow fell heavily in the north of England and, after the final show in Newcastle, Van decided he wanted to head back to the comparative warmth of London. I couldn't blame him. I'd played this show in an overcoat wearing gloves and hadn't need to remove either item during a set where I was usually drenched with perspiration. What this meant was a six-hour bus drive arriving at the Royal Garden hotel at 7am. Van got out a guitar, Beatles songs were sung, and I fell asleep. I woke up around 4am to one of the weirdest moments I've ever experienced: Van Morrison was standing next to me, strumming a guitar, and singing 'Do-re-mi' from *The Sound of Music*! I thought I was still dreaming.

A few months later, a slightly stripped-down band went off to Europe. My old university pal Pete Wingfield had replaced keyboard player Peter Bardens, and I was the only saxophonist. We played a couple of shows on the

French Riviera, then went on to Belgium to play the Bilzen Festival. I've never been a fan of pop festivals but the line-up for this one was pretty special. It included The Police, The Pretenders, AC/DC, The Specials, Whitesnake, Uriah Heep, Nils Lofgren and, particularly exciting for me, Sonny Terry and Brownie McGhee. I gathered they weren't exactly the best of friends, but I had been a fan of their authentic blues since I was a 13-year-old neophyte. So, I was delighted to find myself in a dressing room empty except for Brownie McGhee warming up. He was playing unaccompanied Bach! I listened with my mouth open; as he finished, he looked up at me, smiled, and said, "Don't tell anyone!"

Figure 25: Van Morrison band onstage during the UK tour, 1979. Author's collection.

We went on to Scandinavia. In Denmark I was delighted that when we arrived on the Wednesday in Copenhagen, we were staying opposite the famous Montmartre jazz club. From my window I could see the mouthwatering programme for Tuesday and Thursday nights, plus the fatal words "Wednesday – closed." We arrived in Stockholm, and I went for a walk in the park. Immediately I saw a man running towards me with a briefcase. Behind him was another man chasing him, obviously shouting in Swedish, "Stop, stop!" As the thief ran past me, I thought "I could be a hero here and trip him – hang on a minute I'd have to go to court and we're only here for one day." By the time these thoughts had flashed through my mind he was gone – I hope there was nothing important in the case. (A few years later in Brighton I was able to trip a racist bully chasing a terrified Chinese student and shouting hateful venom. As he passed me, I stuck out a foot, he went flying and three people jumped on top of him to restrain him, while I strolled away in the sunshine.) In Stockholm I developed an inner-ear infection and played seated on a chair, standing only to solo, with two roadies ready to catch me should I pass out. I remember nothing about the show, but apparently I got a great review in the Swedish press!

During our Stockholm stay, Swedish television ran the Rutles movie, *All You Need Is Cash*, with Swedish subtitles. As Van had never seen the show – no video copies were available back then – Pete Wingfield, our interpreter and I crammed into Van's room to watch it on TV. A lot of Eric Idle's hilarious wordplay sadly got lost in translation – according to our translator the subtitle for "A legend in his own lunchtime" read, "He was very famous during the dinner hour." And they say humour is universal!

On we went to Norway. In Oslo my walk took me into a wonderful museum where I was the only visitor, examining the priceless artworks with no sign of staff or other patrons. I took lots of photos both inside and out. When I showed them later to a Norwegian friend, he exclaimed, "That's the Royal Palace!" In Bergen, where it supposedly rains most of the year, the sun beat down and concertgoers arriving early and shown to their seats were astonished to find Van sitting in the stalls engrossed in a book.

Figure 26: European tour jacket – "Into The Music." Author's collection.

Our Rotterdam show in a packed velodrome was something extra special – one of the only times in my life where everything I played seemed absolutely right. Van and the audience picked up on it, and I was featured on solo after solo. A big change from the UK tour where I'd given myself one and a half solos in the whole show!

After we played in Rotterdam, we were due to fly to Edinburgh to headline an open-air festival with Talking Heads and Squeeze, among others. We never played on the day we travelled, so a leisurely evening at the Edinburgh Festival was in store that night. Or so we thought. Due to fog, the flight was delayed by three, four, five, then six hours. Our tour manager had been robbed of all the takings for this European jaunt while he showered that morning in the hotel, so he was already anxious. He saw Van pacing up and down and made an executive decision – to hire a six-seater plane. A couple of the guys volunteered to go with him. As they departed, the tannoy announced our flight was boarding. The airline was East Anglia Airlines – I have never heard of them before or since. The pilot came on the speaker and announced we would have one attempt to land in Edinburgh, if unsuccessful we would try Glasgow, if that was no good it was to be Aberdeen and a six-hour coach trip down to Edinburgh!

The collective groan of the passengers turned to cheers when the fog lifted just long enough to allow us to land in Edinburgh at a deserted airport – no baggage handlers, no passport control, no customs. We unloaded the luggage, located our bags and one enterprising fellow found a telephone and ordered a fleet of taxis to take us all to the one hotel that happened to be open, which luckily was ours. So, crew and passengers all decamped to the hotel bar – there were no other guests as all the roads north were closed. We all got on famously and I think we might even have been indulging in a singsong when, three hours later, an ashen-faced tour manager and a couple of our band staggered into the bar. They had been thrown about in their six-seater, refused landing at Edinburgh, Glasgow and Edinburgh again, and finally found a private airport about 30 miles outside Edinburgh which had allowed them to land. I have to say that their predicament wasn't helped by our gloating.

The gig the following day made up for all the aggravation, with Talking Heads and Squeeze in support and The Chieftains joining us for a few tunes. By now I'd made up my mind that this was the end of my short touring life. I wasn't going to go to the States for the next leg of the tour, but I would try my luck as an arranger and composer in London. I had married in 1977 and decided once and for all that touring all over the world out of a suitcase was definitely not for me. I was replaced by James Brown's musical director and co-composer, saxophonist Pee Wee Ellis and future movie composer Mark Isham on trumpet – not bad choices! But Van and I stayed friends thereafter. A few years later I was playing at a launch party for the Soho Jazz Festival in Central London, closed my eyes to solo and when I opened them, Van and his then-musical director were standing right in front of me. Van said to his young bandleader, "If you want to write anything for me, go to John for lessons!" He also told me I could write anything for him anytime I chose, just to send it in. A nice endorsement.

10 More Legends (2)

(Paul Kossoff, Bob Marley, Peter Cook, Dudley Moore, John Ogdon, Spike Milligan, Mick Jagger, George Harrison)

I first met Paul Kossoff, son of actor David, and later lead guitarist for the band Free and composer of the classic 'All Right Now', when we were both 13-year-olds starting our respective musical journeys. In the earliest days I even had to tune his guitar for him while he held an E chord. Soon he became one of the brightest lights on the rock scene, respected the world over. Unfortunately, he also picked up a terrible drug habit along the way. When I was at Sussex University the blues society would often book Free, and Paul and I would get together to reminisce and grab a quick meal before the show. Success had mellowed his personality considerably and once I'd moved back to London, we re-established contact and started frequenting the jamming sessions that proliferated around town at the time. By now he had quit Free and was busy playing sessions and getting his own band off the ground. He was playing well and apparently thriving.

One evening in 1976, I had taken a first date to Ronnie Scott's club – a girl who later married my closest friend. As we left the club a voice called out, literally from the gutter in the road, "John, John!"

I hoped the John in question wasn't me but looked round to see Paul lying in the road. "Lend me £10," he muttered.

"Sorry Paul, I can't," I replied, shepherding my horrified date away towards my parked car.

"Then can you give me a lift to Notting Hill?"

"Sorry Paul I'm heading north!" I responded, as we made a hasty exit and I explained that Paul was one of the best-known musicians on the scene, adored by millions. I don't think she quite believed me or was too impressed by the company I kept. A matter of weeks later, he passed away on a flight from LA to New York. I was racked with guilt and confided to a close friend, "Maybe this wouldn't have happened if I'd helped him that night?"

"Don't be daft, he would have probably died that night if you'd facilitated him getting his hands on more drugs!" Nearly a half a century later he still ranks as a giant among "rock gods". Gone far too soon.

I can't claim to have known Bob Marley too well, although I was good friends with several of the Wailers, but the conversations I had with him were quite illuminating, once I got used to the Jamaican accent. At that time in the early 1970s, it was quite unusual for a middle-class white Londoner to hear patois. I remember being horrified when I was at Eddy Grant's studio and a guy wandered in and started speaking patois. I assumed he was poking fun at the band, until I realized he was a white Jamaican. Bob told me his father was a white English soldier – common knowledge now, but I don't think anyone in the UK realized then that Bob Marley was mixed race and half English. I remember being backstage at the famous Lyceum show – Bob was then probably best known for writing Eric Clapton's version of 'I Shot the Sheriff' – and I said to my pal Pete van Hooke, "If he can cross over into the mainstream, he'll be the biggest thing in popular music!" We mostly talked about soccer and a bit of cricket – Bob was a terrific soccer player and a Spurs supporter. I played him some of my music – one of his executives at Island Records defined the tracks as "Frank Zappa meets Shorty Rogers" – and he expressed puzzlement mixed with admiration at my cheeky bravery. I think the music had the same effect on Pat Simmons of the Doobie Brothers and everyone else who heard it, including the musicians who played it! It's certainly languished on my shelf for nearly fifty years. I'm often asked the same question about Bob, Nick Drake, Amy Winehouse, John Legend and Freddie Mercury among others that I've been lucky enough to get to know "on the way up", which is "Were you aware that x was going to achieve legendary status?" I can only answer by saying "I was convinced their talents would all be recognized in some way, but then I was certain that other wonderful performers/writers would achieve success – some did, and some didn't. I was lucky to be surrounded by great talents throughout my time in music and I hope it was no coincidence that I was frequently in the musical company of artists who have become legendary.

I met both Peter Cook and Dudley Moore around the same time in the late 1970s. Peter, as I mentioned earlier, appeared in *The Secret Policeman's Ball*. A mark of the respect he garnered was that every other comedian on the bill, from the veterans to young Rowan Atkinson, would crowd into the wings to watch when Peter was onstage. Not being a drinker, I never moved into his domestic orbit, but we would meet for morning tea or coffee at his favourite Hampstead coffee shop, and I still have a cassette tape of songs he wrote with the local Hampstead tramp, Bronco John. It was typical of Peter to find a true eccentric who had at one time been a very competent pianist and now shuffled round his north London patch carrying his own teabags with him. Another Hampstead character, Rainbow George, recorded the first meeting between Peter and Bronco on his reel-to-reel machine – the recording is on YouTube ("Ere you're that bloke off the telly!" says Bronco). Peter always struck me as a very unhappy, lonely man. During his later years he regularly phoned the all-night chat shows on LBC pretending to be a taxi driver or an enraged pensioner. It was funny and tragic at the same time. He was insanely jealous of Dudley's Hollywood success – his well-documented battles with alcoholism were such a waste of an exceptional talent. He once asked my occasional flatmate Craig Ferguson, "How can you be funny when you're sober?" And he genuinely meant it.

Figure 27: *Secret Policeman's Ball*, photocall 1979. Back row: Des Jones, Michael Palin, Rob Buckman; Middle: Chris Beetles, John Cleese, Peter Cook, Neil Innes; Front: John Williams, Eleanor Bron, Terry Jones, Rowan Atkinson. Author's collection.

Dudley Moore was another exceptional talent whose last tragic illness was sadly misunderstood by many to be the effect of alcohol. To me he was a great musician, a very funny man and an unlikely sex symbol after his starring role in *10* catapulted him to sudden worldwide fame. I used to go to his restaurant in Market Street, Venice Beach where he would play the piano, unrecognized, for his own amusement. He was my guest at the LA premiere of the movie *Hear My Song* for which I wrote the score. As we walked the red carpet, screaming and yelling broke out spontaneously. "See," I said to him. "You've still got it!" At that moment we both realized that Madonna was on the red carpet directly in front of us.

His comedic brilliance tended to overshadow his huge musical talent – as a pianist and composer he was and is vastly underrated. (Although Ronnie Ross told me that when Dudley first joined the John Dankworth band his playing was so relentlessly busy that the whole band would glare at him throughout the gigs. He soon learnt.) The last time I saw Dudley, at a Mancini Institute concert, he was in a wheelchair, unable to speak or move his limbs but obviously enjoying listening to the music. All I could do was give him a big hug and a smile. As we would say, a real *mensch*. When he was a huge Hollywood star, he would take bookings for his jazz trio charging ridiculous amounts of money, which he would then split three ways. He is much missed.

One of my favourite pianists was the reclusive and troubled John Ogdon. I had long admired his championing and recording of "lesser known" piano works by British composers of the twentieth century such as Cyril Scott, C.W. Orr, E.J. Moeran and Constant Lambert. A friend had tried to get me to attend her regular dinner parties in North London without much success, and finally I agreed to look in one evening after attending a David Sanborn gig at the Hammersmith Odeon. I should have sensed that there would be problems, as I arrived clad in a leather jacket to find the party attired in tuxedos! I was then subjected to an uncomfortable inquisition by the bejewelled (and mostly titled) guests as to who exactly this David Sanborn was. (One of the great modern saxophonists fluent across the jazz spectrum, from straight-ahead modern jazz to the avant-garde via the fusion genre – certainly a versatile ground breaker.)

Luckily, I was seated opposite John Ogdon and his very talented wife, Brenda Lucas – but sadly he was in his well-documented semi-catatonic state. I attempted to break the ice by mentioning that my regular pianist Simon Chamberlain was the son of his music teacher, and his face lit up as he praised Simon's versatility and wished he could cross the genres as effortlessly. Cheered by this breakthrough, I started discussing some of my favourite British composers and he became extremely excited. "Do you know the Constant Lambert piano sonata? I'll play it for you!" And he ran to the piano – apparently the hostess had been trying in vain to encourage him to play for years with no success. My triumph soon turned sour – the piece was very dissonant and lasted for twenty minutes or so. It made Cecil Taylor sound like

Russ Conway. All the smiles turned to glares and as the last note died away our hostess virtually yelled, "Now play some Chopin!" Thankfully he did but I was never invited back.

I was recording at Air Studios, which was on the top floor of a department store in Oxford Street. I got into the elevator and the only other passenger was the legendary comedian Spike Milligan. We nodded at each other, then I said, "You know, you're a great friend of my uncle." Woolf had conducted the classic *Goon Show* on several occasions and lived next door to Peter Sellers for a while. Spike responded, "That's amazing as *you're* a good friend of *my* uncle!" (Woolf had told me that when Spike rang him, Woolf politely enquired "how are you?" Spike's response was "what are you now, my doctor??") As we reached the ground floor he said, "Shall we share a cab?" We got in and he gave the address in Bayswater where his office was situated. We chatted all the way and, when he got out, the cab driver asked me, "Where to?" "Air Studios in Oxford Street," I replied to his astonishment. My car was parked around the corner, but I couldn't pass up a ride with Spike.

In later years we saw a lot of each other at various jazz events – he was a big fan of jazz and incredibly of mine. One evening stands out – we were both sitting together in the basement bar at Ronnie Scott's where the musicians tended to congregate. (It's no longer there.) On television was a very moving documentary, with Spike talking in great detail about his mental illnesses, while Spike, sitting next to me, was making hilarious comments about the man talking on television. It was as if it was someone else's life onscreen – very unsettling. A true one-off. His tombstone read, "I told you I was ill!"

My relationships with the members of the Rolling Stones are quite varied. I've played cricket with Bill Wyman for over thirty years, been in the company of the late Charlie Watts occasionally for over fifty years, either at jazz clubs or cricket matches, long-time Stones' associates Darryl Jones and Tim Ries are good pals, I've been friends with Ronnie Wood's late brother Ted (and more recently met up with Ronnie himself), have never met Keith Richards, and have played a lot with their original pianist, the late Ian Stewart – a fine exponent of the art of boogie-woogie (once with Charlie on drums). He was a founder member of the Rolling Stones who was unceremoniously dumped from the band by Andrew Oldham because he "didn't have the right look." However, he elected to remain with the band as road manager and offstage pianist. Stu was a very funny man – he once told me of a Stones gig where Mick Taylor joined Keith and Ronnie on guitar.

"How did it sound?" I asked innocently.

"How do you think it sounded? Dreadful racket!"

Days before his sudden early demise, I bumped into him at Cambridge Circus in London and we made plans to play together a few weeks in the future. Sadly, that wasn't to be.

As for Mick Jagger, apart from sitting next to him at the original live performance of *Tubular Bells* and then at the dinner later that evening, and participating in the Rutles movie, I've only ever had one encounter with him. I was at Bryan Adams' Chelsea home discussing a possible collaboration, when I mentioned I was on my way to play a gig that night, hence I had my saxophone with me. As I prepared to leave, Bryan said, "You couldn't do me a favour and play something for my friend?" indicating a closed-circuit TV link to an office obviously in a nearby house (this was long before Skype or Facetime). Obligingly I assembled my saxophone and played rather self-consciously to the camera, assuming that I was serenading a young fan of Bryan's. A head popped up into view and a voice said, "Ooh that sounds good!" It was Bryan's next-door neighbour, Mick Jagger, and I had been well and truly pranked!

Neil Innes was very close to George Harrison. Neil's wife Yvonne landscaped George's gardens and Neil appeared in the video for George's song 'Crackerbox Palace', shot in the same gardens. My own experiences with George were always very pleasant. He produced the original 45rpm release of 'Bright Side of Life', engineered by Steve James (as well as funding the film *Life of Brian* when EMI pulled the plug), and he loved one of the phrases I wrote on the arrangement. He always used to sing it to me whenever we met, instead of saying hello. I'd written something, where the strings went (singing) "Always look on the bright side of life da da deeeeee, da da daa da-da dahhh," a little "Hollywood musical" string phrase behind the whistling. George would always sing that phrase whenever he saw me, "da da deeee, da da daa da-da dahhhh…" and he insisted that they take out the whistle in order for that phrase to come through. So that was George's contribution to the mix of 'Bright Side of Life'. I was delighted to learn that the record featured prominently thereafter on his home jukebox, and he would always point out that phrase and my French horn counter melody to his visitors.

George was the invisible presence on the Rutles, always encouraging and prodding and prompting in the background. He listened to our recordings with a critical ear – once when asked if The Beatles would ever get back together, he responded, "I doubt it, but I hope the Rutles do!" His little cameo as a news reporter with Michael Palin as Apple publicist Derek Taylor stands out because people didn't recognize him in the film! I cherish his response to a journalist's question about whether he appreciated the film. He said "The Rutles sort of liberated me from The Beatles in a way. It was the only thing I saw of those Beatles television shows they made. It was actually the best, funniest and most scathing. But at the same time, it was done with the most love." On another occasion he complained to Neil Innes that Ollie Halsall's guitar solo on 'Love Life' (the 'All You Need Is Love' parody) was a send-up of George's guitar playing. "Well… yes," answered Neil. That seemed to satisfy George! Neil told me that he once visited George at his home, Friar Park, to find George and Bob Dylan playing ukuleles and singing along with a George Formby recording 'When I'm Cleaning Windows'! For those who don't know, George Formby was a very popular Lancastrian comedian onstage and in movies in the 1930s and beyond until his untimely passing in the early 1960s. (My uncle Woolf conducted his last ever TV special.) Possibly the biggest musical comedy star in the UK, he was famous for his innuendo-filled songs. I reference him when I talk about my score for the movie *God on the Rocks* in Chapter 13.

Figure 28: George Harrison with the Rutles ukulele. Author's collection.

I went to many events with Olivia Harrison, George's wife, in the 1990s in various countries in the company of director Hugh Hudson (*Chariots of Fire*), designer Elizabeth Emanuel, and Aninha, wife of the drummer/songwriter Jim Capaldi for the band Traffic. These included a jam session with Vangelis at his housewarming party where we played 'Blue Monk' together, with the roof open to the Parisian skies (with Roman Polanski of all people sitting cross-legged at my feet) and the premiere of a ballet written by Vangelis choreographed by Wayne Eagling in Amsterdam. At the after party one of the dancers brought the assistant choreographer over to see us. Trembling, he asked Olivia for her autograph as he had clandestinely played Beatles records with his friends in the Soviet Union in the 1960s. If caught they could have faced jail. Olivia said, "I'm nobody really, give me your address and I'll get George to write you a letter." The choreographer was in tears, as were we.

A slight (related) diversion – the morning after the premiere, I was due to fly back to London and make my way straight to Lord's cricket ground for that season's Ashes test match between England and Australia. Erroll, the Australian physio, was to leave a ticket in my name on the main gate. At this point in time (1993) the cricket was still shown on BBC1 TV, which was available to view in my Amsterdam hotel room. I was watching the opening overs of the match but thought I should telephone to ensure that I had a ticket. It was easy in those days to get through to the Australian dressing room: you just called the switchboard at Lord's and asked to be put through. As I was connected and someone in the room answered, I asked to speak to Erroll. At that moment the camera panned to the Australian balcony and I saw Erroll get up and walk into the changing room to pick up the phone. The camera stayed on him as I said, "You won't believe this but I'm sitting in a hotel room in Amsterdam watching you on national television talking to me!" Not only did I get to the game later that day, I found myself sitting with Charlie Watts!

When George sadly became very ill, he wanted to watch a copy of *The Point* with the original Dustin Hoffman narration and songs by our old friend Harry Nilsson. I was based in Los Angeles at the time and after vainly scouring many video shops I was able to locate a copy for him in Santa Monica. I was in Hollywood working on a movie when the memorial concert for George was held at the Royal Albert Hall and I was very sorry to have missed contributing to it.

In the early 2010s I got a call from my old friend Martin Lewis who was producing an all-star 50th anniversary tribute album of the songs of Bob Dylan for Amnesty International. Apart from writing a string quartet chart for Pete Seeger's final recording ('Forever Young') my involvement was to write a 1940s style arrangement of the only song co-written by Dylan and George Harrison – 'I'd Have You Any Time'. I put together an amazing band – the Springtimers – consisting of pianist/composer/solo artist Patrice Rushen, Laurence Juber – the former guitarist with Wings, Herbie Hancock's bass player Ed Livingston, Clayton Cameron – the drummer of choice for Sammy Davis Jr and later for Tony Bennett, and George's old friend and colleague, saxophonist Tom Scott. To sing the track Martin made a surprising choice – actress/vocalist Evan Rachel Wood who did a fantastic job. The result was a highlight of the album and a different unique tribute to George and his love of the classic American songbook.

I was a last-minute invitee to the premiere of the Scorsese film on George, as Elizabeth Emanuel's "plus one" had to drop out on the morning of the screening. We ran into two of her clients, Barbara Bach and Ringo Starr, and Elizabeth re-introduced me to Ringo who promptly lifted me up in a bear hug! The movie was a wonderful tribute to a great man.

Oh, and did I mention he was a Beatle?

11 An Intrusion and an Explanation

At this point I make no apology for leaving (fairly) strict chronology behind. The next segments of my story are divided into Records, Television, Movies, Commercials and Live Performance, with a nod to my LA life. The truth is I was so lucky to be able to continue all my activities side by side that they overlap considerably, and to tell the story year by year would mean a bewildering series of dizzy leaps between media. For example, in 1994, I had several hit records, worked on hundreds of commercials, had the most successful television series of the 1990s in the UK, wrote for several movies in the UK, USA and France, and played my saxophone in live music settings with an array of performers from Jeff Goldblum to Prince. And that's just one year out of forty. Did I ever sleep, I wonder? In addition, I had three young children (Bob, Mike and Laura) by 1984. And a fourth (Steve) arrived in 1994 during all this mayhem.

So from now on, it will be the medium rather than the chronology that dictates the arc. And the stories keep coming!

One thing that has remained a constant for me – both watching and playing – is the game of cricket. I've mentioned that my return to the cricket pitch in a charity match coincided with a spell of bowling by possibly the greatest fast bowler in the history of the game, Dennis Lillee. This set the scene for my bizarre involvement in cricket, which encompassed playing for years with David English's Bunburys, with and against Prime Minister John Major, Eric Clapton, Bill Wyman, Richard Thompson, Tim Rice, members of Spandau Ballet, a host of top sportsmen from the worlds of football, horse racing, snooker, and of course cricket, plus many leading actors of stage and screen. Over the years I became accepted as a buddy by most of the international teams too, travelling at one point with the all-conquering Australian team as their honorary social secretary, and building lasting friendships with some of the all-time greats – ferrying them round Los Angeles and hosting them at my gigs in the UK, Caribbean, Australia and the USA. Possibly my greatest feat on a cricket pitch was dismissing four England cricket captains in the space of fourteen balls. I intend to write another volume detailing in full my involvement in the great game. I've certainly been privileged to play a part in the sport I love.

Figure 29: With the Rt. Hon. John Major. Author's collection.

I will mention one amusing tale with a slightly relevant musical tie-in about an early Norma Major charity match. Our batting was opened by England test cricketer Chris Broad and former Rolling Stone Bill Wyman. The Major team's opening bowler was Richard Snell, an international cricketer with the South African side, newly readmitted to the world arena following the release of Nelson Mandela. Richard had been briefed that of our two openers, one was a former world-class sportsman and the other was a rock star. Unfortunately Richard, growing up in isolated South Africa, had never seen the Rolling Stones and assumed that the good-looking long-haired Chris Broad was the rock star, lobbing gentle bowling for him to negotiate. For Bill Wyman, whom he assumed was the former international cricketer, he unleashed thunderbolts that peppered the furious Bill's body until it was pointed out that he'd confused the identities of the two batsmen.

Another constant throughout my career in the studio and onstage, whether it be in the UK, the USA, Russia, Australia or France, is that I've been able to surround myself with the finest musicians every time. Many of them I idolized as a youngster, others I grew up with as contemporaries, some I set on the path to their own musical successes. I've always tried to balance experience and youthful enthusiasm in my choice of musicians which has been especially rewarding. (I remember one session when a 16-year-old saxophonist, Nigel Hitchcock, was demonstrating how he achieved a certain effect on his instrument to two veteran players, Bill Skeat and Tommy Whittle – then both in their mid- to late sixties.) Their all-round brilliance is something to marvel at and I try to find out as much as I can about the thousands of virtuosos I have been lucky enough to collaborate with over the years. Apart from their phenomenal musical abilities many of the players have fascinating back stories. The flautist Eddie Beckett is the nephew of the playwright Samuel Beckett and lived with him in Paris in the 1950s. He now runs the Beckett estate. Violinist Tim Good is the acknowledged world-leading expert on UFOs and author of several best-selling books on the subject. Top LA guitarist Grant Geissman has written definitive studies of the great American comic books. Every single one has a fascinating tale to tell concerning how they arrived at the top of the profession, and all the musicians I've worked with during my many years on the world music stage have inspired and motivated me to always give 110 per cent and go above and beyond the call of duty. I salute them for enriching my life and career.

Figure 30: With The Who vocalist Roger Daltrey at a charity cricket match. Author's collection.

12 Records

After I left Van, I continued playing saxophone on recording sessions. One that I particularly recall was playing baritone sax on the album *Stick to Me* by Graham Parker and the Rumour. Another, for all the wrong reasons, was a late-night session for one of my heroes, Marvin Gaye, who at the time was living in London. Sadly, he wasn't in the best shape and the session dragged on through the night as he changed nearly every bar of music. And we never got paid.

Gradually I phased out playing on my own arrangements, as I found my focus was blurred by worrying about how good – or otherwise – I sounded. There were far better studio saxophonists on the scene and by not playing I was able to concentrate 100 per cent on the overall performance. My first major recording as an arranger, away from Neil Innes and the Python crew, was on *Pearls II* for Elkie Brooks in 1982 – some big band charts on a platinum-certified album, for which I'm still not credited either as arranger or conductor. Unfortunately, this is a recurring tale told by arrangers over the years and it wasn't the last time for me either! Many people aren't even sure what an arranger is or does. It's easier to say you wrote the song than to explain your function on a record, where you may have chosen the chords and string and brass lines, written the intro and hook, booked the musicians, conducted the session, supervised the balance of the instruments, and, in many cases, written the part of the song that immediately springs to mind when the title is mentioned (think 'Tears of a Clown', 'Knock on Wood', 'I Will Survive', 'Sweet Caroline', 'Baker Street', 'Careless Whisper' or 'Dancing In The Street'– all instantly recognizable from parts of the arrangement or instrumental solos, none of which are part of the actual song). Heaven forbid that you ask for credit as co-composer or a royalty on the record – that would surely guarantee that you'd never work with the artist or producer again! Several times, after patiently explaining all this, the question I am most frequently asked after a long pause is, "So do you write the words or the music?"

There is quite an air of mystery surrounding the profession of making music, not just arranging. The other question frequently asked of professional musicians is "so what do you do for a living then?" The saxophonist Olaf Vas and a violinist colleague were in the bar opposite the London Palladium between shows they were playing with Tony Bennett, when a woman came up to them.

"I recognize you; you were playing with Tony Bennett. It must be wonderful to make music with such a legend. So tell me, what do you do for a living?"

Before the violinist could answer, Olaf jumped in.

"I'm a steeplejack and he's my hod carrier."

"Oh really, doesn't that hurt your hands playing the violin?"

"Not really, we're used to it."

"Is there enough work being a steeplejack these days?"

"Well, we keep busy doing general building work."

Before they excused themselves to return to the theatre for the second show, they had taken her card and agreed to quote on re-roofing her house!

I once finished a movie score that kept me writing day and night non-stop for two weeks. When I eventually finished the last cue, one mid-afternoon, I jumped in the shower and, refreshed and feeling great, set out for a stroll. Almost immediately I bumped into a neighbour whose only comment was:

"Hello John, not working then?"

What was my process when I was hired as an arranger? If I was writing for a vocalist my first thought was – what can I do to support and enhance their specific talents? If it was an established artist this was a lot easier. One could refer to their body of work and siphon out the qualities they possessed to make them unique. Generally speaking, I wouldn't consciously try to copy their usual musical accompaniments. If I was hired to write for an artist who had collaborated successfully with another arranger, the last thing I would do is attempt to replicate their style. If they'd wanted x, they'd have hired x, was my rationale. So, I would try to give them what I felt they needed, with enough of my own musical personality to indicate my involvement. I never believed that I had to impose my signature on their record, but equally I didn't court anonymity. It's a fine balance but hopefully one I achieved. Logically of course it would be impossible to write in the same way for Rod Stewart or George Michael as one would for Diana Ross or Tina Turner. I don't believe I would have had much of a career had I tried to impose a "John Altman style," whatever that might be, on any artist or producer. I would always treat each song as brand-new or as yet unheard, unless I was doing a faithful takedown of an existing classic arrangement, in which case I would make subtle alterations to make it sound more "contemporary". In truth that word always baffled me as, if the revival was number one in the charts, how could it be more contemporary?

Over the next couple of decades (the 1980s and 1990s) I was very lucky to have been associated with some iconic artists and songs – as an arranger, conductor and occasional producer and reed player – that are fondly remembered to this day. And there are fascinating stories connected to each one.

In 1985 my old friend and colleague Pete Wingfield called me. He had become a major record producer as well as an in-demand keyboard player and a hit artist in his own right ('18 With a Bullet'). The 24-year-old Alison Moyet was riding high as a vocalist, first with the highly successful synth pop duo Yazoo, and then as a solo singer with her number 1 album, *Alf*. She had decided that she wanted to record an obscure Billie Holiday song that was a favourite of her parents. There was no particular commercial intention in doing this, and Pete recognized my expertise in writing a jazz arrangement and restricted his input to producing rather than his usual hands-on involvement in creating the musical accompaniment. My brief was to transcribe the original chart but to make it sound like the 1980s rather than the 1940s. I reworked the horn parts, went for a more modern recording sound, and replaced the string section with a synth that Pete overdubbed to sweeten the track. My selected jazz-oriented studio ensemble convened at a studio I'd never been to, before or since. Pride of place was given to a Swedish grand piano, the make of which I'd equally never heard, before or since. The piano tuner departed, Mick Pyne sat at the piano and played a chord – it was dreadfully out of tune. With mobile phones still some years in the future, there was no way to contact the tuner and we resigned ourselves to a long delay. But we hadn't reckoned on our artist. "I trained as a piano tuner," said Ms Moyet cheerfully, as she produced a bag of tuning equipment from her case and proceeded to climb inside the piano! By the end of the day, we had the finished track. All the musicians left to pursue their other duties and Pete and I stayed to supervise the mix.

A few months later, something bizarre happened. This "vanity project" song, never destined for release, was issued as a single and within a week sat at the top of the charts! It became her biggest selling record ever – and most of the musicians had no idea they were even involved. For example, Mick Pyne was playing a solo piano engagement at Kettners restaurant in Soho, when Peter Boizot, the owner, walked into the middle of the room, hushed the diners and announced, "Today our pianist is top of the charts, and he will now play his version of 'That Ole Devil Called Love'!" All eyes turned on Mick, who had no idea what Peter was talking about – he had read a chord chart about six months previously, had no clue as to what song he was playing or who the artist was, even the title of the song. "What did you do?" I asked him. "Well, I ran my hands up and down the keyboard playing some florid arpeggios. I did get some puzzled looks from the patrons!"

The worldwide success of the single finally prompted me to organize my own big band (more of that later) and Alison gamely agreed to tour with us. At this point she'd never even sung in public – all her success was on recordings done in Vince Clarke's home. Our first assignment was a charity concert attended by Princess Diana, who confessed her love for jazz to me (her exact words were "I wish I could go to more jazz events, but they wouldn't let me!"). When she walked down the line of assembled performers after the show she spoke a little with each musician and singer. She approached my old friend, guitarist and wit extraordinaire Mitch Dalton, who told her he was playing guitar with Alison Moyet. Diana said, "Oh, from the Royal Box you couldn't actually see if there was a guitarist on stage."

Figure 31: Princess Diana and me at the London Palladium – with members of my band and Humphrey Lyttleton (obscured) introducing us. "I love jazz!" Photograph by Richard Young.

"You'd think they'd find someone of your importance a decent seat!" was Mitch's response. I have a photo of a young Jools Holland and myself, watching this exchange apprehensively. Of course, Diana roared with laughter. She was later to present me with my Anthony Asquith award at the British Film Awards and our paths crossed several times after that.

I got on very well with Alison – I found her to be both modest and talented, not always the case with highly successful vocalists. I was impressed by her willingness to try something out of her comfort zone and how she prioritized her family commitments over the next few years. When she returned to performing, especially with Michel Legrand, her maturity and artistic development were impressive.

Shortly thereafter I undertook an assignment to record a Christmas commercial for Toys 'R' Us. They wanted 'Walking in the Air' from the fabulous Christmas animation *The Snowman*, and they wanted Aled Jones, the sensational 14-year-old choirboy who had become a firm family favourite. We decided that the opportunity was too good to miss, and we would record a full-length single at the same time as the commercial. I wrote a beginning and ending for the song (in the film it had been a part of the score and not conceived as a stand-alone entity). Having got the composer Howard Blake's approval, we booked the session, recorded the backing tracks and then Aled arrived in the studio. Whether it was studio nerves or my presence next to him (I produced the record and commercial and was directing his performance) he could not remember the lyrics at all. I wound up singing the song in a cracked falsetto, line by line, which he then copied. (I'm not telling tales out of school as he wrote about this in his autobiography.) Aled of course has since gone on to become a much-loved television personality and on the occasions we have met in recent years still exudes the same modesty and charm he did as a young lad.

The record became and remains a Christmas classic. We were invited on to the most prestigious music TV show of the time, *Top of the Pops*. The problem was their budget only stretched to about ten musicians – on the record we had thirty! In those days people would do a "tape swap" to circumvent Musicians Union rules. There would be a dummy session booked and the backing track exchanged for the one recorded on the original session. Everyone did it – the only problem was when "Dr. Death" from the Union showed up in the studio unannounced. I got on very well with him and assured everyone that our friendship would mean that he would be a no-show as he tended to materialize at sessions run by people he didn't know well. Ten minutes later he arrived in the studio! All hell broke loose as he demanded a string section instead of a synthesizer. The record company representative cited the number restriction and offered to pay for a string section from EMI funds.

"You can't do that!" said Dr. Death.

We compromised by hiring a string quartet at short notice, but it was now approaching 11pm when the session finished. And our misery wasn't over – the Doctor queried, "Where is the artist? He needs to be here to sing his vocal." Aled's father, who was in the control room, exploded. "He's fourteen and asleep in the hotel, do you expect us to wake him and fetch him here in his pyjamas at midnight to sing?"

The choice was either a possible full-scale standoff and fistfight, or a meekly acquiescent "OK then" from all of us. Of course the latter was more likely, so a sleepy young Aled can be seen on reruns of *Top of the Pops* miming to a specially recorded backing tape while every other artist on the show sang blithely to their original record backing track! Despite this incident, Dr. Death and I remained good friends thereafter and he only showed up at one of my sessions in the future, stayed the whole day and enjoyed my totally above-board big band recording.

I have made three albums under my own name aside from movie and television soundtracks. The first, *Sure Thing*, upon reissue re-titled *Shakin' the Blues Away* (which Dr. Death enjoyed so much) features my orchestra and big band with a terrific American jazz singer living in the UK – Joan Viskant. The album was CD of the month in the UK newspaper *The Observer* and record of the week on the Michael Parkinson radio show. Its fans include Herbie Hancock, Benny Carter and Oscar winning lyricist Alan Bergman, as well as Patrick Stewart and William Shatner (see Chapter 19). The second album, *You Started Something*, recorded in Hollywood, was also CD of the month in *The Observer* and has my LA quartet with either Tom Ranier or Grammy-winner Bill Cunliffe on piano, Sinatra's long-serving bassist Chuck ('These Boots Are Made for Walking') Berghofer, and on drums either Ray Brinker or Gregg Bissonette (Ringo Starr's drummer!). My big band album is in the can and, as of the time of writing, awaiting imminent release.

In the mid-1990s I also recorded a very satisfying project with my longtime keyboard colleague Craig Pruess. He is also a fine jazz trumpeter and a virtuoso sitar player. We gathered together a Pakistani violinist, Indian and African percussionists, among others, and created Terracotta – a very early synthesis of World Music that was definitely ahead of its time and is still a favourite of fellow musicians and producers such as Goldie (see later in the chapter).

I produced several projects with Pete van Hooke. It was always interesting taking meetings with various record company executives, who would lecture us on what was commercial and "what the kids were buying today." I would occasionally chip in, pointing at Pete and saying, "he played drums on the last five number one hit singles, would you like someone more in touch with what the kids want?" Usually, I would bite my tongue while we listened to advice such as "disco is dead" (1974, three years before *Saturday Night Fever*) or "this is what everyone wants to hear" (a Kraftwerk LP played at 45rpm to our amusement – we never let on!).

The phone rang at home one day and it was George Michael (a few days earlier I had answered a call from Paul McCartney which turned out to be genuine, so I didn't swear and replace the receiver this time). George was working on his first solo album after leaving Wham! and said, "You're the only person who can do this with me!"

I arranged and played tenor sax and clarinet on 'Kissing a Fool' on the album *Faith*. I remember telling him that I didn't produce Alison Moyet's 'That Ole Devil Called Love' which had prompted the call, just arranged it, and he said, "Well, we all know you did the important work!" George wanted to record at PUK Studios in Denmark, where much of the album was completed, but I suggested that the musicians I would like to hire wouldn't be that keen on recording in a residential studio in Scandinavia that required a rowboat trip from the mainland and a subsequent long stay on an island. Romantic but impractical. We wound up at the Basing Street Studios, SARM West. (When it was known as Island Studios, I was conducting a large string section recording in the live room when Chris Wood of the band Traffic burst into the session shouting "emergency, emergency!" The take ground to a halt as thirty string players eyed him anxiously, "Anyone got 2p for the telephone?" he asked blithely!) I put together an amazing band for George from the rhythm section of my big band that was about to perform at the Edinburgh Jazz Festival. It was the first ever recording session for our young drummer Ian Thomas, now a mainstay and elder statesman of the music business. "What are you doing next Tuesday?" I asked Ian, Jeff Clyne and Mick Pyne in Edinburgh. Jeff kicked Ian under the table and replied, "We're not doing anything." Ian quickly had to get out of a summer season commitment with Cilla Black and became George Michael's drummer of choice – he loved Ian's playing, as I knew he would.

After endless takes with the rhythm section, we called it a day. We recorded the track over and over again and the session stretched into the evening – I was slightly bewildered by George's apparent lack of enthusiasm and phoned a good friend of both of us, the Grammy award-winning arranger/producer/trumpeter Steve Sidwell.

"You're going back?"

"Yes, we have the brass and woodwinds to do."

"Then he likes it. You'd know soon enough if he doesn't, as he'd pull the plug and send everyone away." (I recall playing an album Pete and I produced for the first time to a record label boss who made no comment at all. "Did you like it?" I stammered eventually. "Of course I do – or I would never have hired you in the first place," was his response.) We did the brass sessions a couple of days later, I played tenor and clarinet on them, something which, as I said, I never normally did on my own arrangements. I am pretty sure I know what motivated me to take this unusual step. I suspect it was a result of some unpaid TV and live shows Alison Moyet undertook after her record climbed the charts. I elected to play clarinet and tenor rather than ask the terrific player who appeared on the record, feeling he would be insulted to be asked to appear for no fee. As it was, he was insulted *not* to be asked, and I vowed that next time I would play the parts on the record myself. I'm very happy I did! (Oddly enough, the instrumental version of 'That Ole Devil Called Love' featured me on tenor saxophone throughout and even more bizarrely topped the UK disco charts.)

Mitch Dalton arrived back in the UK from a Japanese tour early one morning and, like any good studio musician, telephoned the booking service to see if he had any work slated.

"I'm glad you called – go straight to SARM West for a session with George Michael. There's a car waiting for you, your luggage will be collected from the airport and we have hired your favourite guitars. We have also agreed a very large fee for you."

Mitch headed to the studio where he was greeted by George who said, "So glad you could make it – I just have to watch the rushes of my South Bank Show interview and then we will get to work." The rushes lasted over two hours and Mitch found the jetlag irresistible as he drifted in and out of consciousness. Finally, George said, "OK we will get the studio ready and call you in. Grab some lunch while you're waiting." Mitch decided to stretch out for a nap on the sofa. He awoke with a start in total darkness, seeing by his watch that it was now past 2am. He edged his way to the bathroom and washed the sleep from his eyes. Back in the darkness of the main lounge he noticed a light shining under a door. He pushed the door open to find George and the engineer in the control room. "Hi Mitch, nearly ready for you!" When he eventually got set up and ready to record, he played about eight bars before the tape stopped and George's voice came through the headphones.

"Sorry Mitch, I don't think we're ready for you today after all. We'll be in touch."

It's the first and last time Mitch was paid a fortune for sleeping!

During the sessions for 'Kissing a Fool' George sang in the studio every time we did a take. I told him about writing for commercials. (I'd only composed one movie score then.) At one point, while we ate a meal cooked by Lucky Gordon (Christine Keeler's ex-boyfriend who had triggered the chain of events that caused the downfall of the Tory government during the Profumo scandal), he said, "You inspired me to become a musician!" and told the story of how he listened to our schoolboy band rehearsing in the pub next to his father's restaurant (see Chapter 2).

With George happy with how the track sounded, the next step was gathering the musicians for the video shoot. I was recording a commercial on the Wednesday, when his office called and asked if I could get the band together for the Friday of that week. Union rules state that the musicians on the record must be first call for the filming. Somehow between recording the commercial and getting people to juggle their schedules, I managed to organize everyone and rang George's office to confirm. They said, "Oh he's changed his mind, can you all do Monday?"

"Here are the numbers – you sort it out!" I exclaimed. They obviously did to their satisfaction as the male models and members of his touring band in the video looked far more appealing than our motley crew of tired-looking, middle-aged musos!

The album *Faith* became a worldwide bestseller, went diamond and won the Grammy for album of the year. My decision to play was vindicated, as the sleeve states that George Michael arranged the song and played piano and bass. He apparently also arranged the B-side of the single, which was my chart minus the vocals. Certainly, that was news to all of us who were there! I'm sure George wouldn't have sent in those credits. I did get a gold record, but to this day I haven't received any other acknowledgement of my arranging contribution to a classic recording. However, I am proud of what we achieved. In addition, I later learned that on tour George had his backing band miming onstage to a tape of our track, having told them, "You'll never play this as well as these guys." This was the only time we worked together although our paths crossed occasionally in the foyer of SARM studios or at the Novello Awards. A very underrated live performer and someone I found to be charming and in his own way appreciative, I have very fond memories of our collaboration. I only wish I could remember the five-year-old kid running around his dad's restaurant as we ate our lunches on a break from rehearsals. George was a huge loss, personally and professionally.

Back to Paul McCartney's call. I was to meet him about potentially becoming his new "George Martin". I went up to his London office and an assistant said, "He's in a meeting. He'll be with you shortly. Would you like to read this while you're waiting?"

He handed me a magazine which I assumed might be *Time* or *Newsweek*. It was the *Paul McCartney Fan Club Official Magazine*. When the assistant called me into the inner sanctum, I dropped the magazine on the table. If looks could kill! Paul was charming but I guess I was non-committal and years went by before we met again by chance on my birthday. I was on my way to my party at the 10 Room and he was fascinated by my tiny, curved soprano sax and its case. When I told him it was my birthday, he insisted on buying me a celebratory water! Something I felt on my way to and from my meeting with Paul at his Soho Square office, which never affected me in my dealings with George, was a very curious sensation which I wanted to share with the outside world. "I'm going to meet/have just been with a Beatle!" I never met John, although I was told he was a fan of my Rutles arrangements, and in my earlier chapter about George I touch on my relationship with Ringo.

My next record adventure was writing the strings for Prefab Sprout's classic song 'Hey Manhattan'. Producer Andy Richards called me. I was already a huge fan of Paddy McAloon's songwriting and loved the backing track with Pete Townshend's guitar and the evocative lyric. The strings were really prominently mixed on the finished record – quite often you would struggle to hear what the forty-piece string section had played, as they were often way back in the final mix. Like every record I arranged for, I didn't do a demo, just showed up with my music and changed anything that needed altering on the spot – a discipline I honed by doing so much film and advertising writing. Now a quick story about another track on the album that I was not involved in. Paddy had written a harmonica part he wanted played in the style of Stevie Wonder. The session player who was booked to play, struggled with it and told Paddy, "It's unplayable!" Paddy relayed the story to Pete Townshend who said, "Well, why not ask Stevie? I'll get him on the phone." The result was the harmonica solo on the Prefab Sprout album is played, correctly, by Stevie Wonder! Recently I saw a TV interview with Paddy, who now sports a long white beard. He is in his mid-sixties at the time of writing and is recognized as one of the finest songwriters of his era.

By the late 1980s Trevor Horn had become the most successful and in-demand record producer in the world as singers and bands queued up to have him produce their records. His wife Jill Sinclair had propelled my career in the 1970s when she recommended me to write commercials and I would bump into them whenever I recorded in SARM studios, their headquarters. In 1989 I joined my friends Richard Niles and Anne Dudley as one of his "go to" arrangers. For the next few years, until I became increasingly involved in composing, arranging and producing movie music, I would regularly arrange projects for Trevor and these records have endured over the years. My first writing gig for him was on Simple Minds' album *Street Fighting Years*. I had a great time with Jim Kerr and the band – they seemed more interested in hearing stories about my time with Van Morrison than hearing my thoughts on the string arrangements for their latest album – I guess they trusted my judgement. The sessions went really smoothly – I'd heard Trevor could be indecisive, but nothing seemed further from the truth. Thanks to the magic of Trevor and engineer Steve Lipson the strings leap out of the mixes and effectively point up the drama of the tracks.

Our next project was the Tom Waits' classic 'Downtown Train' which Trevor had suggested to Rod Stewart who wasn't familiar with the song. It's no secret to say that Rod's career had stalled somewhat, and he'd hired Trevor to revive interest. Once the key had been set (G) I met with Trevor to discuss the orchestration. He suggested that there should be a sort of other-worldly feel to the orchestration – with a sort of "psychedelic" coda. I wrote for a conventional string section plus two cor anglais (English horns), one playing at the top of his range to give a slightly different texture from the oboe which would have been in the middle of his register. For the outro I wrote a swirling high string figure in 3/4 to wash across the 4/4 metre of the song so that the bar lines displaced to create the desired other-worldly effect.

The recording session (in Angel Studios, London) went very smoothly and I thought no more of the record as I moved on to the next assignments.

The days were long gone when record labels sent you copies of records you'd worked on, so the next time I had any brush with 'Downtown Train' was some six months later in the Virgin Megastore on Sunset Boulevard. In those days they had an in-store DJ who would play an eclectic selection of tracks of which one would occasionally take note if they appealed to you. So, when this introduction started, I was only half listening, but when Rod started singing I realized that this was the finished record that I hadn't yet heard with vocals in place. I started listening closely but then... Wait a minute, there's something up here! I located the DJ booth and asked him if he minded playing the record again as I was the arranger. He duly did so, and it struck me – the song was in the wrong key! I had written in the key of G, but I was hearing Bb. And what caught my ear was the odd vibrato of the strings and English horn. It was several months later, when the record had become a worldwide smash hit, that I learnt the full story. Apparently, Rod had heard the finished backing tracks with my strings and Jeff Beck's guitar and realized the song had the potential to revive his career. He got into shape, went for voice lessons, stopped drinking and when he got into the studio found that our key of G was too low for his newly reinvigorated vocal cords! Now this was the late 1980s – no autotune, pitch bend, protools or logic to alter the key without speeding up the track. Somehow Trevor worked his magic and got the track to move up a minor third to accommodate Rod. The only thing he couldn't do was prevent the string and woodwind vibratos from changing texture. And yet, bizarrely, I think it was this very effect that made the record so striking. It added to the otherworldliness of the arrangement. The English horn and the strings, had they been playing in Bb, would never have sounded that way. More to the point, it would have completely altered the way I would have written the chart – I would have used an oboe (as the top F on the English horn would have sounded hideous) and changed the string inversions. Sometimes serendipity and the odd quirks of fate can be on your side! Whatever the reason, the record was a massive worldwide hit and had the desired effect on Rod's career which still thrives today. Although we are near neighbours and his mother-in-law worked for years for a good friend of mine, retired and then went back, the last time I met Rod was in a college hall at what was then Brighton College of Education for an impromptu soccer kickabout after a Faces gig in 1970. People are amazed that you can make records with folks you've never met, but such is technology! I've been a fan of Rod's singing since the mid-1960s and I'm proud of the work we did together – even if it was at a distance.

My last collaboration with Trevor was a few years later. (He subsequently asked me to work on Seal's debut album, but I was busy in Hollywood at the time.) In the meantime, I had written arrangements for tracks Trevor had produced for Tom Jones and The Pretenders. This final track was with someone I only met once but what an interesting meeting it was! The string chart for Tina Turner's hit record 'In Your Wildest Dreams' turned out to be one of the most enjoyable arrangements I wrote for Trevor. The song was written by Mike Chapman and my occasional writing partner Holly Knight. When I first heard the track, it was designed to feature Tina with a spoken interlude, and I remember on the session mentioning that it would sound great with someone like Barry White. Shortly thereafter I heard a rough mix featuring the voice of... Antonio Banderas. Not quite the same vocal effect, particularly as in those days his command of English wasn't what it is now. Never mind, Tina sounded great and the song was undeniably a hit. The single reached the UK Top 30 and charted well all over Europe. At the time I was represented by Barry White's management, so I was surprised and delighted to learn that he'd agreed to turn the record into a duet – the vocal combination of the King and Queen of sultry soul was guaranteed to be something special. I couldn't help wondering if my prompting had set off that chain of events, but I would imagine that it was in the air already when the thought struck me.

The finished record sounded amazing and the Oscar-winning animator Nick Park (maker of *Wallace and Gromit* and *Chicken Run*) was hired to create a claymation video for the record. I'd worked on many commercials with Nick's company Aardman and knew they would come up with something off the wall. And they didn't disappoint... a hilarious video featuring clay depictions of Tina and Barry suffused with wonderful comic moments from Wallace and Gromit and Antonio Banderas. Everyone loved it... except for Barry White! He immediately slapped an injunction banning the film – I guess he didn't see himself as a large man and objected to the animation. I think that if he'd had more of a sense of humour about himself the video would have propelled the single to the top of the charts. As it was, the album went double platinum, and 'Wildest Dreams' became a one-off collaboration to savour.

Shortly thereafter I attended the New York premiere of *Goldeneye*, for which I had served as arranger/conductor and also composed the classic tank chase sequence through St. Petersburg. At the afterparty I was looking forward to chatting with Pierce Brosnan as I had unwittingly kick-started his movie career (another story for later!) but he was surrounded by fans and back slappers. As I stood waiting my turn, I noticed someone standing next to me who looked remarkably like Tina Turner. I introduced myself as the arranger of 'Wildest Dreams' and all thoughts of James Bond vanished as we sought a quiet corner to chat. She asked me if I'd worked on her song in *Goldeneye* (I hadn't) and after a few minutes of conversation said, "I'm going to find a drink, what can I get you?" I offered to go on her behalf, but she firmly insisted, and who am I to argue with the great Tina Turner? I said, half-jokingly, "Actually, I'd love some tea!"

Astonished, I watched her cross the room to where the tea and coffee urns were standing unmanned, grab a cup and saucer and pour me a cup of tea. She then crossed the room with the tea and a small jug of milk, stopping en route to chat with well-wishers but giving them short shrift as she indicated that I was waiting for my cuppa! Tea duly delivered, she went off again to get her tipple of choice and was soon engulfed by seemingly everyone in the room who wanted to seize a moment with this classy lady. And my admiration for her in every respect increased years later when I learned that she adored the video for 'In Your Wildest Dreams' and had saved a copy from destruction, which she then made available on her own website. And she makes a great cup of tea! (As I write, Tina sadly appears to have retired from public performance and appearances – I'm very proud of my small contribution to her recorded legacy.)

One evening I received a telephone call at home from the notorious manager of the Sex Pistols, Malcolm McLaren, who had reinvented himself as a performer. He had enjoyed great success collaborating with my friends Anne Dudley and Trevor Horn on the song 'Buffalo Gals' and excitedly told me of a new project he had in mind. While he didn't impart any details over the phone, he suggested we meet later that week at a recording studio in Central London and all would become clear. On the appointed afternoon I showed up to find the studio well and truly locked and bolted. After about twenty minutes an engineer showed up – Malcolm had asked him along as well, but he had no connection with the studio, and also no key. In those pre-cellphone days there was nothing for it but to hang around and wait. We repaired to a coffee shop opposite the studio where we could observe comings and goings. Still, no one appeared. After about an hour and a half we parted company and returned home. I never heard from Malcolm McLaren again.

While in Los Angeles I was asked by the composer Richard Gibbs to write two fun big band charts – for the indie band Eisley a 1920s style arrangement of their song 'The Marsh King's Daughter' and for Will Young a roaring big band setting for Richard's song 'Try Again' which featured over the end credits of Disney's *101 Dalmatians.* Another enjoyable big band arrangement I crafted was for the highly rated British band Tindersticks on their song 'Rented Rooms'. Latterly in Los Angeles I was honoured to fulfil the role of King Curtis for a tribute recording by his legendary bassist Jerry Jemmott (Aretha Franklin, B.B. King etc.) with an all-star band that included Guitar Shorty, Mike Finnegan (organist on Electric Ladyland whom we lost recently), David Garfield (George Benson's musical director) and Steve Ferrone (drummer for Eric Clapton and the Average White Band, among others).

I should mention three other record projects that didn't involve Trevor Horn. When my big band assembled in Angel Studios one morning in the mid-1990s, the only thing most of the musicians knew was that they were booked from 10am till 1pm, a standard three-hour recording session to record one track. By our usual standards this was what would be known as a "doddle", uncomplicated and straightforward. All the musicians, including myself, were used to recording three or four tracks in the allotted three-hour timeslot with a 20-minute break in the middle. I was prepared for a tough call – the track which we were recreating had many pauses, slowing down and speeding up, as the lead vocalist drove the performance. And a huge dynamic range, from pianissimo to… well, very, very, loud. I had heard the Betty Hutton 1940s original of 'It's Oh So Quiet', with the Pete Rugolo arrangement, and modified it to suit our artist, Björk. She had been sent the track by a fan who suggested it might fit her quirky style, loved it, and it was forwarded to me by her label. The only instruction – same key, same format. I had yet to meet the lady in question on the morning of the session, but I figured that an hour or so of rehearsals would iron out any gremlins, and then the remaining two hours we could spend laying down multiple takes and fine-tuning the track to perfection.

We began at 10am, getting the sounds and running the chart for possible copying errors. By about 10.30 I was satisfied that the music was ready and popped into the control room to enquire as to the whereabouts of Björk. "She's at home looking for her shoes, and then she'll be on her way," said producer Nellee Hooper. Time for a couple of dry runs *sans* vocals.

By 11am everything was sounding in tip-top shape. Usually, the procedure would be to record a take to a click track and the vocal would then be done at a later stage. However, this song was so "voice driven" this would be impossible except as an academic exercise to fill up time. I asked for an update and was informed that Björk was "en route". As this is a fiendishly difficult chart to play, particularly for the trumpet section, I didn't want to over exhaust the guys so suggested taking an early break so that when Björk arrived we could plunge straight in.

The minutes ticked by, into hours. Midday came and went. My pacing up and down had incrementally increased with every minute lost and I now envisioned three or four takes as the maximum we could hope for. At 12.30 I was told, "Nearly here!" and reassembled the band. Another run through to make sure that no one had forgotten anything and then… nothing.

At 12.50 I had given up hope if truth be told. Suddenly the studio door opened and in skipped Björk with a smile as wide and welcoming as is humanly possible. Wasting no time, in answer to her, "Is everything ok?" I spelt out the situation: "We lose the band in 10 minutes or incur huge overtime costs."

"Oh, I thought they were here all day! Right, we'd better get on with it then!"

She disappeared into the vocal booth, put on the headphones, gave me another big smile. I counted the track in, gave her a nod and four minutes later… we had the finished record! Yes, you read that correctly – no rehearsal, no retake. She sang, I conducted, only the rhythm section could hear her in their booths — the brass and saxes, following my conducting, could only hear the rhythm section — no one cracked a note or missed a cue. And do you know what – it really shows on the record – the thrill of a first take with everyone performing together, vocalist and band at the same time. Ralph Salmins, the wonderful drummer, tells me we did a second take, but it definitely didn't have the magic of take one. It's no coincidence that it was such a huge worldwide hit – I think all the audiences responded to that vibrancy and vitality and energy that was borne of a desperate need to get it right!

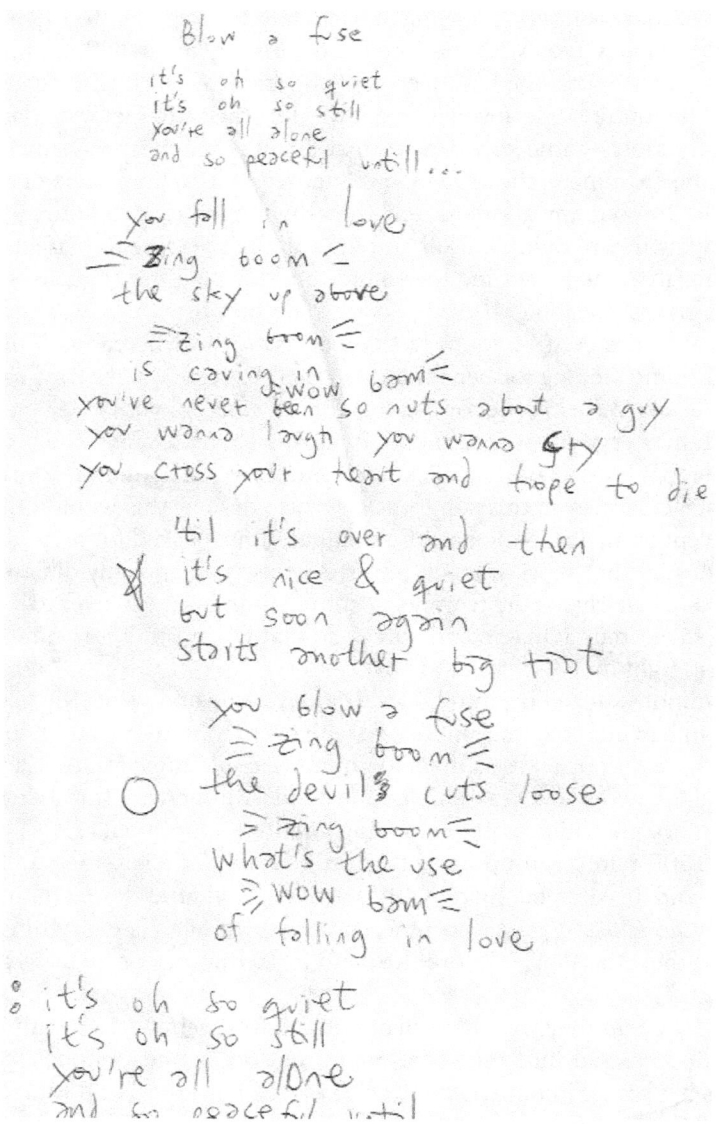

Figure 32: Björk's handwritten lyric for 'It's Oh So Quiet' which I rescued from the music stand in the studio after we had recorded the song. Author's collection.

A while later we went on *Top of the Pops*. After rehearsals Björk was nowhere to be found. A frantic search was launched and eventually she was found lying on the ground in the car park, listening to the earth. The only time we performed the song live was on *Children in Need* – when I arrived, I discovered that the resident band were situated on the balcony quite far away from the brass and woodwind players. And the remaining musicians were seated in a straight line, trumpets, trombones and woodwinds all mixed up, as the floor manager said, "it looks more interesting like this!" I should have been used to this at the BBC – on one music session the engineer had set up one microphone for the drums, pointing away from the drum kit. When we asked if he did a lot of music sessions, he replied, "Oh no, I prefer drama. I did the Grand National on Saturday – that was fun!" In those days the BBC would not allow non-BBC staff to record music. External engineers could be present in an advisory capacity but were not permitted to become involved in the recording process. On one orchestral session booked at Lansdowne Studios the BBC engineer phoned in to say he was stuck in traffic and would be delayed. As the minutes ticked away, the world-class engineer Chris Dibble set the headphone levels for the musicians and balanced the orchestra perfectly so there would be no delay in commencing. The engineer arrived after forty-five minutes, apologized for his tardiness and zeroed all the recording and headphone levels before anyone could stop him!

Another time the engineer proudly told us he had designed a box that gave each musician individual control of what he heard in the headphones. I turned up my saxophone and Charlie Morgan the drummer howled in pain as the guitar suddenly became deafening. Shortly after, guitarist Mitch Dalton adjusted the volume of his guitar in his headphones; I had to hurl off my set of "cans" as the bass drum had suddenly attained the volume of a cannon in the 1812 overture. I don't think we were able to record a single track that day.

Somehow the mix and match big band worked for *Children in Need* although I dropped my hand to conduct the first note of the accompaniment to find the woodwind players all staring at me silently. They weren't hearing the vocalist and were probably unfamiliar with my downbeat. It was only for one second as evidenced on the video I have, but it felt like an eternity. Björk's management asked if I would be able to bring the big band on at Wembley for her encore on her world tour. A great, if expensive, idea that, not surprisingly, was consigned to the trashcan. However, I was assured that her musical director would create an appropriate arrangement for her working band and was sent a ticket to the concert. I offered to send her guy my altered chords for the song but was told he knew exactly what to do. Come the encore and Björk launched into the song. At least she was singing the words and melody – quite what the band was doing remains a mystery to me and the entire audience at the Wembley arena! Sadly, she has disowned the record as a one-off experiment – which is a shame as it's her biggest selling record to this day. I have to say we got on very well – I attended several of the sessions in which I was not involved for the album *Post* and spent some time with one of my heroes Eumir Deodato whom Björk had coaxed out of retirement. Apart from our ten minutes recording 'It's Oh So Quiet' we managed to spend a little time together while the single was being promoted. Certainly, hearing her subsequent work I would have loved to have applied the big band or orchestral sound to some of her original material, but it never happened.

The Xmas market is full of recordings of Christmas songs performed by all and sundry, some appropriate, some not so. When I got a call to arrange and conduct a Christmas album for Diana Ross featuring the Royal Philharmonic Orchestra, I was very excited by the prospect. I soon realized that it was too big a job of writing in too short a time to handle on my own, so I wrote four arrangements and requested some of my heroes to make up the complement of tracks. And they all did – the arrangers' roster on the album is a *Who's Who* of the great contemporary writers. It was a joyous project all round. The only information I'd received from Ms Ross was a list of songs and keys and the footnote – no drums. I think she meant no disco tracks, but I took her at her word and wrote for orchestral percussion, letting the acoustic guitar carry the rhythm. We recorded the tracks in London, they were then shipped to Diana's home studio, and she added her vocals. When I heard the results, I was delighted – she had got into the spirit of the tracks perfectly and the whole album is a joy. I heard from a close friend of hers that it was her favourite album, but you always take these compliments with a large pinch of salt. However, a few years later I was due to meet a friend for dinner at a Thai restaurant in London whose entrance was through a hotel foyer. There was Diana Ross checking in – I went over and said, "Sorry to disturb you but I arranged and conducted your Christmas album."

"Oh my goodness, that's my favourite album, thank you so much!"

So, it was true. Shortly afterwards, seated in the restaurant, my friend whispered, "Don't look now but Diana Ross is sitting over there!" Some time later she said, "She's coming past us any second." Ms Ross was returning to her seat and as she walked past me, she gave me a playful punch on my arm, much to the total astonishment of my friend. I'd heard many stories that she could be tricky to work with – in my experience nothing could have been further from the truth and it was one of the smoothest, most straightforward projects it was ever my pleasure to be involved with.

I was put in touch with Goldie, the drum 'n' bass guru by my friend Isobel Griffiths who had gone from being my advertising producer to becoming the number one musicians' booker in the country. Goldie's management had approached Isobel looking for someone who could get Goldie's orchestral ideas down on manuscript. I met with him and was swept into his unconventional musical universe. At the end of his fanciful explanation of his vision he waited for the usual "I have no idea what you're talking about" dismissal he'd become used to. Instead, I nodded my head and said, "I get it." It made perfect sense to me, and 'Mother', his hour-long orchestral vision realized, made history as the first orchestral marriage of drum 'n' bass and the symphony. There were cameos from Noel Gallagher, Björk and David Bowie too. Now everyone seems to be fusing the two disciplines, but we can legitimately claim to be the trailblazers and he is still a dear friend over twenty-five years later. And still as inscrutable as he was in 1995!

As I became well known as a movie composer, the offers to arrange for recording artists mysteriously decreased. It seemed as if people became wary of you if you wore more than one musical hat – pigeonholing is a subject I will return to in later chapters. I have been very lucky to maintain parallel careers over the years, but I must admit it has been disappointing sometimes to learn that I was suggested for a project, only for someone to chip in, "oh he won't want to do that now that he's so busy in Hollywood!" However, as I point out in a later chapter, this wasn't something I brooded over for any length of time.

13 Television

I was still in demand as a saxophonist, such as when I appeared in a Pop Prom on British television in the early 1970s with Marty Wilde. (An ITV Pop Prom was part of a series of live one-hour popular music shows on British TV starring various artists from the 1940s through to the '70s.) That gig was particularly memorable for me as 1950s pop megastar Frankie Laine was also on the show and we reminisced about his stint at the London Palladium with my uncle Woolf Phillips. We had a visit from top LA session trombonist Lloyd Ulyate who was vacationing round the UK and who noticed, quite by chance, that we were filming in Preston of all places (not the biggest venue in the UK by a long way). So, he stuck his head into the theatre and was amazed to find so many people that he knew. This unlikely venue prompted him to tell me a wonderful story concerning a time when he was doing an afternoon TV show in Los Angeles and an evening show with Frank Sinatra in Las Vegas. Driving to Vegas, he hit a deserted stretch of road, took the car up to 100mph and suddenly a motorbike cop pulled out of a layby and pursued him, sirens blaring. Lloyd pulled over to the side of the road, the cop adjusted his dark glasses and drawled, "I've been waiting for you all day."

"Well, I got here as fast as I could!" replied Lloyd. The cop roared with laughter and let him go on his way.

Saxophonist Ron Aspery was late for a session in Central London and found himself in solid, non-moving traffic on Park Lane. In desperation he switched his car into the bus lane, reserved exclusively for public transport. It was also at a standstill, and while the car was stationary a rookie policeman wandered over and tapped on the car window. In his best Hendon Police College sarcastic tone of voice, he drawled, "Is this a *bus* then, sir?"

Ron eyed him from head to toe and uttered the immortal comeback: "You're new on traffic, aren't you!"

After my stint as a "take-down" expert, I switched in the 1980s to a diverse career in television – sometimes arranging and conducting for other composers, but also composing scores myself for high-end television dramas, and acting as musical director, arranger and producer for TV spectaculars featuring contemporary musical acts. The BBC drama department was possibly the finest in the world at the time and featured actors of the calibre of Anthony Hopkins, Emma Thompson, Timothy Spall, Joss Ackland; great directors like Roy Boulting, Alan Dossor, Tristan Powell, Gordon Flemyng and Sheree Folkson; and great writers such as John McGrath, Troy Kennedy Martin, Alan Plater and Alan Bleasdale. In charge was Michael Wearing who was fiercely protective of all the diverse creatives who worked on BBC drama. I was very close friends with his daughter Catherine, a brilliant script editor and producer, taken from us far too soon.

As an arranger and conductor, I worked on several major dramas and series with composer Ken Howard, including the original BBC recording of *Shadowlands* which predated the Richard Attenborough movie, *Q.E.D.* starring Sam Waterston, and two fondly remembered series, which I will discuss further in this chapter – *By the Sword Divided* and *Miss Marple*. With Neil Innes composing, I arranged the signature tune and incidental music for the BBC series *Jane*, based on the *Daily Mirror* cartoon strip. I also arranged and conducted the signature tune composed by Jeff Wayne for ITV's popular soccer show *The Big Match*. As a composer I scored many award-winning plays for Screen Two and ITV, including *Star Quality*, *Unnatural Causes*, *Selected Exits* (written by Alan Plater and starring Sir Anthony Hopkins), *Ice Dance*, the Emmy winning drama *First and Last*, *The Bell Run*, *Royal Scandal*, *Fair Game*, *Broke*, the BAFTA nominated *The Queen's Sister*, the very first film for Comic Relief *Oliver (Let's Twist Again)*, written by Richard Curtis and featuring an all-star cast, and *The Good Samaritan*, plus several series for both the BBC and ITV. These included the variety show *Time of Your Life* with Noel Edmonds, the cult children's TV show *Tiswas*, the magazine series *01 For London*, and the serialized dramas *Johnny Jarvis*, *No Bananas*, *The Old Devils* (for which I was recommended by my esteemed colleague George Fenton), *Between the Lines* (one memorable episode), *Drovers' Gold*, *Berkeley Square*, *Rich Deceiver*, *Tears Before Bedtime*, *Ellington* and *Peak Practice*, ITV's most successful series of the 1990s. I even wrote and whistled the music that introduced the ITV weather forecasts for a couple of years – evidently my whistling skills were an asset as I utilized this aptitude in *Life of Brian* and *Hear My Song*. I'm afraid that ability has long since departed from my armoury.

If that wasn't enough, I was hired to produce and, when necessary, arrange for the musical acts on the UK's version of *Saturday Night Live* and to be the musical director for various spectaculars – *New Brighton Rocks*, *Lennon*, *Elvis – Love Me Tender*, *Rock Around the Dock* and the *Titanic Commemoration*. And then of course there were three series of the *Innes Book of Records* with the unique Neil Innes. I even appeared in a few productions – my old friend Lenny Henry's series *Chef* ("find him the worst wig in the BBC costume department please!") and his own comedy series, Russell Harty's chat show,

Children in Need with Björk, and several *Top of the Pops* episodes with various acts. I was also musical associate on several programmes, including occasionally the *South Bank Show,* and even, one year, arranged and conducted a Don Black/Geoff Stephens song that came second in the hunt for Britain's entry for the Eurovision Song Contest. One evening I found that my music could be heard simultaneously on all four British TV channels that then existed. I had a play on BBC1, a movie on BBC2, a series on ITV and a commercial on Channel 4. One for the Monopolies Commission I think. I would also appear as a "talking head" from time to time in shows like *The Music of James Bond*, *How Pop Songs Work*, *BBC Breakfast Television* and *The Culture Show*. Sadly, I also became the person to interview across all channels' news bulletins when we tragically lost a major musical figure or colleague such as Errol Brown, Amy Winehouse or James Horner.

Figure 33: Appearing in *Chef* with Sir Lenny Henry who made me wear the worst wig in the BBC costume department. Author's collection.

Just reading this list is exhausting, and when I factor in my commercials, record work, movie writing and live gig schedule, it's no wonder I didn't take a vacation in the 1980s. A few random thoughts about some of these programmes spring to mind. I'm amazed at how popular the *Marple* series continues to be, years after we recorded Ken Howard's music, which I arranged and conducted. I revelled in Joan Hickson's company; she was certainly not the eccentric, slightly dotty old lady she portrayed. As a huge fan of classic British cinema, I was delighted to find the show cast with so many wonderful actors from the golden age of movies – such as Raymond Huntley, Fabia Drake, Helen Cherry and Valentine Dyall. I enjoyed working closely with Roy

Boulting, although he hadn't quite worked out the necessary skills to make a TV drama – his original cut was way overlength and the producers had to resort to a montage of still photographs, of all things, to cram the whole story into the allotted time. It's sobering to think the series is now more distant from today than from the time it supposedly represents – a period piece about a period piece. I still meet people who watch and enjoy the series religiously and tell me proudly that they've spotted my name in the end titles – quite a feat in these days of minimizing the credits, rushing them through and talking over the main theme, frantically plugging the next offering!

My first series for Ken Howard was *By the Sword Divided*, set during the English Civil War. John Hawkesworth, the creator of *Upstairs Downstairs* and a venerated name in the history of television drama, was the producer. As it was my first major TV credit as musical director, I looked forward with eager anticipation to spotting my name in the end credits to make up for the pittance that the BBC paid to arrangers. I was therefore dismayed to receive a copy of the end credits to score, with no mention of me or my involvement. Composer Ken Howard rang the BBC drama department and they said, "It's not our policy to credit musical directors on dramas." When Ken relayed this information to me, I thought, "Here goes nothing," and called John Hawkesworth to inform him of my displeasure.

"We'll soon see about that!" said John. Next thing I knew he had apparently called the BBC and threatened to withdraw the series unless I had a credit. A new end title sequence duly arrived with my name prominent.

The playwright Stephen Lowe told me he wrote a play especially for an actor/musician pal of ours and phoned the BBC contract department to get him hired.

"Oh yes, it says here his fee is £150," said the woman in bookings.

"But I want him to star in my play not work as a session musician."

"Sorry, that's his BBC fee and we can't go against that."

Stephen had another thought. "Who is the most expensive actor on your list?"

"Oh, that will be Sir .... His fee is £30,000."

"Thank you." And that's how Sir .... came to star in a BBC *Play for Today*!

I wrote the music for a terrific TV movie directed by my commercials colleague Ross Cramer, entitled *God on the Rocks*. It was set in the north of England in the 1930s and I travelled up to Harrogate, the location, with the 17-year-old third lead making her first movie, Minnie Driver. We waited at the station while the film company tried to locate our ride, who was looking round the car park for a Mini driver – true story! Minnie has risen to international stardom, and she told me she now owns the rights to the screenplay and hopes to remake it. Certainly, it was a stunning debut and I've since scored three or four projects in which she shines.

One of the questions I'm most frequently asked is what inspires you to make the choices of instrumentation, musical approach and thematic details when you score a movie or television drama? Without wanting to appear too technical, my method for *God on the Rocks* is a good example of the thought process at work. The movie was set in the north of England in the 1930s – an image that immediately and specifically recalled the music of George Formby. Formby's instrument of choice was a banjolele, a hybrid banjo and ukulele that he popularized and it's safe to say became virtually extinct with his demise. The sound of this instrument embedded itself in my mind – but I could imagine three banjoleles playing in unison supported by an acoustic guitar. Added to this a jaunty early 1930s style theme, played by a conventional dance band lineup (including a violin) to reinforce the sunny optimism that ends tragically, some wordless choral voices to emphasize the magical childlike aspect of the plot and a middle section based on a nursery rhyme that one of the characters sings to a little girl, and the template was set – I then wrote around it. The banjolele is such an unusual instrument that two of my three chosen performers had to go and rent their instruments and familiarize themselves with it.

My approach to film composition has remained the same – whether for a multi-million-dollar blockbuster, a small independent movie or a low-budget television drama. I always say that film music is the earliest example of world music, as any instrumental combination is available to the composer – think Ennio Morricone. In addition, I always give the advice that being a composer is like being a painter – if you're stuck in the middle of the picture, go to the bottom right-hand corner. Similarly, if I can't come up with a thematic idea, I look for a rhythmic hook or ostinato that will unlock my creativity. Simple but effective.

I enjoyed the musical spectaculars I took charge of – they don't exist anymore I'm afraid. They were a Who's Who of 1980s and 90s music. Across the shows, among the acts I arranged, occasionally played sax and conducted for, were the Weather Girls, The Damned, Ben E. King (whom I'd first met and bonded with on the Pop Prom I mentioned at the start of the chapter), Meatloaf, Cameo, Run DMC and Chaka Khan. I supervised Frankie Goes to Hollywood, Boy George, Status Quo, Spandau Ballet, the Style Council and many others. Meatloaf came to perform on the Elvis tribute without having learned any of the songs. He proceeded to read the lyrics Brando-style off cue sheets out of the corner of his eye. A highlight for me was having Elvis's TCB Band on the show with Roger Daltrey and Carl Perkins, the great Plas (*Pink Panther*) Johnson and Jim Horn on saxophones and Duane Eddy on guitar. As often happened, Ivor Raymonde who did the string arrangements, and yours truly, who did the brass charts and some of the rhythm arrangements, as well as playing live in the band on camera, have no onscreen credit at all.

Stuart Colman who put the band together for the Elvis tribute then called me to play with Little Richard on a Christmas special. Richard was wonderful, if more than slightly jetlagged, and when he discovered we shared the same birthday, took an instant shine to me! That involved a recurring scenario – the official photographer took a photo of us, and I gave out my usual *cri de coeur*: "I'm never going to see this photo, am I?"

"I'll send it as soon as it's printed," came the reply. I'm still waiting – luckily a friend of Gary Moberley, the keyboard player, took a photo at the same time and I do have that.

Figure 34: With Little Richard at LWT Studios. Author's collection.

After conducting my arrangement of 'Eloise' for The Damned with the Royal Liverpool Philharmonic on *Rock Around the Dock*, I was in the downstairs bar with Dave Vanian of The Damned discussing *Miss Marple* while the symphony players were on the Liverpool Docks throwing various objects into the water and generally misbehaving – surely the wrong way round? The prerecording session was interesting. The Damned, then at the forefront of the new punk wave, were in TV Studio 1 at Granada in Manchester; the Royal Liverpool Philharmonic in Studio 2 with no headphones, just following my conducting. (I could at least hear the band.) The orchestra played an introduction that I'd written, leaving the band on their own to play the first eight bars behind the vocal. The only problem was that the cassette they'd sent me to write from was running fast – they were in the key of B and my chart was in the key of C. Luckily the orchestra immediately agreed to read the arrangement in the difficult key of "Cb", which they did perfectly. After a superb take we all emerged to hear the playback in the control room, punks from Studio 1, symphony players from Studio 2. At the same moment the doors of Studio 3 swung open and Hilda Ogden (played by the actress Jean Alexander), one of the most popular characters from the TV soap *Coronation Street*, emerged wearing hairnet, curlers and apron and smoking a cigarette. We all stood for a moment, marvelling at the incongruity.

Figure 35: Conducting the Royal Liverpool Philharmonic – *Rock Around the Dock*. Author's collection.

There was a jetty into the dock in front of the orchestra and behind my back as I was facing them onstage. Chaka Khan had to walk out onto the jetty while performing 'Ain't Nobody'. She got halfway down in rehearsal before she went flying on the rather dangerously damp runway. As the nearest person, I ran to pick her up and anxiously asked if she was OK. "It's alright John, there's a lot of me back there to cushion my fall," she exclaimed, as I cracked up!

I've already mentioned the three series of the *Innes Book of Records* which we worked on between 1979 and 1981. Neil would send me piano or guitar and voice demos of his songs and left it totally up to me what line-up, style or musicians we would use. We were able to hire the best and had a very quick turnaround. They were "conveyor belt" sessions, four songs recorded in three-hour blocks so that we didn't exceed our meagre BBC budget (which we'd die for today!). Consequently, we made sure that each ensemble was used to the maximum. After two gentle string quartet sessions one morning and afternoon, we somehow scheduled a country and western hootenanny evening, replete with banjos, pedal steel guitars and yee-has. I'm afraid we were all shaking midway through the first run-through. (News of John Lennon's senseless murder filtered through on Neil's birthday, 9 December 1980. Neil was recording a song that day using his Lennon voice and all of us in the studio shuddered at the eeriness. Neil's good friend Terry Jones arrived in the evening, and we left them to telephone George Harrison in private.)

The series anticipated MTV by several years and we had a lot of fun coming up with scenarios for the filming and realizing Neil's intentions with the songs. I managed to appear in several sequences in the shows, usually playing a bandleader – once conducting a cartoon orchestra! The series now has a huge cult following and I will be interviewed at an upcoming screening of some of the episodes at the British Film Institute who have preserved and restored many of the programmes.

For a docudrama aired on the fifth anniversary of John Lennon's passing, I was asked to assemble a band of his contemporaries, all of whom had some connection with The Beatles. I put together a wonderful band including session players extraordinaire Big Jim Sullivan and Clem Cattini, as well as pianist Tommy Eyre who had arranged 'With A Little Help from My Friends' for Joe Cocker. (I had previously tried the ailing Nicky Hopkins, who had played a lot with Lennon, and Ian Stewart of the Rolling Stones, who said "I'll do it but we couldn't stand the guy!"). On bass was John Gustafson who had been in the Big Three in Liverpool, the harmonica player was Paul Jones from Manfred Mann, and among the singers were Carl Wayne of The Move, Helen Shapiro, Edwin Starr and Roy Orbison, all of whom had strong Beatles connections. Peter Cook was there too – playing a vicar! Of course, being the BBC, no explanation was given as to why the band featured a bunch of slightly ageing musicians. Bernard Hill played Lennon brilliantly although he told me he's never seen the show. I'd completely forgotten that I'd written an arrangement of 'Help!' for Roy Orbison and his guitar which was a highlight of the programme – it can be found on YouTube.

I suspect I was hired for *Saturday Night Live* as a mediator between the old-school TV producers and the cutting-edge young musical acts we had on the show. There were occasional flare-ups but in general I enjoyed producing the likes of Slade, Nils Lofgren, the Moody Blues and various young punk bands. I even wound up playing the flute solo on 'Nights in White Satin' as it was taking an age to get a good take. I'd given up the flute some twelve years earlier and this was my only comeback performance – again it's on YouTube somewhere with the Moody Blues' flautist miming to my playing. Some years later, my accountant by accident sent me, along with the actual band members, a breakdown of the Moody Blues royalty payments. I didn't open the attachments but messaged my old friend, their lead singer, Justin Hayward, asking if this meant I was now a fully-fledged member of the band, but sadly not. I have two friends who are fanatical Moody Blues fans so I messaged Justin to see if they could quickly visit backstage after the gig and say hello. He duly invited them to the after-show party – they turned up wearing Moody Blues T-shirts to find all the guests in tuxedos and black ties!

The producer of *Peak Practice*, Tony Virgo, hired me after seeing how I'd scored the movie *Hear My Song*. It was a series about three doctors in the Peak District. The main character was written as a fan of Eric Clapton and had also spent time in Africa, so my theme incorporated all these elements. I wrote the theme quickly and proceeded to mislay the manuscript. I remembered the opening and main theme but couldn't for the life of me recall the middle, or bridge section. Eventually I gave up and wrote a new part, which I was happy with. Months later I found my first manuscript – the show was already on the air and my original bridge was not only awful, I recognized it as lifted from another TV theme! Sometimes things get lost for a good reason. The show ran for nearly ten years and I won the Television and Radio Industry award for the best TV music. Tony told all the directors not to interfere with what I wrote so I was usually left to my own devices, but one director suddenly, to my horror, started suggesting broad slapstick effects. A quick call to Tony nipped this in the bud and all other episodes were a wonderful experience for the regular musicians and engineers.

Apart from the eccentricities of the BBC's payment setup, discussed earlier, in the 1980s and 90s we were able to employ rather large ensembles for dramatic productions and music-oriented programmes. In this day and age, when composers are reduced to paying for extra musicians out of their own fee, I marvel at the fact that we were able to use orchestras of nearly thirty players for one-off dramas and series. Of course, we were all mindful that budgets were smaller than those of feature films but if we really wanted twenty-five players, say, we got them. Added to that, almost all television variety shows had a full orchestra or big band featured. Gradually the number of players was reduced and eventually some bright spark said, "Why do we need a band anyway?" The days when the BBC canteen was full of musicians at lunchtime were no more – Lime Grove Studios were demolished. I used to enjoy the regular mass dash to the street from the canteen during lunch when we were warned of marauding parking wardens patrolling the road in front of the studios (legal parking was impossible anywhere nearby). The car park attendant at the BBC drama headquarters on Shepherd's Bush Green became a great pal and we had frequent long chats about his health, family and vacation plans. All this, however, was no guarantee that he would remember you, or let you park the next time you had a meeting in the building. I fondly recall one saxophone player who used to drive his Rolls Royce Corniche to the BBC TV Centre, be directed into the executive car park, wait for the commissionaire to disappear and then take his sax out of the trunk and head into the studios.

In 2012 I took musical charge of a TV tribute show to the Titanic, broadcast live from Belfast Dockyard, exactly 100 years after the ship was launched from the identical spot. This was a daunting task. Not only was it broadcast live, but the artists ranged from Bryan Ferry and my buddies Joss Stone and Mica Paris to classical virtuoso violinist Nicola Benedetti playing Shostakovich. I had to adjust my musical brain rapidly from orchestral rock and roll, to Alfie Boe singing 'Bring Him Home' from *Les Mis*, to being a classical conductor – something I've never pretended to be – for Nicola and the other wonderful violinist Charlie Siem. Nicola's record company had sent me a recording of the piece played by another violinist, which I became familiar with via the recording and score. Of course, when Nicola arrived on the day of transmission, her interpretation was very different, and I didn't really have the time to adjust to her. I had to cross my fingers and pray. Not only did it all come off admirably, but we also only went 12 seconds overtime on the show. If that is the last spectacular I'm ever involved in, at least I didn't disgrace myself.

Figure 36: Conducting Shostakovich with the Ulster Orchestra and Nicola Benedetti. Author's collection.

14 Movies (1)

The IMDB (Internet Movie Database) tells me I've scored over fifty movies. I'm obviously not going to talk about all of them, but I will pick out some highlights and some fun stories.

I was asked to arrange the score for a John Mackenzie television movie – *Act of Vengeance* – based on a true story concerning the assassination of Jock Yablonski and the corruption in the US United Mine Workers' Union. The movie starred Charles Bronson and Ellen Burstyn, with debuts for the young Keanu Reeves (aged seventeen) and Ellen Barkin. I was introduced to the project by assistant editor Tony Sloman. John Mackenzie, known to one and all as Frenzy, had directed the classic gangster film *The Long Good Friday*. The composer hired was a well-known and well-respected singer/songwriter.

I began work on the songs and then attended a meeting where the composer was due to play his thoughts for the eight-minute sequence that led up to the assassination of Bronson and his family. He began playing an accented bluesy rhythm on the bottom string of his guitar and there were smiles all round. And that's where he stayed for the entire eight minutes! After about two minutes, the producers were looking at me imploringly, and at the end of the demonstration, John and the producers took me to one side and asked if I would score the film. It had everything – love interest, dramatic confrontations, tension and a build up to a brutal murder – so it was a new challenge I couldn't resist. But how would my songwriter friend take this apparent snub? First, he had been told I was there to arrange his music, but now here I was, usurping his role. Luckily his songs stayed in the picture, and he later told me he was relieved to have the burden of scoring the movie taken off his shoulders. He said, "I don't have the first clue as to how to write a score!"

The recording sessions went really well, and we were mixing the music late one night. John was sitting at the back of the control room tutting and sighing, and I asked him if there was a problem with the music.

"Oh no, I'm casting a film and I have a young actor in mind for the role of the bad guy. I used him in *The Long Good Friday*. He's sensational but he's in a spoof detective TV series at the moment and I'm worried the audience won't take him seriously as a villain. I have another on the slate but he's nowhere near as good. I have to decide tonight, and I don't know what to do!"

"Well," I said, "if this actor is as good as you say he is, the audience may snigger when he comes on, but when they walk out of the cinema, they'll all be saying, 'Wasn't he amazing? I'd never have known.'"

"You're right!" said Frenzy. He picked up the phone, dialled and said, "Cast Pierce Brosnan!"

The film in question was *The Fourth Protocol* and Pierce's performance as the villain catapulted him into movie stardom. The TV series was, of course, *Remington Steele*.

Figure 37: With Pierce Brosnan. Author's collection.

Some years ago, I suddenly decided to tell Pierce this tale. We had sat together at the New York premiere of *Goldeneye* and then flew back to London on the same flight but neither occasion felt like the right time to tell him. John Mackenzie has now passed away and the story might never have been told. So, I emailed Pierce and received a response straight away. He was delighted! More recently, we met at a function, and I repeated the story, much to his pleasure.

If I haven't been involved in the filming of a movie in some way – supervising onscreen performing or teaching a song to an actor – my point of contact in post-production was usually the director and editor. It was always odd attending premieres or gala screenings of movies where I really was the Hidden Man – most of the cast wouldn't recognize me at all. This had its advantages and disadvantages. Occasionally this state of affairs would provoke some amusing interactions. I was in a restaurant in London and spotted an actor who had coincidentally appeared in about four movies and TV dramas I had recently scored. I went up to him and said, "Sorry to disturb you, but I'm sick of the sight of you!" I quickly explained lest I were on the receiving end of a well-directed right hook!

I was visiting the legendary movie producer Elliott Kastner one evening in the 1980s. While Elliott and I shared some tea and biscuits, Sir Alan Parker telephoned. He was in South America scouting locations for *Mississippi Burning* – Elliott had produced *Angel Heart* and was producing this new movie; he put Alan on speaker as he read out the international grosses for *Angel Heart* (probably to impress me, I guess). Unfortunately, at that precise moment I choked on a biscuit which went "down the wrong way." With me wheezing, spluttering and coughing and Elliott not deactivating the speakerphone and waving frantically at me to shut up, heaven knows what Alan made of it. He obviously heard the commotion but hopefully never knew it was me – I certainly didn't tell him on the many occasions we subsequently worked together.

Don Black had recommended me as an arranger to the great movie composer Elmer Bernstein, initially to arrange a song for the movie *Honky Tonk Freeway*. Elmer was then scoring a movie called *A Night in the Life of Jimmy Riordan* starring River Phoenix and directed by the author William Richert. He had written quite a few jazz cues for an octet. I arranged from Elmer's (sometimes very basic) sketches. (Orchestrator Chris Palmer told me, "Just write what sounds good – Elmer trusts you.")

When we got to the studio, Elmer said, "You know the music. You conduct and I'll sit in the box with the director." The sessions went very smoothly, featuring the saxophone of Andy Sheppard, and I looked forward to seeing the finished movie, so I was horrified to discover Elmer's score had been replaced, against the wishes of the director. I've recently been in touch with the director, who is restoring the movie with his original cut and Elmer's music. I got to know River Phoenix socially in LA very briefly before his life was tragically cut short, and never worked with Elmer again, although he remained a very supportive friend. During his last hospital stay I spoke at an arrangers' lunch in Hollywood and his manager attended, conveying Elmer's best wishes and a wonderful encomium, which I treasure.

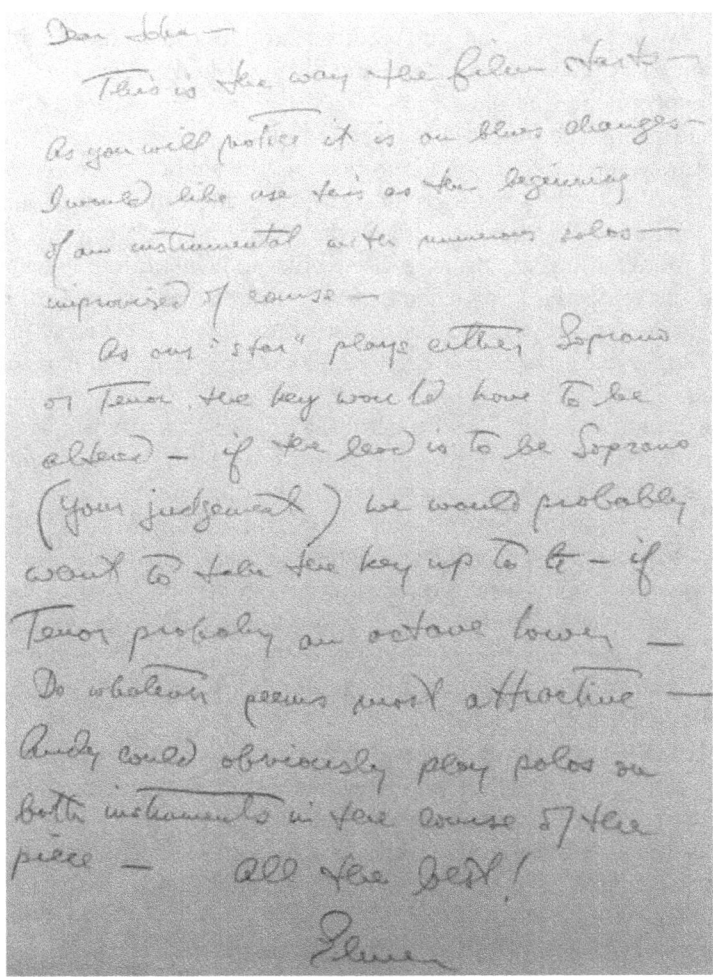

Figure 38: Letter from Elmer Bernstein. Author's collection.

My double bass player on this and many more sessions and live gigs is one of the finest all-round classical and jazz bassists in the world and a member of a very famous musical family in the UK. At the age of seventeen he was playing in a major London orchestra, when he turned to the distinguished harpist and said, "Give me an A, grandma?" The titled conductor went berserk and berated the young lad: "How dare you talk to that iconic lady like that – you should be ashamed of yourself!"

"But she *is* my grandma!"

In the early days of Channel 4 I was asked to score a documentary about the history of Yiddish cinema between 1929 and 1939, *Almonds and Raisins*. The screenplay was by Wolf Mankowitz and the narrator was Orson Welles (see the next chapter for more details). The film was directed by Russ Karel, someone we lost far too soon, and featured surviving veterans of Yiddish cinema, many of whom went on to long and distinguished careers in Hollywood.

My involvement was once again down to Tony Sloman's recommendation. I had been asked to do a five-second burst of saxophone for the ending of a thirty-second *Orangina* commercial. The agency and director of the spot were so disinterested they sent Tony, the editor, to the session. I hired the wonderful Nigel Hitchcock to play the solo burst and Tony and I started chatting about various movies. We discovered we were both movie buffs with a shared encyclopedic knowledge of film music. I pride myself on my love of classic cinema and grabbed the opportunity, when I worked with Ronald Neame, Roy Boulting or Ken Russell, to quiz them about their classic contributions to film history.

Tony remembered our chat and took a chance that I wrote as well as I enthused. Hopefully I didn't disappoint him, as we both became involved in a multitude of movie projects over the years. The documentary won a plethora of awards at various film festivals. Fate brings some strange dishes to the table.

In 1990 I went to a party for graduates of Sussex University. No one else present was from my time at Sussex and the only person I vaguely knew was a younger advertising producer with whom I had briefly worked on a commercial. We started chatting and he suddenly said, "You know, one of my directors is starting a movie about the Irish tenor Josef Locke and the music may well be of interest to you."

I replied, "My uncle conducted records and London Palladium appearances for Josef Locke and Josef was a regular cast member on his radio show—so of course I know his whole story!"

"That's great. I'll put the director Peter Chelsom in touch with you."

"Peter Chelsom? I think he may well have acted in a Noel Coward play I scored for the BBC, *Star Quality*."

The producer passed all this information on to Peter who said, "I've been trying to find out who scored that play, as he's exactly the person I'd want to write the music for this movie."

So, we were off and running with *Hear My Song*. I had to pre-record all the concert material and incidental songs, which went well. For most people involved it was their first film and for me it was the first time I'd been given musical control of the entire movie. I had an idea that didn't seem particularly radical at the time, which was that the various musical themes in the score should be treated in different styles with different line-ups – a big band, a synthesizer, a 1930s style Hot Club Quintet, an Irish band. I was later told by a major Hollywood producer, "Do you know what you've done in this movie?

You've changed the way film music is written!" Needless to say, I never saw or heard from him again.

Everyone involved in *Hear My Song* has gone on to becoming mainstays of the film and television industry: director Peter Chelsom, lead actor and screenplay co-author Adrian Dunbar, debutants James Nesbitt and Tara Fitzgerald, director of photography, the late Sue Gibson, not to mention the Oscar winners behind the scenes – editor Martin Walsh, sound editor Glenn Freemantle and costume designer Lindy Hemming. And I won the Anthony Asquith award for the best score of the year. Princess Diana (who knew me from my jazz gigs she had attended!), along with the real Josef Locke and Stephanie Lawrence (a top star of West End musicals who passed away at a very young age), presented me with the award. Joe saw the movie as his big break back into stardom (in fact a re-release of his 1940s and 1950s tracks, some with my uncle, went to the top of the UK album charts on the back of the movie's success). Sadly, his voice had gone by the time we shot the movie – it would have been a disaster to have used him. He was well paid not to be involved and I used Vernon Midgley who did a fabulous job. I even had a role as the bandleader/pianist in the film, although my acting would hardly give Daniel Day Lewis any sleepless nights. I refer to it as my goldfish role as every time I open my mouth to speak, the camera cuts away leaving the impression I'm walking around in a catatonic trance! We shot most of the interiors in Dublin, in a soon-to-be-demolished abandoned Methodist church which would never pass Health and Safety these days. This was at the same time as Alan Parker's team was filming *The Commitments* on a budget four times larger than ours, and we quite often stayed behind to watch their rushes.

The veteran comedian Harold Berens played the orchestral conductor Benny Rose. Our "orchestra" in the film contained many elder statesmen from the Irish music scene. The lead violinist came up to me with a concerned look on his face during filming. "I just can't follow this man's conducting," he complained.

"Don't worry, you are all miming – it doesn't matter!" I reassured him. There was a joyful camaraderie between cast and crew, and I spent quite a bit of time with Ned Beatty and David McCallum. David's father had led the string section on most of the Beatles' records and David ruefully told me that he had given up learning the cello when his father returned from a day of high-pressured recording (he also led the London Symphony Orchestra) and bellowed, "Stop that dreadful racket!" I vowed never to be that callous with my kids.

I have to say I was never nervous taking on the responsibility of composing my first fully credited score. When I lecture at the National Film and Television School, universities or at the various music academies about composing for film I'm often asked how I broke into movie scoring or what paths I took to become a film composer. My replies may seem flippant, but they are absolutely true: "join a chart-topping band, take down arrangements from records by international artists arriving in Britain who don't have any music with them and go to parties where you may bump into someone making a film!"

Figure 39: With Ned Beatty and David McCallum on set for *Hear My Song*. Author's collection.

With Peter Chelsom as a first-time director I had carte blanche to indulge myself, as I have indicated. I can't say anyone, including myself, was consciously rewriting the rulebook of film music writing, we were just doing what we felt was right and worked. I was very lucky to be onset virtually throughout the filming and that I had the opportunity to control all the music heard in the movie – also that I was able to arrange and produce all the prerecords, to choose our vocalists, and to be at the shoots when the late great Ned Beatty had to mime as Josef Locke (he actually sang along, very well and an octave lower!). I recently attended the 30th anniversary screening of *Hear My Song* in London with stars Adrian Dunbar and Tara Fitzgerald and was delighted to see and hear how well the movie and music have stood the test of time. They certainly haven't dated at all – a great testament to Peter Chelsom and Adrian Dunbar's conception that the film would feel timeless.

Hear My Song was a huge and unexpected success in the USA as well. I had no idea how influential the film had been until I was introduced to Steve Martin and Carl Reiner by Annie Ross, and they carefully analyzed my work and raved knowledgably about the film. Carl Reiner's detailed recount of a hilarious scene with a cow and a well and my musical contribution to the sequence (see the film!) will be a memory that stays with me forever. Another great afternoon was spent eavesdropping on a John Williams session for the movie *Far and Away*. I sat with director Ron Howard and a visiting Dame Julie Andrews in the control room listening to the maestro's wonderful music but found it hard to ascertain how the orchestra followed his unique conducting style.

"Oh, we've played for him for years," responded my friend who was leading the violin section. "We know what he means!"

Offers to score Hollywood cinema and TV movies started rolling in, which meant that for the next twenty-five years I divided my time between London and Los Angeles.

And Russia. My "sponsor," Tony Sloman, who had plunged me into the mix for *Almonds and Raisins* and *Act of Vengeance* was now one of the producers of an Anglo/Soviet co-production, *Assassin of the Tsar*, and I was asked to write the score – the first Western composer to score a Russian film. The alarm bells rang when I arrived in Moscow and was introduced as the composer to the head of music at Mosfilm, Minna Blank, an appointee of Stalin. "We already have music," she stated, fixing me with a glare. (Two cues by a Russian composer in a two-hour movie!) I gave her a present of some teabags, as instructed in those pre-Glasnost days, to receive the response, "I drink Earl Grey!" She then rang Malcolm McDowell in Hollywood, who was starring and co-producing, to tell him the score was awful. Malcolm frantically rang Tony in Moscow (not the easiest thing to do then) to find out what could be done, only to be assured that we hadn't even started recording yet.

The recordings went very well, despite Ms Blank's attempts to disrupt the sessions, and the orchestra enjoyed working with me, although I wasn't allowed to conduct. Her mantra was, "It is not possible," although the opposite inevitably turned out to be the case. Firstly, the recording sessions were delayed because of "technical problems." The main one seemed to be that the multitrack tapes that we had brought from London had been detained by Russian immigration officials, as there was no sign of anyone attempting to fix the "technical problems." At any rate no one seemed too bothered as the old adage "time is money" didn't apply to recording behind the Iron Curtain, and we eventually got under way.

One morning Ms Blank came into the control room and announced, "The contrabassoonist is sick, we must cancel the session!" I explained that it wasn't the worst problem we faced, as the contrabassoon was basically playing long notes in tandem with the double basses. She then suggested, "The pianist will come in and play the contrabassoon part on synthesizer!"

I patiently explained that the concerto-like piano part was infinitely more important than the odd long note on the contrabassoon and we carried on. Later that afternoon I noticed the contrabassoon player in his seat and pointed this out to the engineer. "People recover quickly here," he replied mysteriously. Later in the sessions an important viola line wasn't coming through, and the engineer shrugged his shoulders. I asked Graham, my English music copyist who had flown to Moscow with me (coach class; my music had a seat in first class!), to check the music and he came back asking me, "How many violas did we ask for?"

"Sixteen," was my response.

"There are two!"

I asked Minna for more, but her response, of course, was "It is not possible." At the next session there were sixteen. I took a UREI frame click metronome with me – the engineer and Ms Blank actually had a tug of war over who should operate it ("I'm the head of music, it's my job!" "No, I'm the engineer, I should be responsible!"), with me flapping round them, pleading, "Please don't break it!"

We recorded on the same stage on which Prokofiev and Shostakovich had created their classic scores, and the only hiccup came when the engineer launched into a tirade against the head of music. The inspector of microphones (!) who stood in the control room and didn't understand English called the engineer out to take a telephone call, and from the time he returned he never said another word for the next four days! One afternoon our translator came into the control room and announced, "Now we see spacemen." And everything stopped as four bemedalled Russian cosmonauts entered the room and shook my hand. As "distinguished visitors", we were greeted by the astronauts who were of rock star status then, judging by the appreciation shown by all the musicians and technical staff. As none of them spoke English and my Russian stretched to please and thank you, we smiled at each other. I said through my interpreter, "You are very brave men."

They replied, "Your music sounds wonderful." More smiles and off they went, so we resumed the recording. At one point during the sessions my conductor said to me, "How can you write such expressive Russian music?"

"Because my family came to England from Russia in the late nineteenth century to escape the pogroms. I guess I still have the Russian aesthetic in me!"

Neither the conductor nor any of the musicians he was standing with at the time had ever heard of the pogroms!

Moscow in those days was a very strange place indeed. Americans kept materializing from behind potted plants in the hotel corridors, like a Cold War spy novel. One "communist" who kept surprising us at various venues was, according to our translator, obviously CIA. (People connected with the movie would suddenly emerge from doors at Mosfilm as we walked past.) There was a different elderly lady seated at a desk near the elevator on each floor of our hotel, which apparently had once been KGB headquarters and still had random wiring going nowhere along the walls. The woman's function presumably was to order the hotel staff not to touch my room during my time there, as my bed was never made and my towels never changed during the whole stay. When I mentioned this to Graham, he looked surprised and informed me that his room was cleaned every day – and we had adjoining rooms.

We visited the home of a Russian movie star who lived with her mother, brother, young daughter, and no doubt others, in what looked like a run-down council estate. As it was Easter, I gave the daughter an Easter egg and realized from the look on her face that she had never eaten chocolate before. All the cars on the road kept their windshield wipers locked in the glove compartment to prevent them from being stolen. When it rained, all the cars stopped and the drivers got out and fitted the wipers – it looked like a choreographed scene from *La La Land*. One afternoon during the recordings, we were in an elevator at Mosfilm when a passenger pointed excitedly at Graham. Our interpreter stated that the gentleman was a movie director and Graham was perfect to play the starring role in his current film comedy. Sadly, the language barrier and pressing needs of our sessions prevented him from becoming the Russian Benny Hill.

When I tried to visit Red Square, a soldier blocked our path. The inference was that it was closed. My interpreter showed my pass and the soldier stepped aside. Thus, I was able to visit a church where all the coffins of the Royals were stacked in a huge pile. Apparently, Lenin had ordered them all destroyed, changed his mind, and there they had sat since 1917. The department store window displays were drawings of beach scenes on cardboard. A very different Moscow from today.

It sounds as if we had a fraught, tense time in Russia but I have to say it was far from it. We had resigned ourselves to blips along the way and when they occurred there was a camaraderie that extended beyond the three Brits to our interpreters, engineer, conductor and orchestra. It transpired that the original composer (two cues) was from St. Petersburg (then Leningrad) and was therefore detested by the Moscow-based musicians who performed terribly for him. I heard those cues before we started recording and was horrified by their sloppiness and appalling tuning. Fearing the worst, I prepared for the opening titles recording – it sounded amazing! Even Ms Blank thawed out slightly when she realized that we were going to deliver a successful music score.

The movie went to Cannes, and I went with it. My only real memories of the trip are becoming friendly with the late Oleg Yankovsky, star of our film and the great Tarkovsky movies, being kissed by Juliette Binoche (I still don't remember why!) and the director Karen Shakhnazarov who is now head of Mosfilm, telling me he had made a big mistake cutting a five-minute cue I'd written from the film, as it wasn't the practice then in Russian films to have long musical interludes with no dialogue. *Assassin of the Tsar* was shown in competition and did reasonably well – I had fun sitting in with local jazz groups and gatecrashing studio parties.

Two movie classics I arranged and conducted around this time were Bertolucci's *The Sheltering Sky* with music by Ryuichi Sakamoto, and Luc Besson's *Léon (The Professional)* with a score by Eric Serra.

Sakamoto's music for *Sheltering Sky* won the Golden Globe for best score. I got to spend a lot of time with Bernardo Bertolucci talking film and film music. During one break he mentioned that he had reluctantly just given the prize at Cannes to David Lynch's *Wild at Heart* but was uneasy because of the explicit violence. This led us into a fascinating discussion of one of our favourite directors Fritz Lang and our chat became more esoteric as we both realized the depth of each other's knowledge of Lang's European and American oeuvre. With the Royal Philharmonic waiting for me to restart the session, there appeared to be no desire on Bertolucci's part to end our chat, much to my discomfort as we were wasting producer Jeremy Thomas's money and he was sat waiting in the control room. At that moment one of Bertolucci's assistants sidled up and said, "Bernardo, will you look at these ideas for the poster?" In his best directorial tone Bernardo yelled, "Can't you see I'm busy?"

At that point I bolted to my podium! Ryuichi is without doubt a genius and the sessions at Metropolis and Snake Ranch Studios were a delight. Our tea maker was a young lad whose name was Hans Zimmer – I wonder what became of him? (In actual fact he was already established as a synthesizer expert and keyboard player and co-owned the studio, but it makes a good story!)

I came into Eric Serra's orbit because he loved the *Sheltering Sky* score and wanted the same orchestral atmosphere. Our first collaboration was on Luc Besson's movie *Atlantis*. There was no dialogue, just underwater footage and Eric's music performed by the Royal Philharmonic Orchestra. The film premiered in the old Roman amphitheatre in Orange, France and after the premiere we all went to a restaurant to celebrate. I decided to make my way back to the hotel early and set off down the road. The streetlights soon receded as I set off down the road to the hotel. Then I came to a dead end – I could see the hotel beyond barbed wire and a motorway, but it meant retracing my steps. Just at that moment a posse of motorbikes roared towards me, and I thought, "This is it, I'm going to die, and I will have just vanished from the face of the earth."

I prepared myself for the worst – but just as the bikes got within about 20 yards of me, they turned into a farmyard I hadn't noticed in the pitch darkness. I gratefully set off back towards the restaurant and an hour later burst through the door, to the surprise of Luc, Eric and Ray Williams the music supervisor. This time I waited for a taxi!

When I arranged (with David Arch) and conducted Eric's music for *Léon* (aka *The Professional*) I was blown away by the relentlessness of what I saw and heard, which made me hunger to attend the premiere. I duly flew to LA, stopped at the Chateau Marmont to pick up tickets from Luc Besson, dropped my bags at the Sunset Marquis and headed to the movie theatre with eager anticipation. I settled into my seat, the lights dimmed, the opening sequence began. The next thing I knew I awoke to the sound of the end title song – I'd managed to sleep through probably the loudest movie ever made!

It then took me a year before I could muster enough courage to watch it, and Academy Award winning actor Gary Oldman's performance blew me away, as he usually does. A very unlikely tale – the mother of one of my good friends mentioned to me, when we were in Australia, that she had worked with and looked after Gary Oldman. They were both in pantomime in Southend! When I became friendly with Gary I said to him, "This may sound ridiculous, but were you ever in pantomime in Southend with...?"

His eyes lit up and he said, "Of course I remember – give her my best!"

I'm one of the select few to have composed for a James Bond movie and am lucky enough to be associated with one of the most memorable sequences in the history of the franchise – the classic tank chase through St. Petersburg in *Goldeneye*. My first ever encounter with James Bond was unusual to say the least. I sneaked into our local "fleapit" cinema to watch *From Russia with Love* just after it was released. The projectionist, for some reason, ran reel seven before reel two. Characters began disappearing and reappearing, the story made no sense whatsoever and the overall effect was of watching a French "nouvelle vague" movie of the early 1960s. To add insult to injury the film broke down completely in reel nine and it was years before I was able to watch the movie in sequence.

I had been enjoying a fruitful few years collaborating with Eric Serra. As his orchestrator and conductor, I had already worked on the two Luc Besson movies I mentioned. *Léon* had caught the eye and ear of the Bond producers, who were looking to reinvigorate the dormant Bond series with a new Bond (my "protégé" Pierce Brosnan) and a fresh approach to the music.

Although I was working on my own movie score at the time (*Funnybones*) I was excited to play a role in the Bond adventure. Who wouldn't be? We began work on the score, but it gradually became apparent that the producers weren't sure that Eric's radically contemporary approach was really what they wanted. Matters came to a head when they began dubbing the tank chase – and a decision was made to go for a more traditional Bond approach. I received a call on Friday morning asking me to go to Pinewood Studios for a meeting that afternoon. It became apparent that Eric didn't want to rewrite the tank sequence and that they had decided to change composer for that scene. I was offered the chance to score it but insisted that Eric had to be asked if he was happy with me doing so as I had come onto the project with him. He gave his OK and off I went. To tell you the truth, I knew exactly what I was going to write – every composer working in movies dreams of scoring a top-notch James Bond action scene and the music just flowed out – so much so that I decided to do my own orchestration (I had a couple of orchestrators on standby because of the deadline). Combining the traditional Bond theme with my original composition was an exciting and fulfilling exercise and I never felt under pressure. Writing a major action sequence for a huge movie can be a daunting task. I certainly had no time to panic or feel I wasn't up to the task – in truth (and luckily) it's an emotion, along with stage fright,

I've never experienced. It's a confidence rather than a cockiness – I've never felt smug about my responses under pressure, just that I am lucky to have the ability to rise to challenges rather than be overwhelmed or overawed by them. With the tank chase I was conscious of its excitement, the combination of humour and absurd unreality, and various climaxes, each one topping the previous. I knew I had to use the Monty Norman theme for the major impact points, start big and get bigger, and weave my original composition around it.

I structured the cue and composed for it on Saturday, orchestrated on the Sunday, the music was copied into individual parts on the Monday, and we recorded on the Tuesday evening with 100 plus musicians – a dream orchestra of some of the world's finest (the trumpets alone included Derek Watkins who had played on every Bond score since *Dr. No* and Kenny Wheeler, one of the major jazz soloists and writers). The session was a joy – to hear the Bond theme interwoven with my variations was quite an experience. The dub was finished the next day and the film opened the following week – such was the rush.

At the New York premiere which I attended at Radio City Music Hall, the tank chase received a standing ovation, and it was recently voted the number two all-time favourite James Bond sequence. Although I was uncredited on screen (the credits had already been finalized) word got out via the internet and it is now common knowledge that I was the composer, so I'm not giving away any secrets here. (I have "ghost written" several sequences in movies that everyone is familiar with, but the code of silence among composers prevents me from naming them.) Sometimes even I would be at a loss for words when experiencing the machinations of movie companies. When the charming film *Enchanted April*, with the wonderful score by Sir Richard Rodney Bennett, was ready for release I received a frantic telephone call from someone at the production company.

"The producers have decided there are two sequences in the movie that need scoring before next week's premiere. Sir Richard is unavailable – if we send you the movie and timings could you do something for us?"

I watched the movie and called the office back.

"I know what you're after – I have taken down Sir Richard's themes and can orchestrate them appropriately in the next couple of days, then we can book a studio and the musicians for Friday. It's a push but I'm confident we can do it."

"Oh no, we need something this afternoon – don't you have anything on the shelf you can send us that will fit?"

I resisted the temptation to respond, "yes I have two cues by a heavy metal rock band that would fit the timings perfectly. They shouldn't grate too much in a movie about four women in 1920s England who go off to vacation in Italy!" Thankfully the two sequences remained devoid of music in the final release, which of course was a huge success with critics, audiences and the awards circuit.

'The Tank Chase through St. Petersburg' is performed regularly in concerts of the music of James Bond, there is a chapter devoted to *Goldeneye* in Jon Burlingame's terrific book *The Music of James Bond*, and at the Academy celebration of fifty years of Bond in Los Angeles I was introduced, along with a select group of Bond girls, to a huge round of applause from the audience.

My association with Bond continues in strange ways. I have done a series of live gigs in recent years with jazz vocalist Monty Norman – who originally composed the James Bond theme. I persuaded him to come out and sing in public – something he hadn't done for many years, and we had a blast. Even James Bond himself couldn't think up such a strange twist of fate! Eric's score, which sounded radical then, can now be seen as being very much ahead of its time, and in 2020 I renewed acquaintance with 007 by arranging and conducting some of Hans Zimmer's score for *No Time to Die*.

Getting involved with Daniel Craig's farewell to the role of 007 came about through the terrific composer Lorne Balfe. Apparently, Hans was searching for an arranger to integrate the traditional James Bond big band brass sound with the score he was composing with the assistance of Steve Mazzaro. Mindful of my association with the franchise, Lorne suggested me to Hans as an option, and Hans tentatively reached out to me. Of course, I was delighted to be "back in the fold" and expanded some key cues for the movie – the opening gun barrel sequence and a couple of spectacular chases. While conducting the additional music at the magnificent Air Studios with a brilliant brass section, I was asked if I would stay on board for the rest of the week and oversee the re-recording of all the brass cues in the movie – this ensured the separation of the elements when it came to the final mix-down. I was thrilled to hear the results and to renew acquaintance with the producers – Barbara Broccoli and Michael Wilson – after twenty-seven eventful years! Unforeseen bonuses were bumping into my friend David Arnold who brought so much to the music of James Bond over the years and socializing at lunch with some old and new pals including the Smiths' guitarist Johnny Marr who performs on the soundtrack. As I write these words, the movie is on course to smash all records and I am delighted to have been once again a part of the James Bond story.

15 More Legends (3)

(Classic movie and jazz stars including Orson Welles, Ava Gardner, Fred Astaire, Chet Baker)

The day after the Sex Pistols were on the *Today* show in 1976, swearing volubly (with the encouragement of Bill Grundy and thanks to the machinations of my much-missed friend Eric Hall) I was in Crank's vegetarian restaurant near Carnaby Street. A diminutive, striking-looking older American lady was in front of me in the line and we fell into a conversation about the merits of various dishes. As the tables were pretty crowded, I invited her to sit with me. Not long into our conversation I realized that she was movie icon Gloria Swanson, in London to promote a new cookbook by her then husband. At one point in our lunchtime chat she became very heated about the "disgusting yobs" she'd seen on TV the previous evening – and how they were a disgrace. I looked to my right and sitting at the next table were the Sex Pistols' drummer Paul Cook and guitarist Steve Jones. It was definitely the most surreal moment of my life. Many years later I was able to tell this story to a nattily dressed, three-piece-suited Paul Cook, who looked the image of respectability.

In 1973 my friend Clive Hirschhorn was writing his biography of Gene Kelly and was at my house for dinner. He casually announced, "I'm expecting a call from Gene Kelly so I gave him your number." Sure enough, the phone rang and a familiar voice asked for Clive. I passed on some of the information given to me by Donald O'Connor and Betty Garrett to Clive and was bowled over to get an acknowledgement in the credits alongside the Sinatras, Astaires and other luminaries for what really was very little input.

Donald O'Connor was the reason my uncle Woolf Phillips moved to LA – to become his musical director. I enjoyed his company and his behind-the-scenes tales of classics like *Singing in the Rain*. One thing I hadn't realized was that he was an acrobat and not a dancer. When his days as a child star in the movies were numbered, he joined the Jiving Jacks and Jills and was hidden at the back while he learned to dance. His natural flair for comedy meant that he was pushed further and further forward in the movies and up the credits and within a few years had become one of the best dancers Hollywood had ever produced. Like a later star, Russ Tamblyn, Donald's gymnastic abilities were well to the fore and gave his dancing an extra dimension. He was also a very talented composer – and a charming man.

Another pal from the great days of Hollywood was the aforementioned Betty Garrett who starred in *On the Town*. Betty was very kind to me on my early forays to Los Angeles – she had appeared at the Palladium with her husband Larry Parks during the late 1940s and was delighted that I was following in the family tradition! She told me a wonderful story about a tribute to Gene Kelly in the early 1970s in Las Vegas, which featured all his surviving leading ladies seated in a line. Betty and Vera Ellen flanked the wheelchair bound Ann Miller who had been hit on the head by a steel bar in the safety curtain on the opening night of *Anything Goes* and was unable to walk. Ann asked Betty and Vera Ellen to help her stand up to take a bow when her name was announced. As Ann was introduced, Betty and Vera Ellen stood up to assist her out of the wheelchair. The showbiz gene kicked in and Ann leapt out of the chair unaided, flung her arms out wide, and shouted "I love you all!" sending Betty and Vera Ellen flying!

On my first Hollywood visit in 1972, I actively sought out survivors of the Golden Age of Hollywood movies. One fascinating encounter was with bandleader and early star vocalist Rudy Vallée. My cousin Carole (Woolf's daughter) had appeared with him and Robert Morse in a stage revival of *How to Succeed in Business Without Really Trying*. Vallée had an early karaoke backing track version of his career on tape and did his whole act for me in his front room. Then he autographed a photo of himself from around forty years earlier! One complaint he had was that when he played saxophone in the Savoy Havana Band in 1920s London, they wouldn't let him sing!

In the early 1980s, I met Victor Lownes who was second in command of the *Playboy* empire and ran their London venue. We shared a love of classic cabaret performers and through my friendship with the great Mabel Mercer, I received a free pass to the music room events. I went to hear Mabel on numerous occasions and always sat with her guests. One evening the couple at the table with me looked very familiar. "Are you who I think you are?" I asked the man opposite me.

"Who do you think I am?" he replied.

"Cy Coleman?"

Indeed, it was the composer of 'Sweet Charity', 'The Best is Yet to Come', and many, many more classics. His "date" was Barbara Walters and we spent a wonderful evening listening to Mabel and chatting. At one point I bemoaned the fact that I hadn't lived and worked in the golden era of Gershwin, Porter and Berlin. His response stunned me: "So did I, until I realized I was carrying the torch." My whole attitude virtually changed on the spot – some seventeen years later when I was at a show given by my friend Annie Ross, a familiar figure entered the room. It was Cy Coleman. I went over to him and said,

"You won't remember me, but you gave me some wonderful advice years ago and since then I've won an Emmy and a BAFTA and scored a lot of movies." He looked me up and down and said, "Maybe *you* can give *me* some good advice?"

Figure 40: Photo signed to me by Rudy Vallee. Author's collection.

Another great cabaret performer was Bobby Short. I became friendly with him and one evening he invited me to a live recording session at the Pizza on the Park in Knightsbridge. It was in the basement (formerly a storeroom) of a restaurant, and before it had an expensive makeover in the late 1990s was decidedly gloomy. As I arrived, Bobby said, "You'll be sitting on my table" and led me to the back of the room which was almost in total darkness. At the table he theatrically announced, "Of course you know Liz Taylor, Ava Gardner and Gloria Vanderbilt?"

"Of course I do!" I responded, before my eyes adjusted to the gloom and I realized that was really who I was sitting with! Sitting opposite Elizabeth and Gloria, I didn't really have much of an opportunity to chat, but in the breaks Ava told me some scurrilous tales. In later years I would often run into her near Marble Arch, anonymously walking her dog and not being bothered by anyone. I think she liked the fact that she didn't have to be "Ava Gardner" anymore.

One afternoon Bobby and I lunched with the harmonica virtuoso Larry Adler who had been hounded out of the States by the McCarthy hearings. We started discussing this sorry period of American history and Larry ominously said, "Don't think it won't happen again, because it will, and in your lifetime!" I gently chided Larry about his recently published autobiography. "The trick of course is to outlast all the people you write about so no one can contradict your version of events!" I of course apologize if I have inadvertently fallen into the same trap!

Pizza on the Park is one of those long-lost venues that presented the best in cabaret and jazz. I played there often and attended just as frequently. Some of the highlights of my visits were Harold Nicholas singing and dancing with Mick Pyne's jazz trio, Tony Bennett sitting in with Ruby Braff, and Liza Minnelli seated at the piano with Billy Stritch, without a microphone, softly singing standards. I took the great film director Terence Young there to hear Margaret Whiting in cabaret and Terence entertained me with stories from his amazing career, including directing the first two James Bond movies, rejecting Marilyn Monroe, and a hilarious adventure with Rachmaninoff in the 1940s.

Terence wrote the screenplay for the movie *Dangerous Moonlight* in which Anton Walbrook played a concert pianist. In fact, Walbrook was an amateur pianist and needed to learn the music, which was to be composed by Rachmaninoff in Los Angeles. Of course, this was during the war when transatlantic communication was well-nigh impossible. However, Terence had a very important friend, actress Sarah Churchill, daughter of the British Prime Minister, Sir Winston. She arranged for Terence to place a call from 10 Downing Street to Los Angeles and at the appointed time an army sergeant took him through the correct protocol to be observed. He reached Rachmaninoff and the conversation went as follows over the crackly line:

"Maestro Rachmaninoff, this is Terence Young in London. We need your piano concerto for *Dangerous Moonlight* for Anton Walbrook to practice."

"Huh?"

"We need your music for the film as soon as possible."

"Huh?"

"Oh, this is impossible!" Then a thought struck Terence, "Parlez-vous Francais m"sieur?"

"Ah oui, naturellement…"

At that moment the sergeant slammed his hand on the receiver.

"What???"

"You started speaking in a foreign language. You may have been passing state secrets."

Back to square one. Then Terence remembered that when he was putting his daughter to bed and listening to children's radio broadcasts, there were clever nursery rhymes every evening, arranged as orchestral parodies of the great composers. He discovered that they were done by Richard Addinsell (later to compose the wonderful score for David Lean's film of the Noel Coward play *Blithe Spirit*), so Terence went to see him in Cambridge and, to cut a long story short, Addinsell composed the *Warsaw Concerto* (in the style of Rachmaninoff) which is still one of the best-selling classical pieces in history. Things could have been very different if the soldier had spoken French!

A show I attempted to put on several times at Pizza on the Park, and never quite managed to get off the ground, was a tribute to two of my favourite performer/songwriters of the Golden Age of the American Songbook – Matt ('Everything Happens to Me') Dennis and Bobby ('Route 66') Troup, both at the time still living in Los Angeles. One Friday evening I telephoned both of them to update them on progress. I got through to Matt and he immediately proudly announced to me, "I just won a Grammy!" It was for Sting's version of 'Angel Eyes' in the movie *Leaving Las Vegas*. We had a good catch up and then I rang Bobby Troup. His first words to me were "I just won a Grammy!" (this time for Diana Krall's version of 'You're Looking At Me'). I wish that show had gone ahead as they will always be two of my favourite songwriters.

This chapter reflects some of the heroes I had when growing up. I never imagined I would meet them, let alone get to know some of them well and even work with them. Some, like Harold Nicholas of the Nicholas Brothers and Jerry Lewis I will talk about in more detail in the next chapter. Others crossed my path fleetingly. Often, when I'm asked, "Do you ever get starstruck?" I reply that these are the people in front of whom I'm often lost for words and I have to pinch myself. So please forgive some more namedropping and self-indulgence as I describe my interaction with some of the legends I've encountered, however briefly.

Speaking of the Nicholas Brothers, they appeared in a Palladium Gala Night of 100 Stars in 1990. Memorably, Fayard Nicholas had recently had two hip replacements and not only was he no longer wheelchair bound, but he'd also started dancing again! The brothers did a dance routine mimicking a projected sequence of them dancing in a 1935 movie. Of course it brought the house down, and they had to repeat the whole thing. They invited me to the dinner afterwards where I sat with Hollywood legends Jane Russell, Arlene Dahl, Dorothy Lamour, Gloria de Haven and Georges Guetary (star of *An American in Paris*). Another evening to remember!

Orson Welles looms large in my story as he did in life. Always a fan of his acting and directing skills, I was delighted to work with him (as I indicated in the last chapter) on the documentary *Almonds and Raisins*, a history of Yiddish cinema between the wars. The original choices for narrator were George Burns, who said he was too old to read a script, Mel Brooks who was very interested but busy on his own projects and Woody Allen likewise. Wolf Mankowitz, another legend, who wrote the screenplay for the film, remembered that Orson had directed a Yiddish Shakespearean production in New York! He was approached and was happy to contribute to a wonderful award-winning slice of history. I had to match chunks of music that were on the original soundtracks with a new score to bridge scenes and was delighted with how seamlessly it seemed to work. Some years later I was invited to score Ben Ross's movie on the making of *Citizen Kane*, *RKO 281* produced by Tony and Ridley Scott, for which I won an Emmy. On set for a big scene featuring Liev Schreiber playing Welles and Melanie Griffith as Marion Davies, while watching the filming, I started chatting, joking and laughing with a woman standing next to me. At the end of the shot Liev wandered over and said to her, "I feel very odd playing your dad while you're watching." It turned out that my new friend was Orson's daughter Beatrice Welles. I'm delighted to say we are still great friends to this day, and she manages his legacy with a fierce pride.

In the mid-1970s I was recording at CTS Studios in Wembley, where *Star Wars* and *The Mission*, among many others, were recorded. On a break I headed up to the apparently deserted canteen. In those days there was an L-shaped wall by the serving area so you couldn't see around the corner. I wandered round to check if anyone I knew was hiding out there. What I saw was Fred Astaire and Bing Crosby on a break from their session, both without their toupées and deep in conversation. My first instinct was to rush over and tell them they were my absolute heroes. Then I thought, "Not a great idea, they're enjoying some downtime on their session and reminiscing." So, I went and sat in the main body of the canteen. A little while later the producer Ken Barnes came up and obviously said to them, "We're ready for your vocals now." As they left, Bing nodded to me, but Fred came over, put his hand on my shoulder and said, "I saw what you did there – thank you!" I floated back into my session! Incidentally, my cousin Carole was the dancer who was arm in arm with Crosby at the end of his TV special when he had his well-documented heart attack. My one-time manager dated Fred's daughter Ava and told me how he helped them move house – when the new living room was finally organized, Fred christened it by putting a Count Basie record on the stereo and dancing round the whole room and over the armchairs and settees for an audience of two!

I have many amazing memories of CTS Studios, now demolished as part of the redevelopment of Wembley stadium. It is actually just a hole in the ground, and there's no plaque or sign to commemorate its historical importance. The studios were a complex of four recording studios plus an upstairs canteen, client rooms and offices, and you never knew whom you might run into while there. From sneaking in to hear the recording of *A Little Touch of Schmilsson in the Night* and the first run through of 'Gabriel's Oboe', to bumping into Anthony Newley and Michael Jackson in the corridor, many incidents flood back into the memory.

In the reception area one day I came across my old colleague from Kevin Ayers and the Whole World, the classical composer and conductor David Bedford. After an exchange of pleasantries, I asked him what he was doing there.

"Oh, I'm conducting a score for an Italian composer for a movie. Come in and have a listen – it's very good and there is no one here apart from the engineer and me – no composer and no one from the film."

Accordingly, I went into the control room and heard Ennio Morricone's sensational music, the first performance of 'Gabriel's Oboe' for the score of *The Mission*. The next day I returned for the choral sessions – David had the choir wandering round the studio followed by two assistant engineers holding boom microphones. The effect was other-worldly and uncanny – voices drifted in and out of focus in constantly shifting patterns. I'm pretty sure this would have been Morricone's instruction and I resolved to try it one day – sadly I've never yet had the opportunity.

I produced Eartha Kitt for a commercial in the same studios. She was wonderful and called me "Sir" throughout. I used to lunch with Henry Mancini, a regular at the studios when he was recording the music for the *Pink Panther* films – a very funny man as well as a musical genius. One evening, I took him out to dinner and our table companion asked if he knew a certain cameraman in Hollywood. He said the name was familiar and our friend said, "He's pretty famous, he's won a couple of Oscars."

"Hasn't everyone?" said Hank raising an eyebrow. (Of course *he* had!)

The great saxophonist Plas (the original *Pink Panther* soloist) Johnson was staying with me at the time and I told Hank that Plas was performing at the Dean Street PizzaExpress that evening. Excitedly he asked if he could join me, and they fell into each other's arms. Much later I discovered that Plas had been upset when the recordings moved to London from LA and Tony Coe took over saxophone duties, but there was obvious affection demonstrated between the two brilliant musicians which I was privileged to overhear.

My one meeting with Nelson Riddle wasn't so entertaining. The studio had a video room upstairs. (I once saw a Hollywood movie producer leading a well-known composer there by the ear to show him a video clip he wanted musically copied!) I was doing an interview for a commercials trade magazine and noticed Nelson outside the door pacing up and down and peering in every so often. I guessed he wanted to use the telephone privately – anyway he finally forced the door open and glared at me, "Haven't you finished yet?"

Not the way I'd have wanted to meet one of my musical heroes!

The controversial avant-garde saxophonist and composer Ornette Coleman was recording the Howard Shore soundtrack for the movie *Naked Lunch* in Studio One. Between sessions Ornette, pianist Dave Hartley and I met up in the canteen. Over our drinks (non-alcoholic for Mr Coleman and me) Ornette explained to us his "harmelodic" theory of music – the explanation consisted of turning a piece of music manuscript upside down so a treble clef C became an A.

"There you are!" exclaimed Maestro Coleman triumphantly. I'm afraid he'd completely lost us. There was complete silence for what seemed like ten minutes. Dave took a long swig from his pint of beer, licked his lips, and uttered the immortal words that have served as our greeting thereafter:

"Cheers, Ornette!"

My favourite songwriter of all time has to be Harry Warren who wrote some of the greatest hits of the twentieth century from 'Home in Pasadena' to 'That's Amore' through to 'I Only Have Eyes For You' and 'At Last' among hundreds of others. (Check out his amazing career online.) I wrote an article about him for an English music magazine which printed a photo of Harry Ruby wrongly identified as him. He roared with laughter and said, "That happens to me all the time!" We began a correspondence that stretched over the years from the early 1970s to his passing in 1981, during which time I was privy to some wonderful stories – I wish I'd been able to spend more time with him in Los Angeles.

Chappell Music (now Warner Chappell) is one of the oldest music publishing houses in the world. They had an impressive headquarters in New Bond Street in London with a shop on the ground floor, a couple of recording studios directly above (where we recorded 'Always Look on the Bright Side of Life' and many other sessions) and quite a few "old-style" publishers' offices replete with piano and tape machines. My uncles had a long-standing connection with Chappell Music – uncle Sid had urged them to sign his friend Jerry Gray in the late 1930s when Jerry wrote for Artie Shaw. Gray's work for Glenn Miller during the war years helped consolidate Chappell's reputation as one of the world leaders in music publishing. When I used to write for Chappell in the 1970s, I gravitated towards the "veterans" of music publishing – Jimmy Henney, and Stan Bradbury and Teddy Holmes (who loathed each other) and others who'd been friends of my showbiz family. Here was I, a youngster keen to meet the Sammy Lerners, Johnny Mercers and Vivian Ellises, all of whom were amazed I knew their music so thoroughly. I took in Dave McKenna to collect some Harry Warren songbooks as he prepared to record an album of Harry's songs, and he played 'The More I See You' to an initial audience of three mesmerized souls! As if in a Hollywood movie, all the doors along the corridor opened and we soon had over a dozen gathered around the piano.

I was in Stan Bradbury's office one day soon after we'd lost Johnny Mercer and he handed me a sheaf of papers.

"Look at these – unpublished lyrics by Johnny Mercer which his widow gave me – what am I supposed to do with them in this day and age?"

Around this time the expat Arthur Schwartz, living in Knightsbridge, became a good friend. He regaled me with stories of his long and productive career. One of my favourites was that he and Howard Dietz were working on the movie *The Bandwagon* with Fred Astaire and Cyd Charisse and Arthur Freed came onto the set and asked them to write a new song for the movie along the lines of 'There's No Business Like Show Business'. They departed to an office with a piano and in fifteen minutes had written 'That's Entertainment!' (I do hope that's a true story and not Arthur trying to impress a young fan.)

One of the songwriters with whom I had a long lunch was Sam Coslow, and he told me the following story. He and his composing partner Arthur Johnston were writing songs for Mae West for a movie. One night he received a phone call: "Miss West doesn't like the song we're shooting tomorrow, could you and Arthur come up with another by the morning?" Sam rang Arthur at home to find he was drunk and already incoherent. He drove over to Arthur's place to find him comatose on the floor. No amount of encouragement could wake him, so Sam rolled up his sleeves, sat at the piano, and wrote words and music to a new number. It was presented to Mae West (as a Johnston/Coslow song) who loved it and sang it. It became a standard and a huge hit – and Arthur Johnston has his name as co-writer to this day, much to Sam's dismay! Having incurred Mr Coslow's wrath by admitting my fondness for Spike Jones's 'Cocktails for Two', I didn't dare mention Spike's version of the Johnston/Coslow song for which Arthur Johnston snored through the writing process – 'My Old Flame'.

Gene Cipriano (aka Cip) told me a lovely story about the composer/musical director Johnny Green, who used to amuse himself before recording sessions at MGM by playing some of his compositions on the piano. One day, an early arrival (and well-known joker) stood behind John, as he liked to be known, while he was playing his most famous composition, 'Body and Soul'.

"Still playing the wrong chords I hear," said the percussionist.

Without looking up or missing a beat John replied, as he carried on playing, "Tell it to my bank manager!"

In Los Angeles I got to know four more musical heroes really well. The great Benny Carter became a close personal friend – he was a kind and generous man. I would head up to his house every Thursday, we'd go to lunch at his tennis club and return to his house, where I'd take charge of his CD player and he'd reminisce about the musicians and artists he'd known during his career, which began in the early 1920s.

A favourite Benny Carter story concerns one of my heroes, tenor saxophonist Ben Webster, whom I would often encounter in the basement of Dobell's jazz shop. Ben, nicknamed the Brute, was known to be exceptionally feisty when "in his cups." Apparently, the only person he feared was Benny Carter. Beneath his very gentle exterior Benny had a reputation for being very tough and took no nonsense. Many of his stories attested to his strength and courage. One day a contrite Ben Webster visited Benny and pleaded with him:

"I'm afraid that last night I got into a fight at my gig with [the great jazz violinist] Stuff Smith's group, knocked someone unconscious, and was sacked on the spot. Please would you go and see the manager of the …. Club and see if he will give me my job back."

Benny, for whom this was no novelty, went to see the manager and pleaded with him to restore Ben's gig, pointing out that he was abjectly apologetic and had people depending on his income.

"I'd like to help but there's one big problem there," explained the club owner.

"Which is?"

"The person he knocked unconscious was Stuff Smith!"

I also remember Benny saying to me, "if someone had told me that the shy bespectacled young kid with his head permanently buried in a book who played fourth trumpet in my big band would change jazz history four or five times, I'd have laughed in their face!" The shy kid with glasses was Miles Davis.

On the omission of his interview from the acclaimed Ken Burns series *Jazz* (Benny had played his first gig in 1924 and was a hugely important figure in the history of the music), Benny asserted, "Maybe I said something they didn't want to hear?"

Benny's astonishing stories would fill a book on their own. His humility and grace was exceptional for someone who had achieved so much in his life. One afternoon he rang me to ask how I'd achieved a certain effect in one of my arrangements. Of course, he would have known exactly how I'd done it but wanted to boost my ego!

He passed away on a Saturday in 2003, aged ninety-five, a day after my uncle Woolf Phillips. Some friends came over on the Friday evening to take me out. For some reason I insisted they watch a documentary about Benny Carter – a premonition, I guess. Amazingly he had phoned me from his hospital bed on the previous Tuesday, to apologize for missing my big band concert on the Monday. When I said, "Oh you'll be home in no time," his response was, "John, I've had enough!"

His great friend was composer David Raksin, writer of the ravishing music for *Laura* and *The Bad and the Beautiful*, among others. At a party for the Mancini Institute, a friend of mine sought me out and reported she'd had a wonderful conversation with an ethnomusicologist. I wasn't too sure I knew what this was and asked her to point him out. It was David Raksin who had defined himself as a professor of ethnomusicology!

Figure 41: Exercising with Benny Carter. Author's collection.

Neal Hefti had retired years earlier – his royalties from the TV series *Batman* alone must have kept him pretty comfortable. (The sheet music has the credit "*Word* and music by Neal Hefti.") More interestingly to me, he had changed the history of jazz three times – first with his arrangements for the Woody Herman Band, then with his wonderful writing on *Clifford Brown with Strings* and then as the architect of the classic "New Testament" Basie band sound of the 1950s. Once he pondered whether he should make a comeback. I had told him that I'd recently seen Johnny Mandel leading his big band. "What does he do? Dance around like Kay Kyser?" (Kay was a particularly animated swing band leader of the 1940s who had a long movie career thanks to his ebullient personality). Johnny roared with laughter when I told him. Neal then said resignedly, "I gave away all my music anyway, so it's never going to happen." Johnny did have a late-flowering big band career where he performed many of his great pieces like 'Emily', 'The Shadow of Your Smile (From the Sandpiper)' and the theme from *M.A.S.H*. We often shared the same bill at festivals in California and once cruised the Caribbean together and spent a lot of time chatting. I miss them all.

Speaking of musical heroes, two who loom extra-large are Burt Bacharach and Dave Grusin. Burt is high on my list of all-time idols, with Dave not far behind. One evening I was visiting Dave backstage before a London show and mentioned in passing that I had met up with Burt the previous night. In the concert that evening, with guitarist Lee Ritenour, Dave played a solo piano feature, presumably one of his major movie or television themes. This particular concert he chose to play 'Alfie', obviously inspired by our conversation earlier. I couldn't have been more flattered if he'd chosen to play something I'd written – but I'm afraid that's a very unlikely scenario!

Jazz has always been an important part of my life – it's probably my favourite music to listen to and I have been delighted to play with, and make the acquaintance of, many of my jazz idols. Here's a random selection of memories – again, I could fill a book with the stories they passed on to me.

Chet Baker came to play at a London club during a lull in his career and sat in with my band one night to warm up for his upcoming season. I asked him what he wanted to play and he replied, "Oh you pick anything and I'll join in." Even on an obscure tune he didn't know, his ear was so good he was able to take the first solo and sound like he'd been playing it all his life. He sat on a chair and, while he was playing the beautiful ballad 'Where or When', a woman at the table in front of the band reached over and tugged at his trouser leg. Chet stopped playing and the woman said, "Trumpet player – play happy birthday dear Victoria." I dreaded what might happen, but he immediately started playing happy birthday to a young lady who probably didn't realize that she was being serenaded by Chet Baker! A memorable start to a terrific residency – Chet was on top form throughout the week.

Being a baritone saxophone player, one of my all-time heroes was and is Gerry Mulligan. If Jule Styne's ballet had happened, then I would have been working closely with Gerry but, as it was, a few years later my friend Bobby Rosengarden came to the PizzaExpress jazz club in Dean Street for a week with his trio. Knowing he was a great pal of Mulligan's and Gerry was in town, I asked Bobby to call me at any time if Gerry showed up in the club to sit on or listen. The phone rang at 11pm one midweek night as I got home from a gig of my own. All Bobby said was, "He's here." So, I leapt into the car and roared into London. When I arrived at the club, a very inebriated Gerry Mulligan was onstage propped up against a pillar and conducting the band while playing some rather disconnected notes.

At the end of the set Gerry wandered over with Bobby and said, "I hear you're a baritone player, come in the back room with me." He showed me his horn and mouthpiece – the mouthpiece had a chunk missing. "It was like that when I got it from Harry Carney of the Ellington band in 1927!" The low C# was completely broken and jammed shut and he asked me for some phone numbers of sax repairers. When I said I had some at home, he told me to call his hotel at 8am before he had to check out. He then said, "It's boring here, let's go to Ronnie Scott's and see my old friend Oscar Peterson." We hit the night air and for the first time in my life I realized what the term "legless" meant. Gerry slowly sank to the ground due to the combination of alcohol and fresh night air. I grabbed him with one hand, his sax case with the other and we proceeded thus around Soho Square, Gerry on one shoulder and his heavy baritone case on my other shoulder suspended by a strap. The thought crossed my mind, "This isn't quite how I envisaged meeting my idol!"

Once inside Ronnie Scott's he lurched towards the stage, knocking over an entire table of drinks and an irate patron, who resembled a movie heavy, yelled, "Who the … do you think you are?"

I thought that was a good moment to slip away and with some trepidation rang his hotel about five hours later. I put on my tape recorder as I thought, "This is going to be interesting." I got through to Gerry, now sober, who took down all the numbers, including my number, thanked me and went on his way! Thereafter, he always sent me complimentary tickets to his London shows.

A favourite houseguest was the great American saxophonist and arranger Al Cohn. He always used to stay with me when he played in London and his one-liners are legendary. We spent the evenings watching videos of Jack Benny and Phil Silvers – I think Al would have loved to have been a comedian, he was certainly funny enough. One evening he took me to the Royal Festival Hall to meet Dizzy Gillespie and Woody Herman. I'd always loved Woody's bands and as we shook hands Al said, "This is John Altman, he leads a big band in London." Woody kept my hand in his, gazed into my eyes and said "Why?"

Al noticed that Stan Getz was playing at Ronnie Scott's in London the same week as Al was at the PizzaExpress. Stan had been in awe of Al's playing since they were both in Woody's band in the late 1940s. Al playfully suggested to me, "Let's book a front table and see how long until he gets rattled!"

I took Al round London, with an obligatory visit to Bill Lewington's music shop on Shaftesbury Avenue, the meeting point for all saxophonists until its sad demise. One day I was there when the great Sonny Rollins came in to try mouthpieces, something he did regularly wherever he was in the world. The tenor saxophonist Don Lanphere, then touring the UK, wandered into the shop. Sonny and he hadn't seen each other since the 1940s, when they were both heavily into narcotics. They fell into each other's arms and then Sonny asked, "Are you still… you know?"

"No, Sonny," replied Don. "When I play now, I play for God!"

Sonny thought for a moment and stroked his chin. "Hmmm, maybe I should try that!"

Al introduced me to the great pianist/songwriter Dave Frishberg. Dave told me a wonderful story about Aaron Copland. In around 1976 Dave was playing in the Benny Goodman Sextet, featuring George Benson, at Carnegie Hall. The second half of the concert comprised the Copland clarinet concerto played by Goodman, conducted by Copland. Dave's then girlfriend was a music student – as she stood at the side of the stage watching the Goodman Sextet she became aware of someone standing next to her. It was none other than Aaron Copland. They fell into a conversation and Copland suddenly broke off with a "What's that?"

"Oh, George Benson is playing a guitar solo," she replied.

"No, no – that!" She repeated the answer and got the same rebuff. Thinking that the great man could hear something undetectable to her pedestrian ear she repeated slowly, "George Benson is playing an electric guitar solo."

"*Electric* guitar"? exclaimed Copland. "Whatever will they think of next?" This was 1976!

(I'm a huge fan of the music of the eccentric but brilliant Australian composer Percy Grainger and have conducted some of his compositions and arrangements. When he was well into his eighties in the mid-1950s and lecturing at the Eastman School of Music in Rochester New York, he disappeared one afternoon. A search of the area was organized and as a last resort someone went into the local cinema which was showing *Rock Around the Clock*. There sat Percy Grainger – as the student went to retrieve him, Percy shushed him and said, "it's coming up any minute!" On came Freddie Bell and the Bellboys and Grainger jumped up and down with excitement, pointing at the screen, "Look – a *bass guitar*! Isn't that amazing? I've watched the movie three times already today!")

Dave Frishberg also told me he once worked a one-nighter, and the rhythm section included a teenager who proved to be the best drummer with whom he had ever played. So much so that he asked the young lad's mother if he could hire the kid to tour with him. The mother replied, "Two reasons why not – first, he's seventeen and still at school. Secondly, he isn't really a drummer, he's a pianist." Dave responded, "If he plays piano like he plays drums we are all in big trouble!" The kid was Keith Jarrett.

I still love old Hollywood and watch as many 1930s musicals and 1940s film noirs as I can. When I started working regularly in Los Angeles, I would occasionally attend James Stewart's Christmas carol party and meet up with people like Donald O'Connor, Dick Van Dyke, Carl Reiner, Mel Brooks, Betty Garrett and the next generation – the daughters of Stan Laurel, James Coburn, Peter Finch, Buster Keaton's widow and many more. Some of my favourites would pop up in the most unlikely places – Katherine Hepburn answering the front door at Donald Ogden Stewart's house in London in her gardening gear, Trevor Howard at a screening of a TV drama he wasn't even in where we talked jazz and cricket, Peter O'Toole on a cricket pitch (he was a qualified cricket coach). I reminded him that I'd attended the Brighton preview of *Jeffrey Bernard Is Unwell* with someone sitting next to me in the stalls – Jeffrey Bernard himself – who proceeded to lecture Peter about all the things that were wrong with the play for an hour in the bar after the show. I'd attended as the guest of one of my local cronies, the acerbic theatre critic Jack Tinker (the man who coined the sobriquet "The Glums" for the musical *Les Misérables* – the name now used by all the actors and musicians involved in the show).

And to complete the unholy trinity of hellraisers, a teetotal Richard Harris with whom I hung out quite often at the Sunset Marquis and who attended my Emmy nomination party in Los Angeles and drank copious amounts of Perrier!

16 Movies (2)

The movie *Funnybones* definitely stands out as one of my favourite experiences. Again, my involvement was far more than just writing a score after filming. I had a cameo conducting the orchestra in Las Vegas (actually the Ilford Palais!), I gave Peter Chelsom the idea to use 'La Mer' and its English version 'Beyond the Sea' as a key plot element (so much so that he reworked the script), I engineered the casting of my old friend Harold Nicholas (of the phenomenal dance team the Nicholas Brothers), and I directed the surprisingly malleable and friendly Jerry Lewis in his musical scenes. We shot many of these scenes at the aforementioned Ilford Palais, which answered a question that had been bugging a friend of mine for years – yes, that really was Jerry Lewis walking down Ilford High Street at 9am!

As I mentioned in the last chapter, I'd first met Harold Nicholas when he came to London to appear in cabaret, and we became fast friends. On a later visit he sang and danced with my big band at the London Jazz Festival, after which I asked him to sing some standards in a BBC TV drama, *Ice Dance*. He became a frequent visitor to my house, bonding with my second son, then five years old, who is now a multiple Emmy award winning television producer in Los Angeles. When the part of the MC of the Las Vegas show came up for consideration I thought Harold would be a shoo-in for his singing and dancing ability as well as his "classic show business" reputation. He showed up to pre-record 'Beyond the Sea' with the big band – and couldn't remember the lyrics! "Don't panic," I said to Peter, and wrote out the words for Harold to read off cue cards. He then proceeded to deliver a magical performance that knocked us all out. Come the filming, and the same problem. He was terrific in the miming and dancing but couldn't master the lines at all. Peter ingeniously fed him each line through an earpiece, which he then repeated. The pauses added gravitas until he had to raise the microphone for the considerably taller Oliver Platt. "Move into the mic, Harold," muttered Peter. "Move into the mic, Harold!" declaimed Harold strongly and confidently, and after a pause came the realization "That's me!". For the Las Vegas sequence, members of my big band were hired, dressed as sailors with uniforms covered in glitter and placed in rowboats either side of Harold and the dancers. I stood at the front conducting – in full sparkling naval regalia and began to regret suggesting 'Beyond the Sea' as a motif in the movie. A few of the musicians got some very odd looks when they visited a local public house in costume. I was reminded of the extras dressed as nuns during a break in the filming of *Hear My Song* visiting a Dublin hostelry knocking back pints and chain smoking.

Jerry Lewis was another potential headache. I knew his reputation in the business before we met and was apprehensive that he would eat me for breakfast. On the contrary we got on famously. He did everything I suggested, muttered wonderful comic asides to me throughout the filming (on the Las Vegas set one day, observing the musical sailors in their boats – "No drums, John? Jesus, what a toy movie!") and sought me out whenever he could, even when we attended the Sundance Film Festival for the premiere. One morning during filming he came up to me and said, "I watched this terrific comedian on television last night – Bob Monkhouse. Do you think he'd appreciate a note from me saying how impressed I was?"

"He'd be absolutely delighted," I replied.

I'm not sure he ever did write to Bob, but it showed a considerate side of Jerry that he rarely exhibited on set. I told my recording engineer, the double Grammy winner Steve Price, how delighted I was with Jerry's cooperation, and he told me the only thing Jerry had said to him was, "This had better be good. I put my last recording engineer in hospital!"

For this brilliantly dark look at the nature of comedy that has become a cult movie (although Disney at the time had no idea what to do with it) director Peter Chelsom peppered the cast with real variety performers, many of whom had no acting experience at all. They all give uncannily effective performances. A case in point is George Carl, whose speciality was becoming tangled up with, and extricating himself from, microphone leads and pretending that mics weren't working. By the time we came to film, George was sadly in the early stages of Alzheimer's. After being in Blackpool, filming for six weeks with Jerry Lewis, he got into a hotel elevator with Jerry and exclaimed, "Jerry Lewis! What are you doing in Blackpool?" He also decided to give himself a haircut mid-filming, thus destroying all the continuity. Nevertheless, his almost totally silent performance is mesmerizing.

Another potentially problematic actor they had signed for the movie was Oliver Reed. When Peter and the producer visited Ollie on his farm to interview him for his role as a gang boss, Reed showed them round. Demonstrating his feeding techniques, he proudly thrust the producer's Armani suited arm deep into the pigswill! Despite this, he was cast and gave a great performance. Inexplicably, the studio cut a crucial explanatory scene between Jerry Lewis and Oliver which made his sub-plot rather baffling and nonsensical. I didn't come into contact with Ollie during the making of the movie, but I'd had several encounters with him over the years, most memorably by the exit of the Groucho Club when, in his cups with ballet dancer Wayne Sleep (there's a duo for you!), he grabbed me in a vice-like headlock as I was leaving and insisted I join them for a few drinks. As a veteran "dodger" of Harry Nilsson, Viv Stanshall and Keith Moon's alcoholic adventures, I was able to use a trip to the bathroom as a way to facilitate my escape. I don't think they even noticed!

Peter had cast the wonderful Leslie Caron as Lee Evans's mother in the movie. At one point she had to sing an obscure 1920s British song and I was asked to teach her to sing it, and how to interpret it. I set a rehearsal time on the afternoon of St. Patrick's Day 1994 with the great pianist Dave Hartley and Leslie. My son Steve was born that morning, so I went from the hospital to the studio then back to the hospital to take everyone home. A day I won't forget in a hurry!

Once again with Peter, I was given free rein with the score. I introduced him to the music of Raymond Scott, which became a major element in the film, and suggested the percussion element that became so crucial. I was enamoured of the mysterious percussion sounds that Alex Acuña created with Weather Report and hired him and Mike Fisher to replicate that dynamic. We tried to book every available studio in Los Angeles – but none of them appeared to be able to playback the UK standard PAL video we had brought with us from London. Finally, we got lucky and booked somewhere for the session. The first sign of a problem was that we arrived to find the studio locked. Next, the truck with the percussion equipment couldn't get into the basement car park. When an employee finally arrived, he was wearing a baseball cap backwards – never a promising sign! We got the percussion unloaded to find that no one had any idea as to how a microphone lead would stretch into the studio from the control room – apparently, they'd only ever recorded rock guitar overdubs directly into the mixing desk. The assistant assumed when we had asked for a PAL video that we meant, 'Do you have a video machine, pal?" Of course, it rendered the movie clips useless.

At one point I left the studio for a breath of air to find the engineer and my producer, heads resting on adjacent wheelie-bins, sobbing. On returning, my spirits were lifted by director Peter Chelsom's sarcastically uplifting, "It's all going terribly well!" Luckily Alex and Mike were able to stay for another session, the studio worked out how to stretch a microphone lead, and my timings worked with the picture, so all our recordings could be used. There was one further shock in store. When my producer took the multitrack tape to be duplicated, it was discovered that there wasn't a sufficient gap between the different cues. However, the duplicating facility were able to insert blank tape, so that our London recordings the following week could go smoothly. Despite all those nightmares the sessions in London were a delight. I still get people telling me it's one of their all-time favourite films and movie scores.

As I mentioned, I attended the premiere at the prestigious Sundance Film Festival in Park City, Utah. That is to say *I* did, my luggage didn't. My bags were somewhere between sunny, warm LAX and Utah, so I went to the cinema dressed in shorts, open sandals and T-shirt – in the snow. The assembled crowds must have thought I was either a huge star or barking mad! My cases arrived before we went for dinner, so I was able to rush back and change in time. Our server told our table, which included Jerry Lewis and Leslie Caron, as well as Peter Chelsom, that as the restaurant was busy we had to leave immediately after dessert. Jerry Lewis was not impressed, made his feelings known to the management, and needless to say we stayed for coffee!

Funnybones has amassed a huge cult following over the years and I am often surprised and gratified to learn it's on so many people's lists of all-time favourite films. The late Paul Allen of Microsoft fame owned a special print – plus outtakes – and regularly screened it for friends who had never seen the movie, and the great Robin Williams called it the finest movie about the nature of comedy ever made.

Titanic is arguably the biggest movie of all time. I know its box office gross has been outstripped a couple of times but its impact in movie history is immense. The truth is, no one had the remotest idea that *Titanic* would become the phenomenon it has, and that holds true right up to the original release date. I had been approached by my agent to see if I was interested in acting as the historical (or should that be hysterical) musical advisor for James Cameron's version of the story. The film company flew me out to Hollywood to meet the producers and put me up in the Universal Sheraton (a change from my usual laid-back Sunset Marquis). I was queueing with 300 people for my hired car to emerge from the garage when suddenly 299 decamped onto the tour buses bound for Universal Studios. One morning I found myself in the elevator after breakfast with several contestants from the *Little Miss America* pageant and their mothers. These four- or five-year-old kids were made up and bejewelled and looked like something from your worst nightmare. They exited on the second floor leaving me and James Doohan (Scottie in *Star Trek*) as the only occupants of the lift. Our eyes met in exasperation, and I was able to say, with total conviction, "Beam me up, Scottie!" James roared with laughter. I moved to the Sunset Marquis the following day.

I had the script and the playlist of the White Star Line sent through to me, and once I had agreed to take on the job it was "over to me," while the filmmakers got on with the task of bringing Cameron's vision to the screen. I was pointed in the direction of I Salonisti, a Swiss ensemble who specialized in performing salon music of the turn of the twentieth century. Once I had made my own choice of the material (which would have been learnt by heart by the five-piece band led by Wallace Hartley in first class), my next job was to arrange the pieces I had chosen and head to Zurich, to record an hour and a half of music for use in the film. It was a mixture of popular classics, light music of the period and forgotten tunes from turn-of-the-century Broadway musicals. (Luckily there were sheet music copies in the Library of Congress.) And there was 'Alexander's Ragtime Band' – the first stirring of a new musical sensibility.

A small technical musical point – a ship's orchestra playing the "new music" in 1912 would definitely not have mastered the rhythms and syncopations of ragtime. So, in the pursuit of authenticity, I deliberately had the band play a very stilted arrangement of 'Alexander's Ragtime Band'. That's why, unlike many other "period" films, the music on the ship always sounds 100 per cent authentic.

We recorded in a wonderful residential studio just outside Zurich in the picturesque village of Maur. After about five days of solid recording, I was becoming a little stir crazy and jumped at the opportunity to head into Zurich with the studio manager Claudia to hear some jazz. As we arrived at the jazz club, the band hit a chord and the leader announced, "Goodnight and get home safely!" We hung around for a couple of drinks, and then I was put into a cab back to the studio, as Claudia headed off in the other direction. I arrived back in the village at about 2am to find it in pitch darkness. The cab driver, who spoke neither English nor indeed any variant of Swiss (he was from the Balkans) gestured to me. "Where?"

As I'd only seen the exterior of the studio once, in broad daylight, and five days previously, I was hardly the best person to ask for directions. We cruised up and down the street and found a telephone box. (Mobiles in those days had no roaming capabilities, which meant my London phone was useless.) I rang the studio and got the answering machine. I telephoned the studio manager at home – and got the answering machine. I gestured to a bench in the main square. "Leave me here till daylight."

The cab driver vigorously shook his head. It was his duty to deliver me safe and sound. So, off we set again. Then my luck was in. I'd spotted a gap between two houses. We headed through the gap – straight into a field by a stream! As the driver tried to turn around, I heard shuffling noises outside. Sure enough, we were the objects of interest for a herd of cattle, and the car was soon surrounded in what appeared to be a menacing ambush. The driver revved enough to free the wheels and usher some of the cows away and we eventually regained the road. I was wary of testing out any other gaps, but after about 90 minutes our options were few. I gestured towards the open road beyond the village. My driver gestured back that there was absolutely nothing there, but I insisted. I was right – a sign pointed towards the studio! I paid off the relieved driver but then found myself once again in pitch darkness ringing a doorbell that probably connected to an office that had long been locked up for the night.

Only one thing for it – I started to edge my way along the wall of the building in total blackness, figuring that if I was lucky, I might find an open window or the bedroom of one of the band (luckily, we were all on the ground floor). I had no idea if the studio had a moat or barbed wire round it, but this was my last chance to get at least three hours in a warm bed. That night my luck was in – as I rounded the third corner of the building after about another half hour or so, a door opened as one of I Salonisti made his way to the bathroom. How he didn't get the shock of his life from the sudden tapping on the outside window at 4am I have no idea, but he ran to the front of the building and managed to open the door for me – a fitting end to a "relaxing evening out."

I'm always being asked questions about "that moment." As the ship sinks, the band on deck begins to play 'Nearer My God to Thee' and time (and the movie) seems to stand still for a moment of quiet contemplation. It's probably one of the classic all-time movie moments to rank alongside "Here's looking at you, kid", Ursula Andress emerging from the sea in *Dr. No*, and the Pythons singing 'Always Look on the Bright Side of Life' (oops that's one of mine too!)

Here's how that classic scene was carefully planned by James Cameron and me. Having turned down the chance to play Wallace Hartley in the film (I can't play violin, can't act, and had another movie in the works), I closed the book on *Titanic* and moved on to other things. Incidentally, my decision not to accept two weeks in Mexico proved prescient. Jonathan Evans-Jones who took the role was stuck on or near the set for two years!

One Saturday morning I awoke bright and early. The answer machine was empty when I went to bed at about 1am. So, it was with some surprise that I noticed it blinking with nine messages when I came downstairs some seven hours later. I scratched my head, yawned and pressed "Play."

"John, this is Jon Landau's assistant – could you please ring me on Mexico 1234?"

"This is Jon Landau's assistant, please call me."

Four more of these, each increasing in urgency, then: "John, this is Jon Landau, please call me immediately!"

Three more of these followed, and then there it was: "John, James Cameron, ring me!"

I dialed the number, which after hearing it nine times in a row I now knew by heart. "John Altman for James Cameron," I announced, with a tremble in my voice.

"Ah yes, one moment please."

I heard the sound of footsteps, then nothing, and then… the unmistakable sound of water splashing. A voice: "Hello?"

"James, this is John Altman calling from London."

"'Nearer My God to Thee' – how does it go?"

"I'm sorry?"

"How does 'Nearer My God to Thee' go? I want to film it live and no one here knows it!"

Aaaah – now I realized the urgency and realized that people had been waiting in the water, possibly all night, for this moment. I began to sing (my vocal abilities would not give Bocelli sleepless nights at the best of times, and this certainly wasn't the best of times).

"One moment!" The mighty Cameron interrupted my flow: "OK start again."

I did, if possible, sounding even worse than the first attempt, and realized that there was now a microphone or megaphone held to the mobile phone beaming it out to heaven knows how many cast and crew members. I finished my *a cappella* rendition to total silence, then a perfunctory "Thank you," from the great director, followed by the click of the receiver.

It seems that when they came to shoot the climactic scene, James had decided to shoot the sequence with the band I Salonisti (who had been cast as the ship's orchestra) playing live, and of course they had no music with them. Moreover, there was, it seems, no one else in the world who knew how it went! So, as I sang the band jotted it down on manuscript. My awful telephonic vocal rendition was enough to get the filming back on track and they were able to complete the now classic sequence with no further delays. If the scene in the film seems realistically spontaneous, you now know the secret. It was!

I was very disappointed at the time that the hour and a half of music we'd recorded didn't appear on the original soundtrack release. The truth is the powers-that-be thought the movie would be a gigantic flop and hedged their bets by releasing a single rather than a double album. I was lunching at Fox Studios in Los Angeles a couple of weeks before the film came out and the executives were doing damage limitation: "We'll get Cameron to do *True Lies 2* and *Terminator 3*." Just then one of the studio bosses wandered over, put an arm round each of them and said, "You know, if it wasn't for you two guys – there would be two other guys!" Funny, but true.

It was a disappointment that intensified when the album became one of the biggest sellers of all time! Some justice was done when the 3D version of the film came out in 2012 and I produced part of the 4-CD complete box set but I suspect that this was only bought by completists.

As the release date of the movie in London approached, I was constantly hearing from friends: "See you at the premiere of *Titanic*." This was news to me, and I called my manager, Olav Wyper, to find out more. He contacted the PR company in charge of the event and explained that I had written an hour and a half of music for the film. The response came: "Why would we invite someone like that as a priority?"

Enraged, he phoned my American agent who rang Bill Mechanic, the head of Fox, and explained the situation. Bill called the English PR company and said, "If John doesn't get his invitation today, I'm firing you." A few hours later, a motorcycle messenger arrived with a ticket and a note to the effect that my invitation must have got lost in the post! I attended the premiere to find 6,000 people in two cinemas simultaneously – it was oddly reassuring to discover that there were 5,999 people more important to the project than I was. At the afterparty I found a VIP room where all my collaborators on the movie were ensconced. I arrived at the same moment as my old university chum Nik

Powell, then the head of the British Film and Television School, and we were all refused entry because we didn't have the correct wristband.

"Oh, I see, it's just like the ship then," I said to the uncomprehending bouncer – a line that Nik always repeated thereafter!

The premiere in London of *Titanic* in 3D (to which I *was* invited) gave me a chance to catch up with I Salonisti, stars Billy Zane (an old friend) and Bernard Hill, who had played John Lennon in the BBC show for which I'd been musical director, and to have long chats with James Cameron and the score composer James Horner whom we tragically lost a few years later.

Figure 42: *Titanic* music department – with the late James Horner. Author's collection.

Back in the UK, Film 4 had been at the forefront of independent movie making. Their films were gritty, well written and directed, often by first-time filmmakers, and broke many boundaries. I had become known as the guy who turned things around quickly, so David Aukin, then the head of Film 4, would often watch a finished movie by a neophyte and say, "This needs a score – call John Altman." In that way I found myself working on some wonderful and exciting new movies – including *Bhaji on the Beach*, *Bad Behaviour* and *Beautiful Thing* (and they're just the ones beginning with "B.") I'm very proud of the fact that in none of these cases does the music score sound like an afterthought. For *Bhaji* I came up with a magical theme in 7/4 time, inspired by the cosmopolitan storyline of a coach outing to Blackpool undertaken by a disparate group of Asian women. When it came to scoring *Bad Behaviour*,

I tried to echo the freewheeling aspect of the storyline with a jazzy rock feel inspired by my days with Van Morrison, and *Beautiful Thing* suggested a gentle piano/guitar and string quartet to echo the intimacy and emotions of the scenes I composed for. I can't imagine the movies without my music. In several of these cases the soundtracks have become sought-after collectors' items. *Beautiful Thing*, in particular, was a groundbreaking film in its depiction of gay love in the London of the 1990s.

Two fun projects around this time were *Legionnaire* starring Jean Claude van Damme, and *The Matchmaker*, shot in Ireland with Jeanine Garofalo and my friend David O'Hara, who had appeared memorably in *Braveheart*. For the end titles of *Legionnaire*, I co-produced the brilliant German vocalist Ute Lemper singing 'Mon Legionnaire'. I recorded the soundtrack of *Matchmaker* in Dublin featuring the great Irish saxophonist, Richie Buckley. When I rang the booker to contract a good rhythm section, he responded, "Ah, the good players are all off with the Riverdance!" So, I took a rhythm section from London, whose hi-jinks and playfulness grated with the more serious-minded Irish string players – a contrast to recording the Irish band for *Hear My Song*. They broke for lunch at 12.30 and returned at 5pm!

I was completely left to my own devices in writing the scores for both *Legionnaire* and *Matchmaker* and every few years a communication comes up that someone wants to release the music on CD. I'm always hopeful that one day something will come of these suggestions.

I had become "attached" to the movie version of *Little Voice*, produced by Nik, Stephen Woolley and Liz Karlsen, a wonderful groundbreaking stage play starring Jane Horrocks. The film was to be directed by the great Sam Mendes – however, in the time it took to get everything underway he had moved on and been replaced by the equally brilliant Mark Herman, director of *Brassed Off*. I stayed the course thankfully and set about arranging the songs for Jane Horrocks's performance. Jane had never sung with a piano let alone a 40-piece orchestra, so it was interesting finding the best way to produce her. I realized that if we dealt with each lyric as if it were a dramatic speech, we could achieve the desired effect. I then had to get my old friend Michael Caine to sing (shades of Leslie Caron and *Funnybones*). He was very dismissive of his ability but turned in a riveting piece of cinema. I went up to Scarborough on location and after a great Italian meal with Ewan McGregor, Jane, Bruno Tonioli, vocal coach Jo Thompson and Phil Jackson we set off to try to locate some Friday night entertainment. A local hotel offered a 60s weekend with the Swinging Blue Jeans, and we decided that would be fun. The doorman, however, refused us entry as we didn't have tickets. I wished Michael Caine, the face of the 1960s, had been with us as we were turned away – that would have been one for the papers! I attended the New York and UK premieres and was gratified to bask in the subsequent accolades and nominations for Jane Horrocks's vocal performance and Michael Caine's mesmerizing acting – all those hours of toil had paid off.

Figure 43: With Jane Horrocks and Brenda Blethyn at the New York premiere of *Little Voice*. Author's collection.

Mark's next movie was *Hope Springs*, starring Colin Firth, Heather Graham and my pal Minnie Driver. Set in contemporary Vermont, the first edit was shown in a cinema north of London on a Friday evening to an audience and focus group. Obviously, there was no score composed so the editor had peppered the film with AOR (adult oriented rock) tracks to set the locale. At the focus group after the screenings the fatal words were uttered by one woman: "I didn't like the music!" Although I hadn't yet written a note, these groups can be very influential in swaying the producers and I expected an urgent phone call. When it came on the Monday it wasn't quite what I thought.

"The focus group didn't get the developing romance between Colin and Heather. Could you write a dozen cues and record them on Wednesday to highlight the love story so that we can rescreen the movie on Friday?"

I explained that I had been hired for potentially six weeks to deliver a carefully prepared score to the final cut and now I was being asked to deliver in one day. My response was, "Yes I will do something, but you can't judge it – it's obviously a spur of the moment response to your problem so can I have your word it will never be used?"

"Yes of course."

So, I sat down and began to write the first thing that came into my head. My immediate idea was a country band that would be harmonica led, reflecting the rural setting and I soon had twelve cues prepared. Next day I went into the studio with some of my favourite musicians and we recorded the first cue, not yet heard by anyone including me. At the end of the take I looked through the control room glass at producers, director and editor all applauding (obviously silently as the glass was soundproofed). With only a couple of extra cues for Minnie's character recorded later, my twelve rushed pieces became the score of the movie. There can't be many films that have been scored in one day!

RKO 281 was a momentous score for me. It had a terrific screenplay (basically covering the same ground as the recent movie about the making of *Citizen Kane – Mank*), Ben Ross's direction, an A-list cast and Ridley and Tony Scott in the background pulling the strings. I attended filming on the day they were recreating Bernard Herrmann's score for *Citizen Kane* at Maida Vale Studios. I had transcribed the music for the scene; somewhat disappointingly, although the casting department had hired genuine string players, none of the extras in the brass and woodwind chairs were musicians. Most had never held an instrument, let alone played one. I was there to demonstrate off-camera to the actor playing Herrmann how to conduct a score (he never quite got it right!). I then went round to all the brass and woodwind "players" and showed them all how to hold their instruments in repose and when playing. Luckily, they all picked up what they had to do very quickly and when you watch the movie you'd never know.

Writing the score was an interesting experience. The studio, Ridley and director Ben Ross had different concepts for the music, and I was somewhat caught in the middle. I finally "kidnapped" Ben as the session loomed and asked him if he had any reference points for the score. Ben is very musical, and I noticed that all the tracks he cited were in 3/4 time. I had written a delicate waltz for one particular moment in the movie and as soon as he heard it, Ben said "That's it!" So that became the template for the whole score. Thankfully it was well received by every concerned party.

At this time, I developed alopecia between filming and recording. I also won an Emmy for the most outstanding score for a television movie and found myself at the star-studded afterparty, sat with the cast of *Sex and the City*. The party was held at the famous Los Angeles restaurant Spago, masterminded by celebrity chef Wolfgang Puck, with whom, many years before, I had been involved in a futile attempt to open a jazz venue in Los Angeles. All these delicacies kept arriving at our table, and the surrounding guests complained about the preferential treatment for the *Sex and the City* cast. "It's him!" responded Cynthia Nixon, pointing at me, "Not us!" I spent much of the evening with Joan Rivers. Years later she was a guest on the Graham Norton TV show which my son was then producing. I went backstage and said to her, "You won't remember me, but we hung out at the Emmys one year."

"2000 and you won for best music," came the instant reply – I was stunned.

Three years later I was nominated again for my score of *The Roman Spring of Mrs. Stone*. Once again, I "played" a pianist in the movie and have very fond memories of midnight pizzas in our Rome hotel with Helen Mirren, Anne Bancroft, Olivier Martinez and Rodrigo Santoro. It was Anne's last movie, and I was delighted to spend some quality time with her. I met her husband Mel Brooks in the 1980s through his manager and friend Jo Lustig and used to get invitations to all his advance screenings. Whenever Mel and I met we talked jazz – he would have loved to have been a legendary jazz drummer. One funny thing happened when we filmed on location on the streets of Rome. All four principal cast members were present as were many sightseeing tourists. Now, Helen is English, Anne was American, Olivier is French and Rodrigo Brazilian, so each tourist recognized the actor from their own territories. You could tell where everyone was from by which actor it was whom they pestered for autographs and photos. I deliberately tried to write a score in the spirit of the ominous music written by Bernard Hermann for so many great Hitchcock movies – on a very limited music budget, which seemed to become far more of a "thing" as time went on.

Figure 44: Emmy's dinner party with Kristin Davis. Author's collection.

Around this time, I scored *Fidel*, a mini-series about Fidel Castro with a young, little-known Gael García Bernal as Che Guevara. I was in Mexico for part of the shoot – at the same time *Frida* was being filmed with Salma Hayek, as was a Schwarzenegger blockbuster. A US tourist asked a location manager what was being filmed and told his family, "It's a movie about Castro and Frida Kahlo starring Arnold Schwarzenegger!" That I'd like to see.

That was an interesting trip as I went straight from the airport to a dinner with the legendary movie producer David Picker (who, as the head of United Artists in the 1960s, had revolutionized the studio system) and the director David Attwood. At 9pm they turned in, as they had an early start the next morning, but suggested I spend the time the next day until my evening flight exploring the historic city. I was due to meet up with the boxer Lennox Lewis that night in Los Angeles and head to a party in his honour. I awoke to the sound of a hurricane – you couldn't even open the hotel doors let alone explore – and the hotel broadcast a warning to stay indoors. Everyone I knew on the movie was long gone – all calls to attempt to change my flight proved futile so I settled down in my hotel room to watch endless Mexican daily soap operas on the room TV, not understanding a word and cursing my school for teaching ancient Latin and Greek rather than something useful. Somehow the wind abated slightly and my transport to the airport arrived at around 5pm. A false dawn. After three delayed, hair-raising flights I limped into LAX at around 2am. The series was fun to score and record, although with a wonderful Latin American and Cuban percussion section at my disposal I couldn't help wondering why they'd chosen an Englishman to write the music. At one point I said to the director, "Forget my score, just record the jamming between takes!" Luckily for me they stuck with my music (which I think worked pretty convincingly).

I composed the score for a TV miniseries about the Reagans, inventively titled *The Reagans*, directed by Robert Allan Ackerman who had directed *The Roman Spring of Mrs. Stone*. Nancy Reagan heard about the series and, without having read the script, pressurized James Aubrey at CBS to drop the transmission. It was duly dropped – however, Showtime agreed to transmit it, but we had a major dilemma. I was recording the score that week and the producers were scared that any whiff of portraying the Reagans in a bad light might cause all sorts of problems. So, on the spot I had to neutralize my music to avoid any possible suspicion of ominousness or tension. What resulted was rather bland aural wallpaper and I jokingly told the Academy Award winning producers Craig Zadan and Neil Meron, "You just sanitized my Emmy nomination away!" And I was right. The movie did get several nominations for acting and best miniseries, but the music (mercifully) went unnoticed.

Peter Chelsom's next project was *Shall We Dance*, and I was delighted to score the dance numbers for Richard Gere and J Lo. I would have loved to have written the major dramatic cues as well, but unfortunately someone who is now very much a *persona non grata* stepped in and demanded that his favourite of the moment write the main themes – so we have a joint credit. The same pariah insisted my version of 'Moon River' was "old fashioned" (although it did stay in the film) and insisted on the hiring of a contemporary rapper. Today his is the only sequence in the movie that really jars and has dated.

Having been the first Western composer to score a Russian movie I added another notch to my belt in becoming the first Western composer to score a Malayalam film in Kerala (*Castles in the Air*). The producers wanted a Western sounding score with no traces of Indian music – a first for their industry. I had great fun scoring scenes, quite frequently without subtitles so I had to guess what was happening. I flew to Mumbai en route to Kerala, did some TV interviews and forgot all about them. Just before the premiere – also a first for Kerala – the producer said, "I'm off to see the prime minister to get our motorcade sanctioned." Kerala is a communist state and there was a general strike on. We were told that our cars may be overturned, stoned or worse if we broke the strike! As it was, the crowds in the street were gawking and waving to match any Hollywood premiere.

On my way back to London, via Mumbai airport, I was repeatedly accosted for my autograph. I was completely baffled until it was pointed out to me that the television interviews I'd done were played on a 24-hour loop, so everyone would have seen me. Even more disconcertingly, whenever I entered a shopping mall the tannoy would boom out the music from *Titanic* – word travels fast.

I arrived in Kerala via Mumbai; unfortunately – a familiar story – my luggage didn't! The film company sent me out to buy whatever clothes I needed on their tab. I'm pleased to say I restrained myself. When I got back to Mumbai, I had one night (in the Hotel Taj, just weeks before the dreadful terror attacks) before my flight home, and decided to attempt to locate my missing luggage there and then, rather than trying before my flight. It was just as well I did, as the luggage took four hours to locate with numerous officials in uniform inexplicably joining and leaving me. ("They were looking for you to pay them," said my driver, who waited patiently outside the whole time.) Eventually I found myself outside a room with a sign that said, "Luggage that didn't reach its final destination." I intimated to my latest companion that perhaps my case was in there, but he shook his head. Finally, I got someone to unlock the door and there was one solitary case, placed slap bang in the middle of the room – mine.

Even when relaxing at my London home between projects it seemed as if I couldn't escape the movie world. One early morning I went to my front gate to be confronted by the sight of Jude Law and Ray Winstone ambling past. Apparently, they were filming an interior shot for a gangster film two houses along from mine.

Figure 45: Kerala press and TV conference. Author's collection.

Not quite a movie moment but one evening at around 9pm my front doorbell rang. Standing on my doorstep was the onetime manager of Tottenham Hotspur soccer club, Keith Birkinshaw. I recognized him immediately and as I was pondering if we were in an episode of *Candid Camera* he walked past me into the house, asking "Is everyone in there?"

I replied, "I'm sorry, I know who you are, but I have absolutely no idea why you are in my living room!"

It transpired that there was a Tottenham board meeting at my neighbour's property (my neighbour happened to be the club's lawyer) and Keith had either been given the incorrect address or misread the details. A simple explanation for what could have proved to be an interesting television reality show – celebrities ringing your doorbell and wandering uninvited into your house or apartment!

In 2015 I was asked to compose and conduct a score for the Anthony Asquith silent movie *Shooting Stars* for the BFI London Film Festival Archive Gala to be held at the Odeon Leicester Square. A hundred minutes of music (3,500 bars of music!) to be composed, and then conducted live to picture in front of a red-carpet audience. I scored the movie on a computer using the Sibelius programme which I had possessed for years but only just mastered. When it first came out, and needed an Acorn computer to operate it, the Emmy award winning composer Michael Price came over to teach me how to use it. I wrote a 12-bar nursery rhyme for piano, put a tie-mark on the last bar and it repeated for about a thousand bars, despite all my efforts to switch it off by hitting every key in sight. Finally, I switched the whole thing off for twenty-five years until I felt emboldened to try again and David Tobin, another fine composer, showed me what to do (thankfully the MacBook had by then replaced the Acorn).

Here is the article I wrote for the DVD release booklet of *Shooting Stars*.

> Scoring *Shooting Stars* from scratch (if you'll pardon the alliteration) presented a plethora of problems (there I go again!) to this particular composer. A hundred minutes of continuous score, something I (and the majority of my peers) had never attempted previously. A piece, while of its period, definitely not a period piece. A film so sophisticated it hardly uses any title cards – the emotional and narrative drive are all in plain sight on the screen. What is the modern composer to do? Write a contemporary score that plays against the fashions and mores of the 1920s? Or utilize the rich musical tapestries of an era where music played a crucial role in social custom and change – there are numerous on-screen references to popular tunes and dance and jazz bands? Combine the elements so that the music has no unifying underlying structure? Or maybe attempt something different that might possibly give a new vocabulary to the art of scoring silent films.
>
> I took my cue from a technique I developed when scoring two quirky British movies for director Peter Chelsom – *Hear My Song* (for which I coincidentally won the Anthony Asquith Award for Best Score) and *Funnybones*. In both these films I created musical themes which I was then able to develop in multiple styles within the arc of the movie to enhance and counterpoint the action on screen. Additional binding was created by a consistency of instrumentation – in *Hear My Song* the gypsy jazz violin of one cue became the Irish folk fiddle of another and the conventional string section of the concert hall sequences. For *Funnybones* I utilized percussion, so the tom toms of Gene Krupa became the mysterious rhythmic effects created brilliantly by Weather Report's Alex Acuña.
>
> The twelve-piece orchestra I hand-picked for this project and then wrote specifically for (in the manner of one of my inspirations, Duke Ellington) would become, along with the thematic material, the glue for binding the whole score together and shaping it. In this way I was able to create a varied stylistic palette and to blend dance music and 1920s jazz with modern classical techniques and conventional contemporary movie scoring – often switching from one to the other and back within one scene. I had no idea if

this technique would work until we went live, and to my gratification it seemed to succeed beyond my expectations. I was helped immeasurably by the fact that *Shooting Stars* is a movie about movie making, and the ironic layering of plot (where film echoes real life echoes film) so adroitly manipulated by Asquith, allowed me to use conventional silent movie "chase and danger" scoring techniques which then became the score for the real-life danger. It all helps to cement the bond between music and picture and add a new dimension to the film.

Finally, I cannot heap enough praise on the musicians who performed the score. They are all virtuosi in their own right and that above all gave me the confidence to write anything I felt might work, whether it be complicated solo passages, authentic 1920s jazz, or long form melodic statements. For a composer to have that luxury is indeed a blessing and I thank them all for their enthusiasm and valuable input which on many occasions dramatically improved on my intentions. Above all, they (and I) had a lot of fun and that's something you don't hear often about movie scoring!!

The black-tie premiere of *Shooting Stars* at the London Film Festival was a huge success, and we were asked to repeat the live orchestral performance at the British Film Institute a few months later. In the original packed house were my family, my friend Terry Jones, making almost his last public appearance; legendary record producer Chris Thomas (The Beatles, Pink Floyd, The Who, Elton John, Roxy Music etc.); comedian Simon Amstell; Michael Radford, director of *Il Postino* and of *Van Morrison in Ireland*, my (and his) screen debut; the nephew of Brian Aherne – one of the stars of the 1928 movie – who had lived with his uncle in Hollywood; Colin Vaines, producer of *Gangs of New York* and *Film Stars Don't Die in Liverpool*, and many other old pals. When we recorded the soundtrack for the DVD one of my biggest supporters, the great Hans Zimmer, attended the sessions and wrote a wonderful tribute to the project. I'm sure he won't mind me quoting: "This was truly extraordinary music extraordinarily performed! I couldn't stop smiling! Masterful on every level!" As he jokingly said to me in the studio, "You know the great thing about this project? No director!"

A couple of years later the producers and musical supervisor of a new film musical, *La La Land*, messaged me to source musicians, both for the recording sessions and the on-screen "sideliners" who would mime to the pre-recorded music. Soon afterwards, I suggested a hand double for Ryan Gosling's hands as he purported to play the piano. I was kept in the loop until the film was complete and was surprised and delighted to receive an acknowledgement in the end credits, and to share in the celebrations when the movie was successful at the various awards ceremonies.

On the subject of no interference with your music, I've been writing a lot of production music (known as library music in the UK) over the ten years leading up to the writing of this book. The upside is you get to indulge yourself in composing using any orchestral combination that you choose, in any style you fancy, and the tracks are then picked up and used in the media. Projects I have "invented" myself and then realized include, among others, a history of jazz from the 1920s to today, light orchestral music of the 1940s and 1950s, themes from imaginary movies of the 1960s and 1970s, spy thrillers, a salsa big band, 1960s cartoons and quirky exotic big band music of the 1950s. It's a lot of fun writing and recording them as composed – no last-minute changes! I've had people call me and say, "I heard your recording in that movie yesterday." When I protest that I've never heard of that particular film, they send me a screenshot with my name attached to an unfamiliar title. Eventually I realize it's a library piece of mine that has been renamed, usually because my titles are pretty fatuous. I named all the tunes on one session after my favourite lines in British film comedies of the late 1950s. (When I told this story to the author of many of these lines, Ray Galton, he seemed underwhelmed!) My music shows up in the most unlikely places – *Dancing with the Stars*, *America in Colour*, *The Great British Bake Off*, a Pixar short film, and many commercials and trailers. I hope to do a lot more of these projects in the coming years, once things return to some sort of normality after the pandemic.

17 Commercials

Having worked on over 4,000 commercials worldwide I couldn't possibly begin to discuss them all (in fact, I only know that figure because my producer at Jeff Wayne Music did a count many years ago and told me). They include spots as a composer/arranger/conductor/producer or any combination thereof, and different time lengths, edits and re-arrangements. The influential *Campaign* magazine listed me among the 100 most important people in British advertising, and on another occasion as one of the top five composers in commercials. I have a book of the advertisements I worked on through the 1980s and 90s. Half of the product names mean absolutely nothing to me – were they for shampoo, desserts, cars or cat litter? (Yes, I did a commercial for cat litter – not my finest hour!) More of the cat litter anon.

I was lucky that advertising in the UK had entered a golden age and I was privileged to be a big part of it alongside directors like Tony and Ridley Scott, Alan Parker, Hugh Hudson, Adrian Lyne, Andre Konchalovsky, Elliott Erwitt, David Bailey, Terence Donovan, as well as John Frankenheimer and the younger generation of film makers – such as Tarsem and Jonathan Glazer. And then there was my occasional copywriter and lyricist Salman Rushdie!

Sir Salman was then a copywriter for Grey's ad agency in London. We worked on several commercials together including Anchor Butter and the Burnley Building Society. Inevitably our conversation turned to cricket – he never once mentioned writing novels during our association.

Another frequent collaborator (and a great personal support when my mother passed away in April 1990) was copywriter/creative director Chips (father of Tom) Hardy. I'm delighted to see father and son now co-writing and running their own production company together.

I enjoyed working with the titans of British advertising. They set very high standards for both their own employees and the creative freelancers they employed – the best of the best. It was no surprise to find many copywriters, art directors and animators branching out to enjoy huge success on the world stage as authors, movie directors and major figures in the arts. The sheer volume of work in the industry I undertook, and the speed of the turnarounds, meant I rarely had time to think or luxuriate in my "successes." At one time I could be involved in five or six different commercials a week, as well as television, movie and record commitments.

I also found myself working in and for the USA, as well as many other countries across the world, winning a host of advertising awards along the way. I loved the discipline of 30 seconds to make your point and get out, and many of the ads I wrote the music for are fondly (and some not so fondly) remembered today: B&Q; Burger King; Levi's; BT; BA; Apple Computers (they'll never catch on!); Sheilas' Wheels ("write something that will drive everyone mad" and it did – becoming the most popular ringtone in the UK); Uniroyal tyres (which ran for ten years, became the weather forecast music for Eurosport and which I composed in the car on the way to the dubbing studio); Heineken, with the great animator Chuck Jones; and Addis, the first commercial to allow *Tom and Jerry* to be portrayed. We also had to devise ingenious recording techniques – to get the sound of classic 1940s MGM, we recorded the orchestra on two microphones, fed the sound back into a speaker on a chair in the studio and recorded the music from the speaker. Astonishingly authentic. One client loved finding bizarre pieces of music and located Albrechtsberger's concerto in E major for Jew's harp and orchestra. I transcribed the piece and when the percussionist arrived his face fell and he said, "I have *no* idea how he's playing this and altering the notes." In the days before synth sampling we detuned his performance and pieced together the music like a jigsaw puzzle. To our amazement it worked perfectly.

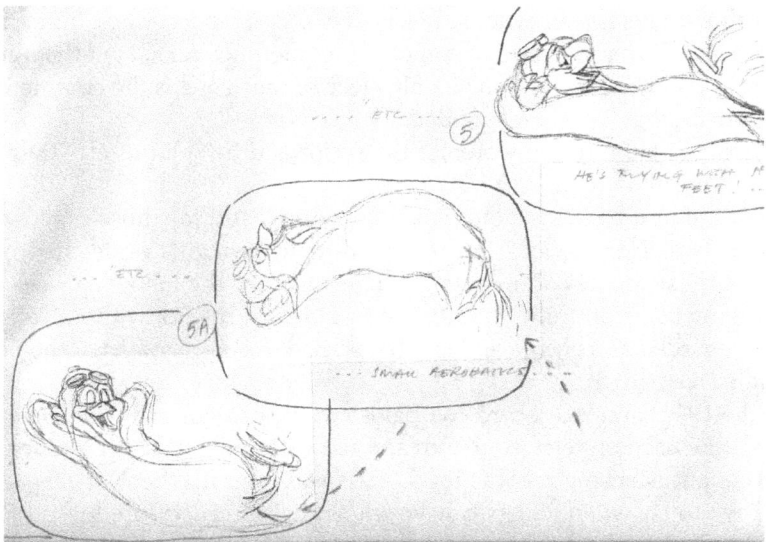

Figure 46: Chuck Jones storyboard for Heineken. Author's collection.

The same creative director had me rearrange Barry Gray's classic *Thunderbirds* theme with *Thunderbirds* creator/director Gerry Anderson sitting in the control room. That was a real thrill. Another time he asked me to "shadow" the eminent classical composer Sir Michael Tippett for a projected commercial. It soon became apparent (because he told me) that Sir Michael had no idea how to write to timings, especially the 28 or 58 seconds of music required for television commercials. After a few anxious conversations with the agency, Sir Michael bowed out and I was left to join together two rather different pieces by Sir William Walton, which I did to the best of my ability. The Walton Estate immediately gave it the thumbs up, possibly more as a tribute to the vast sums of money offered by the agency than a testimony to my brilliance.

I often worked with the agency Lowe Howard Spink, which was considered the finest in Europe. After one BBC session, two of its top creatives came to see me with a script for Heineken lager. It was a direct parody of the *My Fair Lady* song 'The Rain in Spain' and was called 'The Water in Majorca'. I advised that they were safest having no music, as I knew the lyricist of *My Fair Lady*, Alan Jay Lerner, who was then living in London and had told me he spent his days watching TV and looking out for parodies that infringed his copyrights! (I got off on the wrong foot with Alan when I mentioned that Burton Lane had recycled a melody he used in *Kid Millions* for the famous Fred Astaire ceiling dance in *Royal Wedding*. According to Lerner it was the first he knew of it.) The following evening I received a phone call from the much-feared agency boss, the gist of which was "How dare you go over my head and forbid the use of music – who runs this agency, me or you?"

When I protested that they'd be sued, he demanded an immediate conference call with his lawyer who had okayed it and exploded when his assistant told him the phone system didn't allow for conference calls. I got the number of the lawyer, who said, "I think a jolly piece of music helps the commercials."

"Not with that lyric," I responded.

"Lyric?" I read him the words of the script and he spluttered, "They can't do that! They'll be sued!"

I asked if he'd be kind enough to ring the boss and say those exact words. An hour later I got a call from the main man, saying, "I've decided not to have any music in the commercial" and he hung up. The following week I had a charming call from him inviting me to dinner! (The ad, without music, is widely regarded as a classic and is often shown in compilations of the best of British advertising.)

In the 1980s and 90s record companies would categorically not allow their tracks to be used on television, film and radio commercials – it is true to say they thought licensing records for TV use was beneath them. It seems hard to believe today when all labels have whole divisions dedicated to obtaining syncs in advertising, movies and television, but in those days we all had to create "soundalikes" – that's if the artist on the record was deceased, as "passing off" was considered a criminal offence. In the same way that slander and libel cannot be applied in law to the deceased, so if someone copies the vocal style of, say, Elvis Presley or Aretha Franklin there is no legal action possible. If the public believe that, for example, they are listening to Tom Jones or Shirley Bassey then this is grounds for all kinds of lawsuits. The general attitude was typified by Sting confiding in me that a deodorant wanted to license 'Don't Stand So Close to Me' for a television commercial. Richard Branson, who owned the publishing, had given the go-ahead and the contretemps wound up in the courts – certainly the only time I have received a telephone call from Branson. And I wasn't even involved in the commercial!

Advertising agencies would buy the publishing rights and we would set about creating new versions that were faithful to the original records. Tracks like 'I Heard it Through the Grapevine' and 'Sitting on the Dock of the Bay' were re-recorded with vocalists emulating Marvin Gaye and Otis Redding – ironically, the model in a famous jeans' commercial was offered a record deal and secured chart success, while the singer on the soundtrack was unable to get signed. On one occasion we recorded a 1960s hit with the original artist singing and the original musicians playing, only to be told "It doesn't sound like the record!" As the drummer patiently explained, "different equipment, newer technology, we are all thirty years older, and who the hell is going to play them side by side and make a judgement?"

Shooting a Christmas commercial for Woolworths in the middle of July (as per most Xmas advertising) I found myself stood next to three live reindeer, who were to appear pulling Santa into the "store." After about an hour I decided that we had quite a rapport and turned to the lead animal and said jokingly, "Hello Rudolf." His response was immediate – a head-butt that sent me flying across the studio. The trainer rushed over and admonished me: "Don't talk to them or try to pet them – they're vicious brutes and think you're about to attack so they get in the first shot." The joys of Christmas!

One commercial I worked on for the USA was a 20-minute story for Ford, unfolding in five 4-minute episodes to be shown during the Super Bowl. We were booked with a large orchestra on Monday morning, with the head of the agency and the head of the music department flying to London especially for the recording. At 4pm on the preceding Friday, I received an odd, unsettling phone call from the assistant editor in New York. He warned me that I probably had the wrong cuts, with one spot repeated twice and asked me to check. This potentially threatened the recording as I wrote the music precisely to reflect what was happening onscreen. When I verified what he had told me, he then said that he had been fired by the editor but had nonetheless called me with his concerns and gave me the phone number of the head of the agency's country retreat where the assistant's ex-boss was staying for the weekend. I rang the number and was put through to the editor, who was obviously trying to dismiss all my worries, to save face with the boss who could hear the editor's end of the conversation. I then rang the head of music, who said, "Don't worry, just work on the cuts you know are correct and we will do the rest later in the week." When the clients showed up in the studio they were laughing about the number of occasions when the wrong cuts had been sent to the studio. I was trying to imagine what would have been the reaction of some of the UK agency bosses I worked for! We did eventually manage to finish the spot and it remains one of my favourites.

Incidentally, the agency head of music was the legendary big band leader of the 1940s and later the most sought-after Broadway conductor, the late Elliot Lawrence. One afternoon he telephoned me in London from New York about another commercial on which we were working, and the great jazz clarinettist Eddie Daniels happened to be visiting me at the time. Eddie was tentatively booked to do a recording session for Elliot in New York the following week and motioned to me to pass the phone across. I complied with no explanation and Eddie said, "Hi Elliot, this is Eddie Daniels – I'm afraid I can't do your session next Wednesday," and passed the phone back to me. It's quite rare to come across someone who is really lost for words, but Elliot was totally nonplussed!

A remarkable array of voice artists worked on the commercials as well. One we recorded was in the style of a fairground calliope and Bob Hoskins was booked as the fairground barker: "Roll up, roll up!" He could not find his motivation or character at all, and his mood wasn't helped when my producer Alison sat on his favourite hat! I also got to work with some wonderful singers like Eartha Kitt and Mel Tormé as well as the best of London and Los Angeles session musicians and vocalists. I wrote a fantasy Hollywood musical sequence for a soap commercial that was sung on the soundtrack and in the film by the distinguished actress/comedian Dame Julie Walters. Thirty-odd years later, she sang the whole thing to me – words and music! Occasionally things would not quite go to plan. Re-recording 'I'm a Believer' with Davy Jones of The Monkees, I discovered that he not only didn't sing the lead vocal on the original record, but he also couldn't – as he kept switching to his harmony part. Luckily Tony Rivers was on the session performing backing vocals and wound up singing the melody line we all know and love.

The cat litter commercial was unexpectedly interesting. On the Sunday I had played a wonderful concert with Alexis Korner, the father of the blues in the UK. This was the man who had put together the Rolling Stones and encouraged all sorts of talents in their earliest days, as well as being a fine performer in his own right. On the Monday I recorded a track for a cat litter that changed colour when the cat did its "business." The turnaround was such that because it was on air the next day, the voice artist had to come into the music recording session instead of a vocal studio and the mix had to go to the TV channel immediately. In walked the voiceover artist – Alexis Korner. In addition to being such an influence on the burgeoning British blues scene, Alexis's mellifluous voice was much in demand for reading copy on television and radio commercials in the UK. We pretended we didn't know each other. I'm not sure who was more embarrassed.

A favourite commercial to work on, for a number of reasons, was for Renault cars, starring the Arsenal and France soccer superstar Thierry Henry. Directed by Tarsem in the style of the old Blue Note covers, it featured Thierry supposedly playing jazz drums in Ronnie Scott's jazz club. The camera pulls back to reveal the drummer is actually Animal from *The Muppets*. I wrote an appropriate jazz track, and my eldest son Bob dubbed the drumming for Animal and taught Thierry how to look as if he was playing. I can now truthfully tell people that my son is a Muppet! Bob had become a terrific drummer (playing with the likes of a pre-fame Ed Sheeran, Amy Winehouse and Wycliff Jean) and a wonderful guitarist, percussionist and composer. His teenage school band, with his brother Mike on bass and a schoolfriend on guitar who is now Head of English at Eton College, was heard and subsequently managed by Mark Owen of Take That. We were all invited to Mark's own show at the Shepherd's Bush Empire – a girl seated behind us tapped me on the shoulder and asked, "Are you Mark Owen's grandad?" Since I was twenty-three when Mark was born, I pointed out that it was quite unlikely! Bob started playing drums on most of my commercials, including Sheilas' Wheels, and did a fine job – these days he concentrates more on the guitar and composing.

A few years later, I took my driving test in California. I'd been told not to talk to the examiner and follow the instructions to the letter. The cars queued in a line and the car in front landed the sternest-looking examiner I'd ever seen, who almost certainly failed the driver on her attempt to exit the parking lot. My examiner appeared at my passenger door, wearing an Arsenal football shirt. As he got in the car his first words were, "Who do you support then?" (I guess the paperwork said I was English.) When I told him my son had taught Thierry Henry the drums, I think I passed before I'd even started the car!

Another award-winning commercial was a well-remembered spot for Levi's. I had a history with Levi's. I had done quite a few commercials for them over the years and was once asked to form a band to perform at a launch for a new Levi's product. They had indicated that everyone in the band would get a sample as a bonus gift. There was no shortage of volunteers for the band and we duly played at the launch. Sure enough, we were all given the new product – a pair of stay-pressed white skin-tight jeans that no one, including the general public as it turned out, would be caught dead wearing. (The only other items I was ever given as freebies in my entire career in advertising were an aftershave that smelled like dead skunk and a crate of miniature Baileys that Count Cinzano – yes there really is one – sent to me after a recording session for Baileys Irish Cream, when I complained that no one ever sent me anything!)

Figure 47: Thierry Henry and Animal. Agency press publicity shot for Renault commercial – photographer unknown.

The award-winning Levi's spot I mentioned above was directed by Jonathan Glazer and at the time was the most expensive commercial ever made in the UK. It involved the hero and heroine running through walls and up a tree at the end – all totally convincing special effects. Someone had found a piece of Vivaldi, which I orchestrated perfectly to fit the changing pace of the ad. Everyone loved it – the director, the agency team, the client – everyone except the boss of the agency. He thought the music should be detached from the film rather than commenting on the action. Someone came up with the Handel Sarabande and we duly recorded my orchestration, again tailored to the film. The spot won every award going and the agency boss was totally vindicated – however, the director's showreel pointedly utilizes the Vivaldi!

The great photographer David Bailey was a memorable, if unpredictable, client. One day he stopped a large string orchestra in mid flow to ask what the music would be like if played by a jazz trio! And this with three minutes left in the session. Another day he complained that the first synthesizer layer in a complex piece requiring about twenty overdubs didn't sound right, although we explained there were still many sounds to be layered on. However, all his sessions were great fun. I remember him approaching me on one session and saying, "Here John, have a chocolate. Women love fat men who eat chocolate."

I replied, "No David, women love fat men who eat chocolate and take wonderful photos of them!" The stories I heard from the three great photographic chroniclers of the Swinging Sixties – Bailey, Donovan and Duffy – still keep me laughing today.

Several spots cashed in on topicality. When my old nemesis Oliver Reed and Paula Yates had a famous boozy spat on the Michael Aspel chat show that went viral, Paul Masson Light Wines (99.5% alcohol free) immediately signed them both to appear in and voice a deadpan sober advertisement for their product. I wrote and produced the music for the commercial and was delighted that Ollie was on his best behaviour, showing me respect and taking my direction as if I were Carol Reed or David Lean! The same unfortunately can't be said for Paula who flirted outrageously with the film director, sitting on his lap and unbuttoning his shirt much to his and our embarrassment. The commercial was very funny though.

I saw the commercials I usually worked on as mini movies – often directed and written by the best of the best. I never really thought of myself as a "jingle writer." There were those who did that far better than I. However, I did come up with one or two earworms. "*You can do it when you B and Q it*" ran for over twenty years, and it's no exaggeration to say that Sheilas' Wheels swept the UK in the mid-noughties. I heard people whistling and singing it in the street, countless parodies on YouTube and it launched a brand-new company into the position of market leader within a few months. In other words, it ticked all the advertising boxes, but I had mixed feelings when I was introduced at events as 'the composer of Sheilas' Wheels'. At least mention some of my movie scores or hit records, please! Not that I'm putting down creating a monster – the fact that this happens so rarely attests to the difficulty of coming up with just the right vibe to appeal across the board.

When I composed or arranged to picture for movies, television and commercials, before the advent of digital files, I would have a VHS tape (later a DVD) in the muted machine, switch to the AV channel so the screen was usually blank, or sometimes leave the terrestrial channel playing silently in the background while I wrote. One afternoon while writing I happened to glance at the screen, where my student lodgings were displayed exactly as they were in 1968. Convinced for a moment I was in an episode of the *Twilight Zone* I watched as the camera travelled along the Brighton seafront, again as it was in the late 1960s, before cutting to a living room I remembered vividly and a couple whose names immediately sprang to mind.

"I sat in that room with them on that very sofa a quarter of a century ago," I muttered as I frantically searched for the remote control, which of course had gone missing at that precise moment. Finally, I was able to restore the sound to the visuals and what I'd stumbled on was a documentary titled something like *Twenty-Five Years On*, where an aspiring Brighton band of the late 1960s who never made the big time were reflecting on a documentary, shot in 1968, about their hopes and aspirations. Their then manager was the owner of a Brighton record store with whom I was quite friendly, and I used to visit his flat above the shop for dinner. A down-to-earth explanation of a surreal moment.

Once in the late 1970s I flew to Bavaria to begin preliminary work on a commercial, arriving in the hotel, in the middle of nowhere, the night before my meeting – at around 9pm. With no prospect of doing anything but channel surfing I was idly flicking through the television channels when to my amazement I happened upon a live feed from the Berlin Jazz Festival. The next morning the director asked me what I'd done the previous evening.

"Well, it was quite something – I watched the Berlin Jazz Festival live. You'd never see anything like that on British television."

"Oh, we have jazz on TV all the time – I'll tape some and send you the VHS."

A few tapes arrived but, since the director wasn't really a jazz fan, they were a mish-mash of jazz and unlistenable (to me) avant-garde posturings. I mentioned to my friend and fellow jazz fanatic Eric, who worked throughout Europe as an accountant, "Wouldn't it be amazing if we could find one person in each country who videotaped jazz from the television and set up some sort of system of global tape swapping?"

The next week Eric headed to Stockholm, visited the local jazz club and asked the host if he knew anyone who taped televised jazz.

"You're in luck – that man sitting there has directed every jazz programme on Swedish television since the 1950s! He has all the unedited footage in his possession."

Sure enough, a treasure trove of broadcasts arrived days later, complete with outtakes, conversations and onstage routining. Eric had found contacts in Germany and Italy as well and, to cut a long story short, this grew into a worldwide network of jazz fans swapping rare material. Our joint collections swelled to over 10,000 videos and Eric later made DVD copies of what was basically an alternate history of jazz. Eventually we showed or made tapes for Stan Getz, Herbie Hancock, Carlos Santana, the Miles Davis Estate, Art Farmer, Gil Evans, Al Cohn, Jerome Richardson, Eddie Daniels, Jimmy Heath and many many more. Some got a commercial release, many of the artists had never seen their performances, and I delivered dozens of lectures and hosted screenings at jazz festivals and academic institutions all over the globe. When Eric sadly passed away, I bequeathed his collection to Sussex University and when I "downsized" I donated the homemade DVDs to the Hamilton College Archive in New York and my VHS collection to the National Jazz Archive in the UK. And all because I decided not to watch *Starsky and Hutch* dubbed in German!

I've worked on many commercials with Sir Ridley Scott over the years, but none was as complicated an idea as the spot for a British bank in the early 1990s. The bank's motto was "the listening bank" and the creative team at Saatchi and Saatchi had come up with the idea of a 90-second TV and cinema spot that would trace the history of music through a series of vignettes, from a caveman banging two rocks together, through ancient Rome and medieval music, culminating in a full symphony orchestra and choir performing

Beethoven's *Ode to Joy*. The problem was all the vignettes were to be filmed to playback in the Mojave Desert in mid-summer!

I recorded a guide track in London using synthesized music for timings that could later be stretched or shrunk depending on what transpired during filming and editing, and then re-recorded with full orchestra and (sadly, due to budgetary constraints) synthesized choir. It was shaping to become, as indeed it did, the most expensive commercial ever shot (superseded by our Levi's ad which was widely reported at the time to be the most expensive commercial ever made).

I flew down to the desert from Los Angeles in a six-seater plane with Sir Ridley and the creative team. We were due to stay for several days shooting. The daytime temperature was expected to hit 50 centigrade (122 degrees Fahrenheit), but I was warned to expect the night temperature to drop to freezing. And in addition, to watch out for desert snakes! I travelled well prepared with layers of clothing to warm me at night, and brand-new cowboy boots to protect me from the venom. The first morning on set I rather stood out amidst the throng in T-shirts, shorts and flip flops – more fool them, I thought, as I sweltered safe in the thought that the snakes weren't going to get me! At least I wasn't in full evening dress like the poor symphony players stuck out in the relentless hot sun. I soon discovered that there was some amazing talent in the ranks of our miming orchestra. The bass section alone contained the great Al McKibbon, who pioneered Afro-Cuban jazz in the Dizzy Gillespie band of the 1940s; Eugene Wright, the last surviving member of the Dave Brubeck Quartet (who sadly passed away at the age of ninety-seven at the end of 2020); and Harvey Newmark, who has played with all the jazz giants.

I survived the first day of filming by constantly replenishing with water, although my dress code now seemed totally ludicrous, particularly as the snakes seemed to have got wind of our presence and taken a vacation. Nevertheless, by 1am the temperature had dropped to an icy 40 degrees centigrade (104 degrees Fahrenheit) as I surveyed my totally useless bag full of thermal underwear.

The next morning was to provide my real test. Sir Ridley had set up some amazing breathtaking shots, and I could only marvel at his artistry. He likes to operate the camera himself on advertising shoots, so he set up the first shot, and then turned to me. "You'll direct this shot."

"I'm sorry, I thought you said I will be directing?"

"Yes, that's right. I can't operate the camera and direct, so you take the megaphone and shout 'action', then give me a countdown for when the music starts, then thump me on the back when I need to start my pan, then thump me again when I stop panning, then shout 'cut'."

I carefully digested this information, and on the first run-through managed to co-ordinate my actions. Was Ridley happy? No. "You'll have to hit me harder than that, I didn't feel anything!" So, this is how it's done, I thought to myself as I yelled action and walloped the Oscar-winning director between the shoulder blades, again and again.

The commercial went on to win several awards but I've always regretted not being nominated for best director. And Ridley still hires me from time to time so I can't have hurt him that much! (Most recently we did an atmospheric five-minute mini movie for Prada that he directed with his talented daughter Jordan – it's on YouTube.)

Figure 48: Ridley Scott operating the camera under my direction. Author's collection.

In the golden age of British advertising there were surprisingly few composers and music producers at the heart of the industry. This wasn't a deliberate monopoly – it was more a testament to our speed and versatility. During my career I saw many major names in the world of pop music enter the business and exit ignominiously soon after. Writing tracks for commercials not only requires an encyclopedic familiarity with many diverse genres, it also entails a fair amount of diplomacy. Quite frequently you are dealing with people who have no musical knowledge. Sometimes you are with people who do know something about music. Both can be recipes for disaster and one can dine out on some of the true tales – those who had lengthy careers in this industry have wonderful stories, which are shared to this day.

Director to me (after the first run-through when asked if he liked the music): "It seems to start at the beginning, carry on very nicely through the commercial until the end – when it stops."

Me: "I'm sorry that's the only way I know how to write music!"

Ad agency rep to guitarist Mitch Dalton (asking for trouble!): "If I hear a noise in my head, could you play it?"
Mitch: "I had five years at medical school. I could probably cure it!"

Client: "What's that cheap noise?"
Me: "It's a £5,000 bass marimba."

Worried-looking client before the session for Age Concern: "How loud are you going to have those castanets?"
Me: "It's 'Morning Has Broken' for flute and strings with Dame Thora Hird's voiceover. There are no castanets."
Client: "There – I hear them clearly!"
Me: "That's the engineer's assistant, scratching the microphone to see if it's working!"

American client on hearing the pulse used to synchronize our recording with the film: "What's that?"
Engineer: "It's the synch pulse, you won't hear it on the finished track."
Client: "I love it – give it to me on a separate track so I can bring it in and out of the mix!"

My friends were mixing a composition of theirs while the client sat at the back of the control room reading a newspaper. He folded it up and said: "I think I'll head back to the agency now."
"Right," replied my pal. "We'll finish the mix and send a messenger over to you with it."
"I wouldn't bother," said the adman!

I really enjoyed my 40-plus years stint in the advertising world. My encyclopedic knowledge of musical genres allowed me quite often to "change horses in mid-stream" and suggest pieces and styles of music that no one had thought of using. (I should point out that this knowledge was not something I strived for; I was, as I explained earlier, exposed to every style at a very young age and grew to appreciate them all.) Some people thought of me as a jazz musician, some as a classical music expert and some as an ex-Van Morrison sideman. I was happy to encourage this ambiguity and refused to be pigeonholed. Quite frequently in my earliest days as an arranger I would be told by older studio players, "Oh yes, I know how to play jazz/funk/country/rock/reggae." They would then deliver a grotesque parody of the style in question. String players in particular were notorious for non-cooperation. I suppose they saw us as threatening the well-established status quo. I witnessed one viola player (not on one of my tracks, thankfully) pack his case and walk out in the middle of a take as the clock struck one – he was wearing his watch so he could see the minute hand while he was playing. Incidentally this was totally against union rules – takes begun before the hour were supposed to be completed even if the time ran over. I never saw that musician again but on a later session the violins were having problems articulating a rhythmic figure I had written. One player even suggested I rewrite the part. At the back of the violins sat a 17-year-old Christopher Warren-Green and a young Gavyn Wright. Chris, now a world-famous soloist and conductor, beckoned to me and said, "You don't need this – let us book your players!" I happily agreed, and the next two string sessions produced 'Always Look on the Bright Side of Life' and *The Rutles* and from then on, with Isobel Griffiths handling my rhythm, brass and woodwind bookings and Chris or Gav my string sections, I was secure in the knowledge that every musician on my sessions could play convincingly in every style.

One afternoon I was in a bookshop in central London and a young woman carrying a cello case was looking at me. Eventually she came over and said, "I know you, you're our conductor." At the time I was conducting a lot of movies and record dates with the Royal Philharmonic Orchestra. That remark certainly boosted my ego, especially as I had begun conducting as a necessity not as a vocation. I'm often asked, "Do orchestras actually follow the conductor?" All I can say is, one afternoon rehearsing with the Royal Philharmonic, I switched off for a moment. I suddenly snapped out of my reverie, which probably only lasted for a few seconds but felt like an eternity. My right arm was still waving in what I assumed was the correct tempo; however, I glanced at the viola section and was met with an incredulous stare from the second row of the violas. I vowed never to let my mind wander again on the podium.

18 Going Live

Throughout my writing career I never gave up the desire or the opportunity to play music in live shows. I remembered a conversation I had with my uncle Woolf Phillips in the early 1980s when I was beginning to establish myself as a composer/arranger.

"Have you given up playing saxophone yet?"

"Of course not, why do you ask?"

"You will sooner or later – it's impossible to keep up the playing once the writing takes over."

That conversation made me more determined than ever to keep my playing up to a level that satisfied me. After I left Van Morrison, I quickly shed the flute and clarinet as they needed too much time to maintain any standard of performance, and started to concentrate on saxophones, becoming particularly enamoured of the curved soprano and baritone saxophone, although still playing tenor when and if required. I began the 1980s by undertaking a weekly residency at my local jazz pub, now sadly demolished, at which I welcomed the finest UK and occasionally US musicians. I was also still in demand on the British blues scene, undertaking tours, recordings and regular gigs with Lowell Fulson – composer of 'Tramp' for Otis Redding and 'Reconsider Baby'. He had been a huge, acknowledged influence on B.B. King, who also sat in with us one night.

Lowell told me I reminded him of one of his early saxophonists Stanley Turrentine – high praise indeed. He also told me how he hired a young Ray Charles to be in his band. I played with Little Willie Littlefield, too, who recorded the first version of 'Kansas City' and I recorded and gigged with two wonderful vocalists – Dana Gillespie and Maria Muldaur. I was featured on tenor and baritone sax on Dr. John's *Live in London* album, and I once had to leave a session with the veteran R&B singer Nappy Brown and pioneer rock and roll saxophonist Big Jay McNeely, as I was conducting Elgar the next morning in the studios! My big band formed in 1985 and I quickly wrote a whole book of arrangements, to which I'm still contributing. I've fronted different line-ups in the UK, USA and Australia over the years which have appeared in many festivals worldwide.

At the Soho Jazz Festival one year at the Piccadilly theatre, I peeked through the curtains about thirty minutes before our set to "count the house." The entire theatre was deserted except for my mother and father in a middle row. My heart sank, but there was a simple explanation which I discovered at the interval. The stewards were preventing the audience from entering the theatre, but my mother had said to the commissionaire, "It's my son's band!" So, a rope was lifted, and my parents got pride of place. Thankfully we eventually had a full and appreciative house. My good friend Mitch Dalton, our brilliant guitarist, had recently returned from a sold-out tour of Japan with the great Henry Mancini. Their first show in the UK was in Nottingham and as Mitch peered through the curtain at the sparse audience before the show, he became aware of someone behind him. Henry Mancini surveyed the three-quarters empty room and whispered to Mitch, "Where are the Japanese when you need them?"

When we played at the Wigan Jazz Festival, Mitch got stuck in traffic on the M1. As we went on stage, I jokingly announced, "I apologize for the absence of our guitarist – please try not to notice when he sneaks onstage in the middle of the fifth number wearing a totally different outfit to our tuxedos." There was a roar from the audience when Mitch sneaked on in the middle of the fifth tune dressed in T-shirt and jeans!

My big band began with the success of Alison Moyet's 'That Ole Devil Called Love' and over the years I tried to use the band in movies and on record as often as possible, as well as playing live shows. I used to kid, "This is our 25th anniversary show – 25 years and 25 gigs!" The band provided the backing for Bjork's 'It's Oh So Quiet' and the soundtrack for several of my movie scores – notably *Funnybones*, *Little Voice* and *Shall We Dance.* On tour with Alison, we played at the televised Cork Jazz Festival. We had a camera run-through in the afternoon and the director and continuity person mapped out the solo order to ensure a smooth transmission that night. On one song, Mitch Dalton was due to play a guitar solo after Mick Pyne's piano solo. The camera duly zoomed in on Mitch and stayed there for the entire chorus. Unfortunately, the inexperienced Alison began singing her next chorus just as Mitch started soloing. We were treated on camera to Mitch stopping his solo, shaking his head and laughing, and obviously – to even the most inexperienced lip reader – uttering the words, "What have I done to deserve this?" All this time the camera stayed resolutely on him until the chorus was over.

I had a press screening in London of a television movie I'd scored the morning after our show in Cork, so I was booked on the 8am flight to Heathrow. The plane was full of American and British jazz musicians who had appeared at the festival. As this was 1985 and still at the height of the Troubles in Northern Ireland, all arrivals from Eire and N.I. were sent by bus to a special terminal. On the way the bus was hit by a baggage van and everyone went flying. I had been sitting with my arm resting on a rail and moments before the impact had moved my arm to my side. The impact of the crash, were I still seated as I had been, would have sent my ribs at high speed into the rail – as it was, my arm immediately went numb. An airline official asked that anyone injured stand to one side – eight of us were immediately transported to the local hospital and told our luggage would be left by the terminal for us. A long day in casualty ensued in the company of many jazz greats like Benny Golson, Buddy Tate, Carrie Smith and "Smitty" Smith and when I was finally bandaged up with my arm in a sling I was taken back to the deserted terminal. There was no sign of my luggage so I asked an official where I might locate it. He pointed to a door that read "cleaning staff only." It seemed unlikely but I pushed the door open to be confronted by the sight of six soldiers in full uniforms with machine guns pointed at a two-way mirror on the other side of which were unsuspecting arrivals from Ireland.

"I was in the accident on the tarmac and was told my luggage would be here," I stammered.

One of the soldiers nodded towards a back room, where an army major was seated. I repeated my nervous request, and he retrieved my case from a pile. "Don't drive," was the medical advice but by then I'd had enough of Heathrow and as my car was parked there ready for my trip to the screening, I got in, took off my sling, and headed home. Not only did I miss the screening, my letter of complaint to the airline was never acknowledged or answered. That was the last I heard of it until Mitch Dalton, affecting an Irish accent and pretending to be from the airline, pranked me on the telephone into relating in detail the whole sorry story.

The band was playing at an outdoor festival in the late 1990s. Our pianist had borrowed a DX7 (an early portable synthesizer with built-in orchestral sounds) to do the gig but was totally flummoxed by its workings. On one tune he decided to play a Hammond organ solo which kicked off with a 2-bar pick-up following a powerful hit and stop by the band. However, he'd pressed the wrong setting and come up with the flexatone, the "boiiiiiing" usually reserved for the moment when a 10-ton weight lands on Bugs Bunny's head. All hell broke loose as a series of "boingy-boings" filled the 2-bar break and the band couldn't resume for laughing. Only the drummer, who wasn't near enough to the PA to hear the full impact, carried on playing as the keyboard player struggled to continue his solo. He started playing again at the end of the bridge, but sadly all his efforts came to nothing as a new succession of "boings" rang out and the whole tune collapsed amidst hysterics. At least we got a standing ovation!

Technical glitches in retrospect do seem to be a source of great mirth. I'm reminded of a tale told to me by a pal who was asked to play the organ at a cremation. The crematorium had hired a keyboard and my friend got there early to set it up ready for the solemn moment at the end of the service when the coffin departed through the curtains. Moving to his seat during the last reading he discovered that someone had pulled out the keyboard's plug from the socket. He quickly restored it and switched on the machine. To his horror it began playing a prerecorded samba backing track which ploughed on through all his efforts to silence it. After the ceremony he was inundated with congratulations from the mourners who affirmed that that was obviously the way their happy-go-lucky friend and relative must have requested his final exit to be accompanied! I remember a TV recording where the band, led by Stuart Colman, was accompanying various stars of the 1950s and 60s. We were backing the great Del Shannon on two of his biggest hits – 'Hats Off to Larry' and 'Runaway' – and Pete Wingfield played the famous keyboard solo. Unfortunately, someone had pulled the plug on his synthesizer and quickly restored it, so what we got was a fairly avant-garde solo several musical keys removed from what we were playing, and what Pete actually played. Mortified, he rushed with his keyboard to the sound van where, luckily, they had a multitrack machine and repaired his solo. What we had all forgotten was that the whole solo was shot in close up, which transmitted with Pete grimacing and furiously trying to reset the keyboard and Del Shannon and the band laughing hysterically. Of course, what we heard was perfect!

Around this time a friend was touring as Tom Jones's drummer. He was very particular about the microphones used on his drumkit and carried a long list of technical specifications relating to every drum and cymbal for the sound department. It listed every make of microphone and the precise settings for each input. At one provincial show he started reading out his ideal set-up in great detail in a loud voice to the sound booth located at the back of the theatre. After a few minutes he noticed the sound engineer marching down the aisle of the theatre towards him. Under his arm was a pod from the mixing console, and as he reached the foot of the stage, he pointed to the equipment he had wrenched from the sound booth and exclaimed indignantly: "Look here, it says tone – on or off!"

In the early 2000s, a cache of negatives of phenomenal photographs of the golden age of Hollywood by the photographer Frank Worth was discovered in Los Angeles. Large prints were created of some of the best pictures and for the London launch of the exhibition, hosted by Stephen Fry, my big band, with vocalist Joan Viskant, was hired. The invited audience included several surviving veterans portrayed in the photos, including James Whitmore, Noreen Nash, Patricia Neal, Peggy Cummins, and my friend Betty Garrett. I was particularly excited that the reclusive Doris Day would be attending and hoped she'd be able to circumvent the appallingly managed crush outside the theatre. Indeed, as her car drew up and she saw the mayhem, she instructed the driver to take her straight back to her hotel.

Sadly, I never met her, but I relish a tale told to me by a director I worked with. Apparently, Doris Day had seen a commercial he'd helmed and wanted him to direct a spot for her favoured animal charity. He arrived at her Carmel residence, carrying the storyboards for the intended advertisement and sat at the bottom of a double marble staircase, nervously awaiting her appearance. And she didn't disappoint, elegantly descending the staircase, dressed from head to toe in white. He stood to greet her and as he did so the storyboards fell from his hands to the floor. As he went to pick them up, he noticed she had also bent down to retrieve them. She spotted him at the same time and they both stood up simultaneously. Unluckily, his head came into contact with her jaw and she fell poleaxed. All he could think was, "I've killed Doris Day – that will be my epitaph after all these years of hard work and awards!" Luckily her assistant was able to quickly revive her and, because we love happy endings, he wound up directing the spot and isn't reviled as "The man who killed Doris Day."

A great protagonist of mine was the late Derek Jewell, who had discovered and championed Andrew Lloyd Webber and Tim Rice. Together we put on a show dedicated to the life of Duke Ellington that debuted at Lloyd Webber's Sydmonton Festival. During the run-up to the show Derek invited my compadre Mitch Dalton and myself to a party at his house, which is how the two of us found ourselves in conversation with Andrew and Julian Lloyd Webber, Alan Parsons and Sir Stirling Moss – a varied assortment. Andrew was complaining that the Sunday paper reviews were useless if your show opens on the Monday. "Especially if it closes on the Tuesday!" retorted Mitch – I'm afraid Andrew didn't find that funny. Tim once joked to me, "There's no truth that Andrew and I had a falling out. Why only last week I went to see his last show – at least I hope it was his last show!"

One of the strangest gigs I undertook in the early 1980s was a Warner Brothers convention in Brighton. I was booked to play sax with a bunch of 1950s British rock and roll stars in Brighton, including my old friends Marty Wilde and Vince Eager, who told hilarious tales in the bar after the show of their days as pop stars in the 1950s. We were interrupted by Phil Carson from Atlantic Records: "Jimmy Page of Led Zeppelin wants to jam; anyone play piano and drums?" I volunteered my services as pianist, and we took to the stage. Jimmy was in his "out of it" phase and we played an endlessly loud, slow 12-bar blues. Suddenly one of the Warner Brothers female staff who had somewhat over-indulged climbed onto the top of the piano and proceeded to disrobe and writhe in ecstasy in front of my disbelieving eyes. Only the prompt action of Warner executive, former pop star and one-time policeman Dave Dee prevented a full-scale riot, but curiously – although there was a photographer there from *Music Week* – I've never seen any photos. Jimmy apologized to me for the fact that he was used to playing guitar with a vocalist and kept losing his place. I don't think he noticed the cabaret on top of the piano – Vince and I still talk about it frequently.

Speaking of strange gigs, one afternoon I received a telephone call from Robert Maxwell's PA. The mysterious entrepreneur and possible triple agent, who has achieved the dubious distinction of new notoriety as the father of

Ghislaine Maxwell, had decided that he wanted to learn to conduct 'Land of Hope and Glory' at the BBC Proms and somehow my name had been suggested as someone who could teach him! I was told I would be collected at the appointed time from the roof of the *Daily Mirror* building by a helicopter loaned by Andrew Lloyd Webber and transported to the imposing Maxwell residence at Headington Hall which, true to form, didn't actually belong to him. I was intrigued to see what he was like – at the time he and his family hadn't yet fallen from grace – although I was convinced he would be totally unable to conduct an orchestra. Evidently, he felt the same as he cancelled on the morning of the day I was due to visit him. A great pity – I'm sure I could have written a tell-all exposé about the encounter.

My Australian trips were interesting. On my first visit to Sydney, I arrived on New Year's Day from Melbourne and having ascertained where to find the famous Basement jazz club, I wandered down with my saxophone case in hand to take a look. When I got there, a man sitting on the wall outside said, "Are you playing tonight?"

I replied, "Not really, as I don't know anyone here – I just arrived in town for the first time this afternoon."

He responded, "Well it's my band this evening, so why don't you come up and play a bit?" I made my way onstage, suspecting I'd get one solo, a thank you and goodnight. The band must have enjoyed what I did as they asked me to remain onstage for the rest of the show, and I had a great night. The next day I was out to dinner with an old friend from London who said, "I'm known as the unofficial Mayor of Sydney and I'm going to take you to this great club, the Basement." I didn't say anything and after dinner off we went. When we reached the club, I hung back as he greeted the guy on the door, who said "I'm really sorry, we're sold out."

"But you know who I am, surely!"

"Yes, but we're still sold out – there's no room inside!"

At that moment the door person spotted me lurking at the back: "Oh hi, John, I didn't realize it was you with them – of course you can all come in as our guests."

The bewildered look on my friend's face was priceless – I never let on!

I did a wonderful series of big band and quartet gigs in Melbourne, Sydney and Brisbane with the much-missed composer/keyboard player Allan Zavod, stellar sideman for Frank Zappa and Maynard Ferguson and revered by George Benson and the late George Duke among others. It was also my pleasure to play and socialize with Motown legendary arranger/musical director Gil Askey.

And then there was Slim Gaillard. I first became aware of Slim in the 1960s via *Slim's Jam* featuring Charlie Parker, the great sides cut by Slim & Slam, and the chapter featuring him in Kerouac's *On The Road*. When I was with Van Morrison, we often discussed Slim and wondered where he was. He suddenly showed up to perform for a week at the Canteen in London. I went down to introduce myself, was immediately co-opted into the band and wound up performing with him at all his gigs when he spontaneously decided to relocate to London.

We became very close, and I often found myself in his company for dinners with Dizzy Gillespie, Johnny Griffin or Kenny Clarke. Dinner with Dizzy was fascinating – one conversation went something like this:

"Hey Slim, remember when I pulled a knife on you?"

"Oh yes, but I knocked you unconscious before you could use it!"

Both collapsed into helpless laughter. Slim became the darling of the young swing revival scene that exploded in the UK in the mid-1980s, and we played to packed crowds everywhere. We even travelled as far as Bermuda for a week one Christmastime in order to play a 30-minute corporate gig on the last night for BMW's top salesmen (two of whom gave us a sales pitch for a car in the taxi from the airport). Slim fell asleep at the piano during the second number! The show also featured Eartha Kitt, Mel Smith and Griff Rhys Jones – by the time we went on, late in the evening, the BMW elite were too drunk to notice or care.

I spent a crazy week being driven around the island at an average speed of 80mph in Luis Bacardi's Rolls Royce. (The island had a 20mph speed limit!) The eccentric Luis Bacardi (yes, that Bacardi!) was a huge jazz fan, took a shine to me and regaled me with tales of his imprisonment by Castro in post-revolution Cuba. One excursion we all enjoyed was a boat trip following the potential US entry for the America's Cup. I spent an agreeable afternoon with the great American broadcaster Walter Cronkite, only marred by the potential contender getting soundly beaten by a second-string yacht. On our final day in Bermuda, I decided to participate in the Sunday lunchtime jam session and the hotel concierge told me where it took place. I took a taxi way out of the capital's centre to the venue, paid the driver who departed and made my way into what appeared to be a deserted club. There was a janitor mopping the floor and I asked him where the jam session happened. Obviously not there – he scratched his head and responded, "The only place I can think of is the x club in the centre of town."

I asked where I could get a taxi and he laughed, before asking me what my driver looked like. When I told him, he replied, "That sounds like so and so – he's probably visiting his sister on such and such road while he's here." I noted the directions and set off in the noonday sun, saxophone in hand. I reached the house, saw the taxi parked outside, knocked on the door and asked the startled homeowner if her brother would kindly take me to the club! Fortunately, he agreed and dropped me by a deserted shopping mall with no sign of life. I climbed a staircase next to a closed jeweller's store, pushed a door and found myself in a room full of people with an organ trio in full flight! It was like a scene in a Western as the music and conversation suddenly stopped and all eyes were on me! Then the bandleader said, "Is that a saxophone? Get up here!" At the end of a couple of hours I said to the bandleader, "I have to go and pack and get to the airport now."

"Don't worry, we'll take you."

And that's how a convoy of cars arrived at our hotel, much to the amazement of Slim and the other musicians who had lazed by the pool soaking up the last of the December sunshine before our return to freezing-cold London.

Slim and I drifted apart slightly in his final years, although he would show up at my big band gigs and disappear before I could find him. That seemed to be the story of his life. I still booked him to record several vocals on commercials that I'd written or arranged, and he always delivered the goods for me. He became a legend once again during his extended stay in London; however, he remained just as exasperating as he'd been through his whole career – on the day he was due to shoot his part in the movie *Absolute Beginners* he was nowhere to be found. He'd taken another movie role for that day!

A favourite Slim moment occurred after the passing of Marvin Gaye, his son-in-law. (Yes, he really was – like so many other apparently tall tales he told, it was completely true. Another story was of his radio show with Sinatra and Dietrich as guests and Ronald Reagan the announcer. I scoffed until I heard the transcription of the broadcast.) Slim arranged a benefit show for his daughter and grandchildren and the flyer advertised everyone from Bob Dylan to Eric Clapton as appearing. Knowing Slim, it was quite possible that they might make an appearance but at showtime there was just Slim and his trio – sax, bass and drums – and a full house no doubt enticed by the mouthwatering flyer. After one tune Slim announced, "And now the trio will entertain you!" leaving the stage to saxophone, bass and drums. There followed the longest ten minutes of my life as we struggled to perform in front of what we were sure would soon become an unruly mob. Luckily at that moment, George Melly entered the club and I beseeched him to join us onstage. The evening turned out to be a great success although of course none of the billed superstars showed up!

One evening I had just got home from the BBC after an exhausting day of recording. On the kitchen table was a note: "Slim rang – gig." That was it – no cellphones then and no information about when and where. I guessed it was probably that night, so I rang the drummer's home and got his wife. "Oh, he's out at a gig."

"Any idea where?"

"Putney, I believe."

Apart from Putney being on the other side of London and about five minutes from where I'd been all day, I had no clue if this was the gig with Slim or not. I called all the venues in Putney and asked to speak to the drummer. I got lucky at the Half Moon – Robin confirmed he was with Slim and asked why I wasn't there yet! Having told him, to his surprise, that it was literally five minutes since I'd learned about the gig, and I was at least 45 minutes away, I promised to do my utmost to get there in reasonable time and asked him to keep my whereabouts from Slim so that he didn't panic. Luck was with me – I got every green light on the route and arrived as the band made their way onto the stage for the first set. Slim didn't even bat an eyelid and I'm sure never knew the hoops he'd made me jump through!

A surreal experience occurred just after Slim passed away. I received a call stating that in his will he had requested that I play at his memorial, and the concert had been fixed for a Friday afternoon at Ronnie Scott's. I was in the middle of recording a big movie score and was conducting a largish orchestra all day long – it was a wartime drama with very sombre and melancholic music. I worked out that if a car was sent for me at 1pm when we took our break, I would assemble my curved soprano sax in the car, run straight on stage, play a set and rush back to resume conducting at 2pm. All went to plan, and I ran through a packed club to the bandstand; as I arrived on stage the rhythm section kicked off a mid-tempo blues. It felt so good that I had to look round to see with whom I was playing – there on piano was Les ('Compared to What') McCann and on bass was Percy Heath of the MJQ! I'd never met either of these heroes and they had both flown to the UK to take part in the memorial concert. As I finished my first solo I looked over to the piano where Les was comping with his left hand and videotaping me with a camera held in the right! I played two tunes, hugged Percy, waved to Les, ran out of the door to the waiting car, packed my horn and five minutes later was conducting some sad dramatic scoring for low strings, thinking to myself, "Did that really happen?"

I've been friends with the other John Altman (Nasty Nick Cotton in *EastEnders*) since the late 1980s. I frequently got his pantomime offers and frenzied phone calls from TV researchers pleading, "Can you be on *Wogan* tonight?" Meanwhile, he claimed to receive my royalties! It was always fun presenting our credit cards to nonplussed cashiers in restaurants – one even pointed out that John only needed to use one card. Occasionally we do shows together under the banner John Altman Presents John Altman – we never clarify who's presenting who! We performed several times at the PizzaExpress in Dean Street, one of my regular performing venues since the mid-1970s. You never quite knew who would be in to hear you – one evening my audience included Marlon Brando, enjoying the jazz and a pizza. I'm still not quite sure how he got down the narrow staircase to the club. On another occasion my old boss Van Morrison showed up to a Hoagy Carmichael tribute. When our trumpeter made the mistake of introducing the Man to the audience, Van was out of the door before the introduction was complete! A regular at my gigs there was Sir Eduardo Paolozzi, widely considered the pioneer of pop art, who designed the cover of Paul McCartney's *Red Rose Speedway* album, and whose mosaics still decorate the platforms at Tottenham Court Road underground station.

The great jazz organist Jimmy Smith came into the Dean Street club, where by chance I happened to be working with my quartet. His right arm was in a cast and sling – apparently, he had fallen and broken it a few days earlier, bringing his European tour to a premature end. I happened to know his drummer Frank from LA and sat chatting with them for a while on my break. I can't recall exactly how it happened, but Jimmy was persuaded to sit in with us on piano, playing left-handed. I must say he played more piano that evening than most pianists with two hands!

A memorable PizzaExpress gig was with the pioneer of modern jazz clarinet Tony Scott. During the interval he proudly showed us the only extant photo of Billie Holiday and Charlie Parker together (backstage with Tony). It was carefully wrapped in cellophane and Tony told us: "I have been asked by innumerable film makers and publishers for this photo and I won't let anyone have it for less than $25,000!"

Tony is long gone and I'm afraid the photo is all over the internet – I guess he never got his $25,000.

A fixture around the British jazz scene, seemingly forever, was guitarist Allan Leat. He seemed to be the embodiment of the old gag, "How do you become a jazz millionaire? Start out a multi-millionaire." He had a fabulously rare pre-war Gibson guitar which he'd "modified" with a penknife. I took the great jazz guitarist George Barnes to look at the instrument – his words as he examined it were "what a beautiful guit – AAAAARGH." Allan (not his real name as I believe the taxman was after him), who came from a wealthy background, invested and lost his money in buying houses that accommodated disreputable people who did moonlight flits without paying their rent, and opening jazz clubs doomed to failure. Until his cash ran out, he drove a Rolls Royce, which he managed to reverse over one of his rarest guitars. We used to hide him away at the back of the stage where he happily strummed away four beats to the bar, except when the spirit really moved him, at which point he would unleash his sopranino saxophone, turn red from the top of his bald pate to his neck and emit the noise of a wounded animal. Fortunately, these outbursts were few and far between, but on one memorable PizzaExpress gig he was sat unobtrusively within a swinging group consisting of sadly missed wonderful musicians – Keith Nichols on piano; Dick Powell, violin; Neville Skrimshire, guitar; Ron Rubin, bass and Bobby Orr, drums. I looked up and spotted the then London resident jazz star Bud Freeman descending the stairs with the unfortunately named World's Greatest Jazz Band in tow. There was Bob Haggart, Yank Lawson, Billy Butterfield, Vic Dickenson and Eddie Miller – all giants and heroes from the USA. Our band was on fire, but, as Bud's foot hit the bottom step, from behind us emanated what resembled a cross between a hyena caught in a trap and an ear-splitting fire alarm painfully drowning out the whole band. As one man, all on the stairs turned and departed hurriedly. However, I do miss Allan, a genuine character who seemed to know as many obscure 1920s songs as me!

After the club was enlarged, I played there many times and attended some wonderful shows – the debut of Diana Krall, Gregory Porter and a marvellous evening with my good friend Jon Batiste where I joined him on an exuberant New Orleans encore that eventually wound its way, audience and all, into Dean Street pursued by a large number of waiters fearful that their "tables" would vanish into the London night without settling their fairly considerable bills! I had been introduced to Jon in Hollywood by the larger-than-life Jeff "The Dude" Dowd, the inspiration for the Jeff Bridges character in *The Big Lebowski*, and we immediately gelled both musically and personally.

Once I started writing and working in Los Angeles, I actively looked for places to play. One stop was the China club where my bandmates might include Bruce Willis and Harry Dean Stanton on harmonicas, Herbie Hancock and Chaka Khan. One particular night the band was full of musical superstars from the likes of Michael Jackson's band, Steely Dan, and the Average White Band. We had to accompany movie actor Gary Busey who played and sang 'Not Fade Away' for 20 minutes with no solos. I guess no one had the courage to wind up the number and he finally left the stage to sit at a table with his three bodyguards. I would also jam at venues like Drai's on La Cienega where the audience might include Arsenio Hall, Uma Thurman and many other movie names. Arsenio brought in an extremely tall young man who was obviously a professional basketball player. Our drummer Vince Wilburn, Miles Davis's nephew, was a basketball fanatic so I said to him, "It must be a thrill seeing this guy here?"

"Oh, I don't know him at all, he's a benchman for the Lakers."

I had no idea what that meant, so Vince explained that he was a rarely used substitute.

Curiously I asked, "What sort of money would he be earning?"

"Several million dollars a year," came the reply. In the words of a stand-up comedian I saw at the Comedy Store: "Why don't they just lower the baskets, so we all have a chance?"

I always used to sit in with the excellent blues band that played between scene changes at *Seinfeld* so I was able to watch many classic episodes being filmed. When I got to know various cast members in later years, they all had fond memories of those jam sessions. Around the same time, I started playing jazz with Jeff Goldblum, an association that has continued for over a quarter of a century. (I guested on his last two UK appearances, and he also wrote some wonderful words about me for this book.)

Jeff has always taken his music seriously, and since I've known him, has surrounded himself with the finest jazz players around. Whenever he was on a talk show promoting a new movie or talking about his life and career, he never failed to mention music and often the musicians with whom he performed. In the last few years his music has suddenly become commercially viable instead of a fun thing to do in downtime from shooting a movie. From the early 1990s around Los Angeles to the immediate past when his music has gone global, I've enjoyed his musical and social company. He attracts a huge youthful crowd at most of his gigs – many of whom have never experienced live jazz and all of whom seem to react with enthusiasm. When our Green Cards came through, my son Mike had turned twenty-one during the process and therefore had to fly immediately to the USA to validate his card. Mike now produces *The Late Late Show* with James Corden after a successful UK career producing Graham Norton (during which time he was responsible for the Will Smith *Fresh Prince of Bel Air* reunion which has to date garnered over a hundred million views worldwide) and, after relocating to California in 2015, has had a multiple award-winning career in American daytime television. Back in the early 2000s we landed at LAX, were whisked in a courtesy car to my apartment, changed clothes, and I headed out to play with Jeff that evening. As we pulled up in the car park next to the club, Jeff arrived simultaneously. I introduced him to Mike and Jeff put his arm around him and said, "Welcome to America!" I pointed out that this wasn't how people normally had their Green Card activated! (Nearly twenty years on, Mike and Jeff are occasional work colleagues and good pals.)

I've already mentioned the Original Comets' set at the Viper Room on the night of the 50th anniversary of the movie *Blackboard Jungle*, organized by Martin Lewis. It was a thrill and an honour to be asked to play with them and one could hear right away why they made such an impact. Their music really was Western swing combined with a rock and roll sensibility and it was that swing element that really hit home with the whole audience. Another great memory for me was guesting with the fabled stars of the Wrecking Crew as they performed and talked about all their hit records with the Beach Boys, Marvin Gaye, Sonny and Cher, Nancy and Frank Sinatra, the Jackson Five and the tortured insane genius, the late Phil Spector. The Comets and the Wrecking Crew, along with Little Richard and Muddy Waters, were seminal components of the beginnings of my musical journey – I'm blessed to have been able to play and hang out with all of them.

Later Los Angeles informal jam sessions saw me in the company of many greats – Albert Lee, the much-missed veteran blues guitarist Roy Gaines, Lawrence Juber from Wings, Johnny Echols of Love, the great bassist Jerry Jemmott, Blondie's Clem Burke and many more.

I played regularly all this time with the great jazz singer Barbara Morrison. At one festival, where I also performed with the LA All Star Jazz Caravan, top of the bill were the legendary Crusaders. Their saxophonist (and top studio bassist) Wilton Felder said to me, "I love your sound on the curved soprano sax – I think I'll get one!" Encouragement and praise like that, which I received from my jazz heroes such as James Moody, Jimmy Heath, Plas Johnson, Red Holloway, Houston Person, Jackie Kelso and Teddy Edwards certainly boosted my confidence in my jazz credentials. I started playing at jazz clubs and festivals around California, both with my small group and big band, and back in the UK I had another project in mind.

It's a Monday night in a London club – onstage Lionel Richie is singing his greatest hits. Waiting in the wings is Chaka Khan. Listening and watching with total absorption are Amy Winehouse and Joss Stone. On a sofa in the corner, baseball cap pulled down over his eyes, is Leonardo DiCaprio, in the middle of the room are Tim Robbins, Cuba Gooding Jr, Orlando Bloom and Brad Pitt. In the corner sit Justin Timberlake and Christina Aguilera. By the bar the US Olympic athletics team (including athletics legend Michael Johnson) is chatting with English soccer stars and being entertained by resident magician Dynamo. Behind a pillar lurks Spike Lee. Straight from the airport comes Samuel L. Jackson, pausing only to dump his suitcases in the cloakroom. Fantasy? No, just an encapsulation of eight exciting years at London's most exclusive and little-known Monday night entertainment at the legendary 10 Room.

Figure 49: Chaka Khan at the 10 Room. Photo by Tim Holt.

From 1999 to 2006 in an upstairs room in the heart of London's West End, an unbelievable array of superstars performed with a handpicked house band for an invited audience – and none of them were paid a penny. And if you think I'm exaggerating, here's a partial list of performers who graced the stage – John Legend (his first ever showcase appearance), Lionel and Chaka, The Roots, Pharrell, Black Eyed Peas, Nas, Sean Paul, Narada Michael Walden, Shalamar, Chic, Roy Ayers, Sugar Hill Gang, Will Smith, Chris Tucker, Eddie Griffin, Macy Grey, Joss Stone, Wyclef Jean, Blu Cantrell, Angie Stone, Shaquille O'Neal, Mario, Tyreece and of course Amy Winehouse. Plus, the best of British soul and pop.

So how did this all start? As I discussed in an earlier chapter, back in the 1960s I cut my teeth jamming in various clubs around London. In those days it was very easy to play with the likes of Peter Green, Jimi Hendrix, Kevin Ayers, Keith Moon. Either you would be playing in a club, and they would ask to sit in, or you would go to their gig and ask to sit in. Having a saxophone made it easier – they were still rarities on the rock and blues scene. You'd get maybe one number as a test, then if they liked you, an invitation to stay for the whole show and to return for the next gig – sometimes even to appear on record. Bands like Kokomo and Gonzalez continued this jamming tradition in the London club scene of the 1970s, centred around the Speakeasy Club, which actively encouraged off-duty rock stars to let their hair down and jam alongside their peers. However, sometime in the mid-1970s, things began to change. Managers and minders appeared on the scene, the bands moved up a gear into the "Enormodomes" of *Spinal Tap*, and interaction between bands virtually ceased.

The arrival of the synthesizer seemed to toll the final death knell for the jamming scene – quite often in the 1980s I came across pop stars who had never performed live, let alone interacted with other musicians. So, by the mid-1990s I found that, apart from the jazz scene, there was nowhere I, or other like-minded players, could go just to jam with each other. A chance meeting in Amsterdam with one-time Michael Jackson choreographer and dancer Patrick Alan (he's one of the "leaners" in the 'Smooth Criminal' video) lit the fire again. Patrick had run successful singers' nights in both Los Angeles and New York, and I was ready for a live music adventure in the UK. Out of our meeting was borne a plan – to revive the jam session in London.

We approached the 10 Room in the heart of central London, and they were willing to give us Monday nights – traditionally the deadest night of the week for nightclubs. For the first couple of weeks, we pleaded with our friends to come along (which was tricky) and then to return the following week (which was well-nigh impossible). But we were in luck – the show *Top of the Pops* filmed on Wednesdays, which meant that most US acts appearing were flown in on Mondays. It just needed some good word of mouth, coupled with the best band that could be assembled at the time, and soon the club became the must-attend for all visiting US artistes. After just three weeks the door staff had to turn away Madonna and her 33-strong entourage as we were at capacity. Then the word got out – others turned away included Jon Bon Jovi, while Prince was ambushed at the door by the staff of the club next door, China White, and lured in there while we awaited his arrival. Attendees over the years included TV presenters Louis Theroux, Gerry Kelly and Ade Adepitan, major music and movie names such as Bob Geldof and Armand Assante, and chart-topping pop bands such as Westlife, Blue, Atomic Kitten and the Spice Girls, numerous sports and media stars, many young unknown actors and musicians later to become world famous, and "personalities" such as Paris Hilton. Just how much of an institution we became was brought home to me by a friend who flew from Edinburgh to London on a Monday morning seated behind the US athletics team. One was heard to ask, "Where are we going tonight in London?" An old hand, probably Maurice Greene, responded, "There's only one place to be in London on a Monday, the 10 Room of course!" Sure enough, when she arrived at the club that night, there was the US team.

Spike Lee would arrange his London visits to arrive on a Sunday to make sure he could be at the club, while Samuel L. Jackson used to come straight from Heathrow airport. I was able to introduce Spike to Orlando Bloom one evening. And no one would turn down the chance to perform with our amazing house band. (Amy Winehouse, a regular performer before and after her fame, took the band *en masse* to be her touring group, and they stayed with her till the end.) Only Dave Matthews tried and failed (too much hospitality!) but everyone else managed magnificently, instantly gelling with the band and our talented backing vocalists. Kanye West brought in his protégé to showcase – a young lad named John Legend (I particularly enjoyed duetting with him on 'Let's Get It On'). I have a video recording of that night – as Patrick tries to explain who John Legend is to a noisy crowd, he loses patience and calls out, "OK Kanye, please take him back to the hotel if these people aren't prepared to listen!"

I invited Herbie Hancock and his band – in London for two nights – to be my guests at the club. I called Herbie at his hotel at 8.30pm to give him directions and, with the resident band, eagerly awaited his arrival for a very special night. Then… nothing. No one showed up, much to our disappointment. The next day Herbie called to apologize and explained he was on the verge of leaving the hotel when a courier brought in a master test pressing of his new album. Herbie listened and was horrified with what he heard – he spent the whole night on the telephone to the record company trying to rectify the mistakes. I then spoke to his bass player who was all ready to leave the hotel, then lay down for a minute for a nap to take care of the jetlag and awoke at 11 the next morning! The happy postscript to this story is that the remastered album in question, *Gershwin's World*, won the Grammy for Best Jazz Instrumental Album.

I was at lunch in Los Angeles a few years ago with Erin Davis and Vince Wilburn Jr (son and nephew of Miles Davis, and two of my closest friends). As we waited for the elevator, I excused myself for a bathroom visit. When I returned they were deep in conversation with Lionel Richie. I stood on the fringe of the conversation, not wishing to intrude, while Lionel kept shooting glances in my direction. Finally, Vince said, "You know John, he used to run the nights at the 10 Room." A huge smile broke out on Lionel's face and turning to me he said, "Oh I really *miss* the 10 Room!"

We were the best kept secret in the UK – guestlist invitations only and no paparazzi outside. The club ran its course and is now part of a luxury hotel catering to the tourist trade. But our nights didn't stop – we moved to the Pigalle and hosted Prince and the New Power Generation and helped kick-start more young talents – the mercurial Jessie J, and the multiple Oscar nominee Cynthia Erivo, who was one of our backing vocalists.

For around ten years in September from 2000 to 2010 I led a band at a sports charity gala at the Royal Albert Hall. Over the years the band included such luminaries as Bill Wyman, Paul Carrack, Ray Cooper, Eddie Chacon (of Charles and Eddie) and many musical sportsmen, fronted by England cricket captain Mark Butcher who, since his retirement as a cricketer, has successfully pursued a musical career. In the next chapter I will talk about the 2000 and 2001 shows but one memorable year I decided to save time by wearing my stage outfit to rehearsals and thus travelling light on the train, since parking the car was a nightmare around Kensington. I had to make a stop in the West End to pick up some music and entered a store under clear blue skies. I emerged to the biggest storm I'd ever seen that seemed to come from nowhere. It didn't look as if it would last long so I waited under a shop awning. Sure enough, the rain stopped within minutes, and I set off towards the station. Somehow, I managed to trip and fall into the only puddle on the street, soaking my suit and ripping my trousers in the process. Luckily at that time there were still men's clothing stores in the area, and I ran into the nearest one. "I need a suit," I exclaimed and charged into the changing room with the first suit that fit.

Figure 50: Lionel Richie with Patrick Alan and me at my 10 Room birthday bash. Photo by Harrison Funk.

"It just needs a few alterations, and we'll have it for you on Thursday."

"You don't understand – I need it now!"

The salesman realized the urgency of my predicament and rushed off to the tailor's workshop while I sat in the changing room. Twenty agonizing minutes later I had my suit and was on my way – no one was any the wiser! From then on, I have always taken a change of clothes to important shows.

Immediately after 9/11 I was asked to lead a band at Windsor Castle for the Royal household's annual party. We were all vetted thoroughly in the week prior to the show but amazingly when we drove up to the castle there was no security anywhere in sight – perhaps there were snipers hidden along the way! We got a tour of the private apartments, out of bounds to the general public, and apparently the Queen was just outside the party, enjoying the music. Or so we were told. One of the classic lines of all our careers was delivered by an on-duty policeman to our keyboard player as he attempted to leave the ballroom to put his synthesizer in his car.

"Not this way sonny, the Queen's gone to bed!"

One of my most memorable live experiences came when I arranged for and performed at a celebration of my old friend Michael Caine at the Royal Albert Hall. Michael's birthday and New Year's Eve party were held at Langan's restaurant, which he co-owned with the notorious and ill-fated Peter Langan, who would inevitably make a drunken attempt to sing with the band. His vocal would consist of repeating the song title instead of the lyric three or four times, before fading away and either falling to the floor or dropping the microphone and wandering off. Michael's 50th birthday was fun, as the relief pianist, who obviously had no idea what he'd been booked for, wandered in, lit his cigarette, sat down and wearily "cased the joint." Next to him was Barbra Streisand; across the room were Steve Martin and Jack Nicholson. He played for all he was worth! My band at the party included two venerable characters in the history of British jazz – violinist George Hurley and pianist Gerry Moore. On a break they were trying to work out when they'd first played together. The consensus was 1923!

Sir Michael's New Year's Eve party was eventful – my coat, with my house and car keys, was stolen from the dressing room and at 4am I was standing in the snow in a tuxedo with nowhere to go. Luckily our vocalist took me to his place and let me sleep on his sofa. The coat never showed up. A few years later I taught Michael to sing for his role in *Little Voice* and he gives a mesmerizing, award-winning performance. For the above-mentioned Albert Hall tribute, I wrote some arrangements for the LSO, Joss Stone and Quincy Jones, and appeared with all three. I'd always been friendly with Quincy, but this was the first time we had performed together. Believe it or not we sang, with Lance Ellington and the LSO, my orchestral arrangement of 'Get a Bloomin' Move On' by Quincy and Don Black from *The Italian Job*, which of course starred Michael Caine. A few years later for the same producer, Tommy Pearson, I got to transcribe Quincy's entire original score for live performance with orchestra (with the movie being screened simultaneously).

Figure 51: With my "star pupil" Sir Michael Caine at the Royal Albert Hall. Author's collection.

Screenings of classic movies with a live orchestra performing the score simultaneously have become very popular over the last few years – sell-out "concerts" of classics such as *Star Wars, Star Trek, Titanic* and *James Bond* have become much loved and anticipated events. Although technically I wasn't going live in these performances, I was audible in the prerecorded "choir" singing the classic 'Get a Bloomin' Move On' – this time exactly as heard in the movie. I obtained some original scores from the film company and found many discrepancies with the final dub. Some cues were missing completely, some began or ended halfway through, some were crudely spliced into the middle of others with different instrumentation, tempos etc. One cue included a complicated orchestral fugue which must have taken a long time to compose and orchestrate – the finished movie has a harpsichord playing a jazzy version of 'Greensleeves'! Of course, one expects these changes to occur on the soundstage and at the dub, but my remit was to duplicate exactly what was heard in the cinema. By chance I had a lunch during the takedown process with Howard Blake, the composer of the music for the classic animation *The Snowman*, who verified that he was in fact the harpsichord player on the soundtrack sessions, and it was a spontaneous suggestion of the director after he had heard the fugue. The whole writing process took a couple of months and really exercised my long-dormant takedown skills. The premiere at a packed London theatre was a huge success and the musicians did us proud with minimal rehearsal time. Once again, a career highlight and hopefully we will see and hear it many more times in the years to come.

Figure 52: With Quincy Jones at the Royal Albert Hall. Author's collection.

A couple of years ago I was invited by my friend Sophie Christophe to bring a jazz quintet to the amfAR Gala at the Cannes Film Festival. Usually when one is booked on an event like this the musicians are shown to their dressing room, given some curled-up sandwiches or the classic "band lasagna" and told not to emerge until showtime. As we arrived in our cabin by the sea, the organizers presented us each with a pass – enabling us to go wherever we liked! We were delighted to find that we were sharing the bill with Grace Jones and Sting. Grace's son and musical director Paulo is one of my closest friends and I've known Sting forever. As we stood outside Grace's trailer chatting with her brother and Paulo, Sting emerged from his trailer. "What are you doing here?" he asked me.

"We're playing jazz," I responded.

"I thought I could hear some jazz," he said. Just then a photographer asked, "Could we get a photo?"

"Sure," said Sting and flung an arm round my shoulder.

"I'm never going to see this photo, am I?" I asked the photographer.

"Give me your email and I'll send a copy straight away." I have never seen that photo! (Fortunately for all, Sting agreed to pose with the band backstage and my phone camera *did* capture that shot.)

Figure 53: My jazz quintet with Sting at the amfAR Gala at the Cannes Film Festival – Andrew McCormack, Andy Cleyndert, Mark Mondesir and Quentin Collins. Author's collection.

I've been very lucky and delighted to have participated in two special all-star celebration concerts in recent years. One was the great guitarist Albert Lee's 70th birthday weekend with an incredible roster of wonderful musicians and singers (I really got to know Albert well thanks to the LA jam sessions). The other was a memorial for my old friend Jack Bruce, again with a star-studded line-up. Both events were a great chance to catch up with many old friends and to play music with a mind-boggling collection of men and women who have shaped popular music over the last sixty years. I've also been playing live with the legendary Zoot Money, who was the first person in the UK to meet Jimi Hendrix, who came to his London apartment directly from Heathrow airport! And Jimi played his guitar too.

Jimi had toured and become friendly with the Soft Machine, especially their charismatic bass player and vocalist Kevin Ayers. He asked Kevin to be the bass player in The Experience, but Kevin passed on the opportunity. Once Kevin formed his own band The Whole World in 1969, which included a 17-year-old Mike Oldfield, I began sitting in with him regularly, a habit which lasted until the mid-2000s on stages around the world, and on record. A wonderful songwriter and performer, we became very close, and he even introduced me to the joys of Chinese food. Some of the gigs were pretty chaotic – Kevin and Mike Oldfield collapsing under the effect of too much alcohol, Robert Wyatt before his tragic accident playing the drums while lying on the floor – but they were always huge fun! After Kevin's sadly premature demise I played at his funeral and memorial in Deia, reuniting with my old musical friend and colleague Bridget St. John, and subsequently had the honour of standing in for Kev and giving his talented daughter Galen away in marriage.

Talking of Mike Oldfield reminds me I was on possible standby for the original *Tubular Bells* concert. They didn't require me in the end and, as I mentioned in an earlier chapter, I sat next to Mick Jagger at the Queen Elizabeth Hall for the premiere. I didn't see Mike for quite a few years, then randomly bumped into him in the Gloucester branch of W.H. Smith newsagents! With long hair, a straggly beard and an ankle-length fur coat he looked every inch the reclusive rock star, and true to form disclaimed any knowledge of me or Kevin Ayers. I assumed he had withdrawn from the gaze of the public following his success so when, a couple of years later, I was booked to appear at a Greenpeace benefit concert on the South Bank and suggested they might approach my old Kevin Ayers bandmate David Bedford (who had recently composed a classical work about saving the whale), I was surprised to learn that David had agreed to perform and was bringing Mike Oldfield, who was very much looking forward to seeing me again! As we arrived at the South Bank and were searching for our designated dressing-room area I was smothered by an unseen friendly assailant and firmly kissed on the cheek. Having no idea if this was a male or female I was astonished when a white-suited, short-haired Mike Oldfield sprang backwards and greeted me with a hearty hello! The wonders of the programme of Exegesis – a now discredited self-help cult. A few years thereafter, for a brief moment, he joined the commercials company I composed for. I recall bumping into him near the offices, carrying a very smart briefcase and looking like the ad men he was off to meet. Our next point of contact was at Kevin Ayers' memorial in Deia when he appeared via Skype from Nassau in the Bahamas where he now lives. A far cry from the shy 17-year-old I first came across onstage with Kevin in 1970.

A few years ago, I met an extraordinary young man named Jacob Collier. Although still in his teens, he immediately struck me as one of the most brilliant musical minds I'd ever encountered. I asked him if he would play piano in my jazz quintet and he was astonished, "No one has ever asked me that!"

"Well, I am," I replied.

We played at the Dean Street venue and of course he was wonderful – the rest is history. Multiple Grammy awards later and thanks to Quincy Jones's support and Jacob's incredible talent, he has become a superstar of contemporary music – and I still boast that once upon a time he was my piano player! I've really enjoyed playing with and learning from some wonderful young musicians like violinist Nora Germain; the aforementioned Golden Globe, BAFTA and Oscar winner for the brilliant animation *Soul* and bandleader on the Colbert Show, Jon Batiste and his band Stay Human; Chinese virtuoso pianist A Bu, with whom I first played when he was thirteen years old; and saxophonists Kamasi Washington and Xhosa Cole, the BBC Jazz Musician of the Year 2018 whom I first encountered when I wrote an orchestral piece to feature him as soloist with the Birmingham (UK) based People's Orchestra. The future of music is very bright with these marvellous musicians in the vanguard.

Figure 54: With Joss Stone and Jacob Collier at the Royal Albert Hall. Author's collection.

19 LA Life

I spent twenty-five years "commuting" between the UK and California and somehow managed to divide my time to work effectively in both places. On my frequent flights between Los Angeles and London and vice versa I met up with a fascinating array of people. One flight was spent hearing Herbie Hancock's wonderful anecdotes – he also would have been a great stand-up comedian.

My favourite Herbie story concerns the time he made the Grammy winning album *Gershwin's World*. He had recorded a jazz version of Ravel's Piano Concerto and the record label told him that any alterations to the original score had to be sanctioned by the notoriously difficult Ravel Estate. A tape was sent to them, but no word came back. Another call came from the label nearer the release date, the gist of which was that the track had to be pulled from the album unless permission was granted. Herbie rang Edition Durand, Ravel's publishers in Paris, and was put through to someone in authority. Haltingly he explained the urgency of the situation and exactly who he was. There was complete silence on the other end of the phone and Herbie's heart sank. After an interminable delay a voice spluttered, "WOW – HERBIE HANCOCK." Of course, the track was a highlight on the CD.

We've remained good friends for over a quarter of a century, and I always attend his UK concerts and those in California when I'm there. One night in London he performed an entirely electronic show with seventeen iPads and no instruments on stage. Inevitably the whole thing crashed and with no acoustic instruments to hand, we watched Herbie and a technician frantically trying to get the whole show going again. I went backstage to greet him afterwards and found I was the first person there. Herbie came over and whispered sheepishly, "Don't tell anyone – I turned off the main iPad and crashed the whole lot!" Even the great Herbie Hancock can make a silly mistake.

Figure 55: Herbie Hancock and I, delighted to see each other as usual. Author's collection. Photo by Aaron Liddard.

Just before the flight with Herbie, in the departure lounge, I'd bumped into Sir Stirling Moss, the legendary racing driver, whom I had met and bonded with at Derek Jewell's party. I'd recently spoken with Allen Eager, a terrific saxophonist and contemporary of Charlie Parker. He had married a wealthy socialite in Paris and took up motor sport, neglecting his sax playing, although at the time we met he was attempting a comeback (with not that much success). Allen had boasted to me that his claim to racing fame was that he'd once beaten Stirling Moss, so I asked Stirling if he remembered Eager. "Oh yes, he was one of the wealthy, fast-living set who dabbled in driving racing cars."

"He says he beat you in a race."

"*In his dreams*!" was the immediate reaction of one of the greatest figures in motorsport history.

Another flight was spent reminiscing with Lemmy of Motorhead about the late 1960s and early 70s. We had appeared on the same bills with a variety of different bands. A trip with Nile Rodgers was spent swapping stories about David Bowie, another with Ian Dury and actress Pam Ferris involved telling amazing tales at the bar on the plane until I said, "I think I'll get some sleep before we land in London." At that moment the pilot announced our descent into Heathrow – we'd talked away the whole nine hours. On one flight, I knew everyone in Virgin Atlantic upper class, either through music, movies or commercials. On another I thought I recognized someone I'd played in a band with years earlier. He turned out to be a business manager, and he still looks after my US interests twenty-eight years later (as of 2021). However, the most memorable trip I nearly didn't make at all, but it turned into a tale to dine out on.

In those days Virgin Atlantic sent a car to collect you from home and take you to the airport. All very civilized and the car picked me up at home at 8am. An hour and a half later the driver passed my front door again – all the roads into London were closed and the traffic barely moving. So, I asked him to drop me near an underground station and ran through the rain with my cases to the platform. The underground took forever, and I arrived at Heathrow airport with minutes to spare. In those pre-9/11 days they would let you board a flight with your luggage and so I leapt on board around midday. I sank into my seat, and the cabin crew brought me a glass of water, which I proceeded to spill all over myself, saturating my trousers. This is before the plane had even started taxiing. I called one of the cabin crew over and she offered to take the trousers and hang them in the cockpit to dry (again pre-9/11 when rules were far laxer). I was given a tartan blanket to wrap round me and realized I hadn't visited the bathroom since before 8am, so when the seat-belt sign was extinguished, I ducked my head and made for the front bathroom. "At least I don't know anyone on this flight," I thought as I opened the door to return to my seat – to be confronted in the first row by Billy Connolly. I first met Billy when he was a member of the Humblebums with Gerry Rafferty, then worked with him on the *Secret Policeman's Other Ball* and scored his movie with Sharon Stone, *Beautiful Joe* (for which I wrote the song 'If You Believe in Me' sung beautifully by Paul Carrack).

"Oh John, which clan are you from then?"

I stood with head bowed while Billy did a hilarious spontaneous routine about my tartan blanket. Shamefaced I returned to my seat – to find my now dry pair of trousers carefully laid out!

Once I flew to the UK from LA via Houston and New York. For the Houston – New York leg I was upgraded to first class and sat next to an obviously very successful Texan businessman. It was the first day of the first Gulf

War and during our conversation he said: "By the way I think you're very brave."

"Oh, London is used to being on alert because of all the IRA bombs of late."

"No, I mean personally you are very brave."

"How so?"

"Aren't you afraid the Iraqis will drive up overnight while you're asleep and invade your country?"

I'm afraid I was left speechless.

After my Emmy victory I was given a Green Card – when I relinquished it, I travelled on an O-1 visa (alien with extraordinary ability or achievement!). By the time I was virtually commuting to Los Angeles it was definitely not advisable to echo Peter Cook's flippancy. When filling out the entry form, to the question "Are you or have you ever been involved in a plot to overthrow the government?" he wrote, "Sole purpose of visit!" On one arrival the immigration officer congratulated me on my Emmy win – on another, when I was asked the date on which I had left Los Angeles, I thought for a moment and responded, "It was the third of September." Without missing a beat, the officer came back with "That day I'll always remember!" We both burst out laughing at our mutual fondness for Temptations' lyrics ('Papa Was a Rolling Stone'), albeit my quote was delivered completely unintentionally.

For most of the 1990s, my "home from home" was the Sunset Marquis hotel in West Hollywood and my nightly haunt was the Whiskey Bar situated in the hotel. There was a noticeable absence of paparazzi and the clientèle was almost exclusively A-list Hollywood. Regulars included George Clooney, Pedro Almodóvar, Jeff Beck, Sean Penn, John Entwistle of The Who (with whom I had a drink a few days before he passed away), Drew Barrymore and various members of big rock bands. It was where I headed after I won my Emmy – a young lad I didn't know asked if he could hold it. ("Heavy, isn't it?") As I circulated, another friend asked me, "How do you know Eminem?"

When I lost out at the Emmy's three years later, I repaired to the hotel with Sacha Baron Cohen and company, who had also won nothing. The photos around the bar were by the great Jim Marshall, who would often join my party and voice some of his outlandish opinions. One evening I introduced Barry Gibb to Mickey Rourke, and they discovered they were both staying in the same part of Florida at the same time. "Did you know my house?" asked Barry.

"Know it? I burgled it!" replied Mickey. We weren't convinced that he was kidding.

The self-styled "mayor" of the Whiskey Bar was Billy Bob Thornton who can still be found around the hotel most days. We hit it off, thanks to our mutual musical interests and I spent many fun evenings in his company. I was the first person to know he and Angelina Jolie had married. (They told me and then said, "Don't tell anyone!") One year I was leading an all-star band at the Royal Albert Hall and had to fly back to London. Billy Bob offered me a lift in a private plane he was taking to the UK. A tempting offer, but there was a stopover in New York, and I had to be back for rehearsals. I suggested he might like to sit in on drums at the concert, with the likes of Bill Wyman and Paul Carrack and he was fired up. On the day I duly phoned him at his London hotel, they told me he had already checked out and they didn't know where he'd gone. So much for that bright idea.

The Whiskey Bar closed at 2am but someone always came round with pieces of paper bearing the address of afterparties, usually in the San Fernando Valley or the canyons. Not being a drinker, I always drove, so one night found me chauffeuring a very eclectic cargo – in the front was R&B superstar Rick James, in the back actors Vince Vaughn and Kevin Spacey (before his fall from grace) and one-time child star Leif Garrett.

I have some great memories of my time at the Marquis. Here are a few in no particular chronological order. One afternoon I was practising my saxophone in my room, figuring that everyone in the hotel would be out and about. I finished, put the horn away, and exited the room. At the same moment the door of the adjoining room opened and, as the guest spotted me, he nodded and said, "Sounded really good!" It was Al Green. I spent a lot of time with another regular resident Peter Boyle, who told me fascinating tales of his friendship with John Lennon. Peter was a great actor whom we lost too soon. At Sunday brunch I would find myself exchanging greetings with the likes of Gene Hackman or Lou Reed. A week in the company of 11-year-old Charlotte Church, in LA to sing for then-President Clinton, and her family was memorable for singing Charlie Parker solos with her grandfather in the Whiskey Bar!

The hotel was often full of British filmmakers, actors and commercials production teams, so breakfast by the pool was often a big reunion. One morning I spotted Nik Powell, my university chum, Stephen Woolley and Neil Jordan, with someone else who had his back to me. I went over to say hello and Nik said, "You've met Tom Cruise, haven't you?" Tom stood up to shake hands, I extended my arm and realized as I said "Hello" that my raised hand was a little too high! The tables by the pool were very close together and one morning I sat next to producer Norma Heyman and my old boss John Mackenzie, deep in conversation. Neither had noticed me but I could hear every word that was said. They got onto films that never had the recognition they deserved, and John started saying how good *Act of Vengeance* was and how it got rather lost in the shuffle.

This had to be my moment and I suddenly spoke up, "I wrote the music for that movie!" The expression on their faces was priceless. I pulled the same stunt at Mr Chow in Beverly Hills. I'd gone to dinner with my pal, actress Brenda Bakke (star of *Hot Shots Part Deux* and a memorable Lana Turner in *LA Confidential*) and we were next to a table of Australian television executives from Channel 9 over for the pilot season. It was the day after Brian Lara had broken the world record for test cricket runs scored in an innings, and one of the execs loudly declared, "I've no idea how anyone in the world can get this guy out." It was too good an opportunity to miss – I chimed in, "I can tell you – I've got him out!" The jaws dropped. (Incidentally Brian Lara, the world record holder for both the highest test and highest match score in cricket, has been a close friend for thirty years and we have spent many happy moments around the world.) Many years later I repeated the feat a third time in London when John Malkovich was on the next table in a Soho club. Someone in his party professed their admiration for the score of *Sheltering Sky* and John very kindly pointed me out as one of the collaborators!

The late great photographer Terry O'Neill was sitting with me one night. We were having so much fun reminiscing he decided that we would stay seated by the pool chatting rather than head out to our intended rendezvous with Hugh Grant (yes, it was that night!). Hugh's then-fiancée Liz Hurley was (and still is, I hope) a pal and in fact when she moved out of her house, I was offered her old room (sharing the house with my friend who lived there). It was a fun time. As well as working hard we played pretty hard. I remember one very competitive game of pool at the Hollywood athletic club with the Baldwin brothers – Stephen and Billy, random nights out in the company of Trey and Matt, creators of *South Park* and *The Book of Mormon*, and Chuck Lorre, who came up with *Two and a Half Men* and *The Kominsky Method*, among others. And playing cricket under the Hollywood sign with a whole host of expats. (Two locals arrived at our ground a few minutes after the match had started, bouncing an American football. One said, "What are they doing?" The other replied, "Playing cricket I think." "OK we'll wait!")

Figure 56: Cricket under the Hollywood sign – teas courtesy of Elizabeth Hurley. Author's collection.

I met some fascinating people while based in Hollywood – a great character whom I became very friendly with in my early days in LA was the legendary record producer Lee Magid. Then in his late sixties, he had worked with nearly everyone from Big Joe Turner and T-Bone Walker through to Della Reese and the Clara Ward Singers. His many anecdotes of a vanished era in the music business often kept me entertained at lunches and dinners.

My agent at the time arranged a meeting for me with the amazing Lew Wasserman. Once known as the most powerful man in Hollywood and President of MCA, he had just opened a new office as his career wound down. Our entire meeting consisted of him and me moving his desk from one office to the other – hardly the glamour of Hollywood. Several meetings for imminent movies seemed to end with, "We'll be in touch with some dates for you to start work." I'm still waiting – no one likes to say no to a potential major player! One meeting with two very powerful Hollywood agents didn't happen because, as my then-representative and I sat in the waiting room, the shouting and yelling from the interior office intensified and we soon became aware that they had come to blows. We beat a hasty retreat.

For a while after that, every trip I would stay with Craig Ferguson as he moved around LA. Craig had arrived from the UK an unknown in the USA and I met him on his first night in California. He soon found his feet in movies and on television, and eventually became the iconic personality he is today, a constant presence on American television with awards galore. One evening we were forced to leave a lavish Hollywood ceremony as we had a fit of the giggles. It started when Michael Jackson made a spontaneous effusive speech of thanks to all and sundry including the Lord. The whole speech was on the teleprompter next to us. The next award went to country star Vince Gill – we decided it was meant for the very MOR British vocalist Vince Hill, whose big hit was 'Edelweiss' from *The Sound of Music*. That was the point of no return. Craig used to enjoy attending my jamming sessions with LA's finest blues musicians – however, his career was taking off on American television and I realized I would have to get my own place as my workload increased with more major movie projects coming my way.

Eventually I rented an apartment with a friend. I called it the House of Doom as most of Hollywood's "bad boys" seemed to congregate there. I won't mention any names but they're all the usual suspects from the early 2000s and all friends of my then-roommate. One visitor who *was* very welcome was the magnificent Luther Vandross. I once asked him how he made a certain notoriously untuneful diva sound good in a Grammy duet. His response could apply to a lot of arrangers and musicians that I know. "I spent years as a back-up vocalist, I know how to make anyone sound good!" When he was sadly hospitalized for a while in those pre-YouTube days, I made him a DVD of concerts by Aretha Franklin, Ray Charles, Curtis Mayfield, Marvin Gaye and James Brown among others, which he loved. A tragic early loss – sadly we were never to work together but Luther remains one of my favourite vocalists and everyone I know who did write, record or tour with him holds him in the highest regard.

I moved out of there into an apartment found for me by Michael Richards, Kramer in *Seinfeld*, who was dating my soon-to-be new roomie. I was due to fly to the UK on 10 September 2001, but my agent rang and said, "Sylvester Stallone is interested in you scoring his new movie, *Avenging Angelo*, can you meet this afternoon and change your flight to tomorrow?"

My response was, "Sure, one day won't make any difference." The movie wasn't great and to cap it all, I got a flat tyre on the freeway home in the rush hour. "Well, things can't get any worse," I thought. The next morning, I heard my roommate on the telephone at 7am. I thought this was slightly unusual for her, then she knocked on my door and said, "You're going nowhere today!" With mounting horror we both watched, along with the rest of the world, the events of September 11th unfold. Teresa, my flat mate, eventually went round to a friend and I sat alone in the apartment, feeling numb. Eventually I realized I had nothing to eat in the place and all my clothes were packed for a flight that wasn't going to happen and I went down to Larchmont Village to see if I could get some takeaway food.

Larchmont was unusual for Los Angeles in that it felt like a British village. You would see the same people every day and bump into locals like Diane Keaton, David Schwimmer and Sophie Dahl. On this early evening it was totally deserted except for one Japanese takeaway. I went in and ordered some food. The only other customer was Cameron Diaz who looked as shell shocked as I was.

I spent the rest of the week in limbo, not daring to unpack in case a flight suddenly materialized. Indeed, I wondered if any flights would ever happen again. I was due to lead the band in my annual charity concert at the Royal Albert Hall and had all the music with me in LA. The concert was on the following Monday so my cut-off for calling the organizers and pulling out was realistically the Saturday. On the Saturday morning I rang the airline and was told "no flights" so I decided to get some shopping done. I went to the Beverly Centre and my cellphone rang. This is 2001 when mobile phones weren't that common in the USA and reception was very poor. (I was frequently stopped in the street by people enquiring what was that strange object I was speaking into. After the invention of Bluetooth, I was outside the Dolby theatre in the Hollywood and Highland complex trying to locate a friend arriving for the awards ceremony we were attending, speaking into the cellphone via the earpiece. I was interrupted at least twenty times by arrivals showing me their tickets, asking where the bathrooms were situated, or where to validate their parking!)

At the Beverly Centre, a faint voice on my cellphone said, "Could you be at the airport for 2pm – we have a flight to London?" I rushed back to the apartment, begged a lift from a generous friend, and was dropped at the car park quite a way from the airport. The authorities were not allowing anyone near

LAX for obvious reasons. A fleet of buses stood there, plus literally hundreds of people. I stood in the sweltering heat in my suit with my two cases – no one was making a move of any kind, including the police and airport staff. I took matters into my own hands and went over to a bus driver. "Airport?"

"Jump in," he said, and off we went to the kerbside, where an airline employee was standing with a clipboard.

"Follow me please," she said after she'd checked my name, and literally three minutes later I was on a packed flight. The man next to me was a "security expert." I felt pretty sure that this would be the safest flight I ever undertook and wondered how many more of the passengers were security experts. Moreover, this was the first international flight post-September 11th and my inconvenience paled into insignificance next to the magnitude of the tragedy. The following Monday there I was at the Albert Hall where one of the performers dedicated a magnificent version of 'Amazing Grace' to all the victims of 9/11. Everyone has their own story of how they reacted to the awful events of that day – I'll always remember saying to my agent, "What difference will one day make?" Sadly, that day changed the world forever.

As life returned to "normality," within months I had resumed the pattern of intercontinental commuting. While I regularly travelled between the UK and USA, my family remained in London. In order to maintain contact with the UK at a time when transatlantic calls were pretty expensive, I signed up for an AT&T scheme. Instead of a dollar a minute, calls to the UK cost 10 cents. I happily utilized the reduction until I received my first bill – $500 for overseas calls. On calling to query the amount, I was met with the classic response: "Just because we sent you a letter welcoming you to the scheme, it doesn't mean you are on the scheme!" I refused to pay the amount, which reappeared on my bill every month thereafter. A year later I switched phone provider and alerted them that I disputed the $500 that would appear on my first bill.

"What $500?" asked the phone company. I never heard of it again!

My English accent caused some problems along the way. Once I had to change a flight time on American Airlines that I'd booked with American Express. Amex said this would be no problem, then called back to say I had to do it myself, so I rang the airline and got the dreaded computer automated service.

"Which airport are you flying from?"

"Los Angeles."

"I'm sorry, I didn't understand that. Which airport?"

"LAX."

"I'm sorry, I didn't understand that. Which airport?"

(Puts on dreadful fake American accent) "Los Angeles, LAX, LA!"

A pause: "I think you said Oxumoxu Airport" (whatever that is!) Sound of phone flung across the room!

My English accent certainly confused a number of native Angelenos, and I was frequently asked where in South Africa or Australia I was from. One local asked a Swedish friend if she lived near Zurich, but I think the experiences of an Austrian pal stand out. She was often being told of people's trips to Perth or Sydney, but I cherish this encounter she had in a Hollywood grocery store:

"Where are you from then?"

"Austria."

"Oh, that's interesting – I know someone who comes from Austria."

"Who's that then?"

"Hitler!"

I'm afraid there's no answer to that!

In the UK I had often been confused with well-respected saxophonist/session musician Johnny Almond. He was occasionally credited with projects I had been involved in and vice versa. When I began composing and recording in Los Angeles, I found a new "nemesis" – Academy Award winning composer/editor John Ottman. As our names sounded similar when pronounced with an American accent, I began getting calls from musicians apologizing for having to miss their session the following week. I was mystified by the regularity of these messages until I realized the sessions were for Mr Ottman. He jokingly suggested taking out a contract on me – I'm still alive so I guess it's no longer such a big problem! John is a very talented all-rounder, and I have followed his career with great admiration. (The actor John Altman, the novelist John Altman, and I, once discussed marketing ourselves as a triple threat!)

A television movie I did score at the time, *King of Texas*, was produced by and starred Patrick Stewart who is still a great friend to this day. After we'd finished the film, he invited me and some friends to his house for dinner and to watch the finished movie. At dinner I found myself seated between Patrick and William Shatner! Two captains of the *Starship Enterprise* and no camera – oh (again) for an iPhone! To add to the irony of the evening Patrick put on my big band album with Joan Viskant as background music. "What's this?" asked Captain Kirk.

"It's my latest CD," I responded apologetically.

"I love it – can I have a copy? Tell us all about it!" My fanboy dinner turned into me giving a blow-by-blow account of my album, its conception and realization, to the two Captains!

After ten years and many memories in that apartment, my third flat mate Sandra, who stuck with me for the next fifteen years, and I moved to a house in Hollywood. On the first night an apartment in the block next door hosted a raucous party with Balkan music playing till around five in the morning. "What have I done," I moaned as I buried my head in the pillow. Thankfully, it never happened again. We didn't need security cameras as some of the residents of the block sat outside all day and evening, and although the most common wake-up call in the early days was "He's got a knife!" our area eventually became the location for the encroachment of gentrification with hotels, clubs, restaurants and luxury apartment blocks springing up all around us. Despite the violent reputation of Los Angeles, I have to say I felt safer there for twenty-five years than I ever did walking through the streets of Central London at night. My next-door neighbour in London at the time ran a successful betting company. One evening, while watching TV and relaxing, I was suddenly confronted by the sight of my jacketless neighbour pressing up against the garden patio doors and gesticulating. Apparently, he had been robbed at gunpoint by two thugs who were waiting in his driveway. He had thrown his jacket at them, vaulted the fence, and while I dialled 999 his wife called to say she had seen the whole incident from her kitchen and called the police. She assumed the robbers had knives, so the police response was immediate. They intercepted the felons making their getaway on a motorbike, both ran, and one was caught with a shotgun stuffed down his trouser leg! The police told us, "You're very lucky – if we'd known they had guns we would have had to wait for an armed response unit, and they'd have got away!"

Ironically, Tom next door got his jacket back intact and when he counted his cash, he found he had more than had been stolen – he got his assailant's money as well! I don't think anyone was too concerned.

One night in LA before my move, I got back to my apartment after a gig in Orange County at about 2.30am. As I parked on the street near my place, I noticed someone approaching my car. I had a snap decision to make – drive off immediately, lock all the doors or get out of the car as if unconcerned. "Fortune favours the brave," I thought as I blithely stepped out of the car and faced my potential mugger.

"Was that Charlie Parker with Sarah Vaughan I heard on your stereo?" he asked.

"Yes, indeed it was!" I replied as I strode confidently to my front door (which I then quickly double-locked behind me).

I was invited to a party in honour of a vocal duo, the Opera Babes, at a house in Bel Air which made Buckingham Palace look like a garden shed! The event was very "old Hollywood." I sat for dinner with Mrs Gregory Peck and Mrs Frank Sinatra who spiked my cranberry juice with Tequila. "Cranberry juice is no drink for a man!" she muttered as I choked. I was subject to a Don Rickles' "put down" as we met in a doorway, and shot the breeze with Quincy Jones. Across the room I spotted Suzanne Somers and Joan Collins. I couldn't wait to call a pal in London to tell him about the evening and I drove down the hill while chatting on the phone. Suddenly the road wasn't there anymore. "I'll call you later," I exclaimed and hung up. I had got myself onto a horse trail on the side of a mountain in my new car and in the pitch darkness I somehow had to reverse back to where I'd come from. Fate was with me that night as I was convinced either the car or I, or both, would topple over the mountain edge. I've still no idea how I got back to the slope, but I couldn't then turn the car or reverse it up the hill. I had visions of having to hire a helicopter to rescue the car in the morning, but then a thought crossed my mind. If the house and guests were so monied, there had to be security dotted around? I walked up the slope and found a guy with a walkie-talkie and explained my predicament. "Are you drunk?" was the first thing he asked. When I assured him I was perfectly sober, he radioed the house and soon another security man appeared and together they headed down to my car. After about 40 minutes, the car reappeared unscathed, except for a couple of scratches from the foliage on the underside of the chassis. "How did you…?"

"Don't ask – just remember you leave by driving up the driveway, not down." I learnt the next day that everyone left at the party had been thoroughly entertained by reports from the security as to the progress of the rescue mission.

Speaking of opera, I love this story told to me by the late Derek Smith. Derek was on call for *Good Morning America* on US television should they need a pianist and accompanied everyone from Tony Bennett to Dusty Springfield. One Christmas eve he received a call that Pavarotti was on the next day and needed accompaniment. Nervously he arrived there two hours early to practise reading music from short operatic scores, eventually to be presented with a song copy (store-bought sheet music) of 'We Wish You a Merry Christmas!'

An unlikely effect of living in Hollywood was running into major movie stars and celebrities in the most bizarre circumstances. I was shopping in Rexall's drug store and a customer was stooping to take something off the bottom shelf. As he stood up he connected with my chin, thankfully not very hard. Sir Roger Moore was most apologetic though. As we queued to pay for our toothpastes and ointments, I spotted him in the line behind me and gestured three ahead, where Joan Collins was waiting to check out. He nodded and soon the "darlings" were echoing round the checkout till. I had my car washed at the Celebrity Car Wash on Vine – one afternoon I found myself waiting with my old friend John Malkovich. "Are you the celebrity in Celebrity Car Wash?" I asked. Zsa Zsa Gabor's daughter (and Paris's aunt) Francesca Hilton was a very upbeat "bag lady" on Beverly Boulevard – she would always pop into the AT&T store and bid a cheery good day to everyone.

Spotting celebs was fun, but far more rewarding for me was meeting up with Hollywood veterans, especially performers who had worked with my uncles in the 1940s and 1950s. They all had fond memories of working with my relatives and were usually amazed at how well I knew their work. I would see Dean Martin in his wheelchair every Friday at Hamburger Hamlet but never got beyond a friendly nod of recognition. In the early 1990s many veterans of the Golden Age of Hollywood were still alive if not active. As I stated earlier, I attended James Stewart's Christmas carol gathering, and also made sure I was at the big band society's annual reunions, arrangers' lunches and events at the American Society of Music Arrangers and Composers in Hollywood (I wound up on the board of ASMAC with many heroes such as Arthur Hamilton, composer of Julie London's 'Cry Me A River', Billy May, and Johnny Mandel), the Radio Pioneers' award ceremonies – and a visit to Nate 'n Al's delicatessen, Dan Tana's or the Musso and Frank Grill would usually yield an encounter with a movie or music favourite such as Artie Shaw. The "other" Ray Charles (of the Ray Charles Singers and *Muppet Show* fame) once asked me how I knew so much about the golden era of American showbusiness. "You're talking to a man whose first contribution to the business was giving half his milk ration to John Boles!" I replied. John Boles, the star of early talkies like *The Desert Song*, *Rio Rita* and *King of Jazz*, appeared at the London Palladium nursing an ulcer for which I provided some consolation!

Figure 57: Quartet with Emmy award winning composer Sean Callery. Author's collection.

During my time in LA, I kept busy playing live music – both jazz and R&B. The esteemed critic Don Heckman wrote in the *LA Times* that I was "one of the few movie composers with authentic jazz skills." My jazz quartet performed at many now defunct jazz clubs and festivals around Los Angeles. It usually included world-renowned pianist Mike Lang, bassist Putter Smith, who memorably acted as the villain Mr. Kidd in *Diamonds Are Forever* (cast for his only movie role while playing a jazz gig with Thelonious Monk and spotted by the director), and drummer Frank De Vito, who played with Sinatra, Billie Holiday and Charlie Parker among others. Another quartet I co-led with composer Sean Callery (*24* and *Homeland*). My occasional pianist was the wonderful Theo Saunders whose father Nick was then one of the last surviving regular cast members of my all-time favourite television comedy *The Phil Silvers Show* (he was Captain Barker). I enjoyed his tales of Bilko days as much as the gigs themselves. A terrific regular gig was at the Desert

Rose restaurant in Los Feliz with drummer Mark Z. Stevens – many friends would drop by to sit in. The audience one evening apparently included two Oscar winners and an Olympic gold medallist – my former cricket teammate Audley Harrison. One evening playing at the fashionable W hotel jam session, my sax solo was enthusiastically applauded by Selena Gomez and various Kardashians and Jenners seated at a front table. Of course, I had no idea who they were, it was pointed out to me by another younger musician!

An annual event in which I participated was the Sweet and Hot jazz festival. It ran over the Labor Day weekend and was the brainchild of the late Wally Holmes. An archetypal jazz trumpeter – beret wearing and goatee sporting – and a contemporary and friend of Chet Baker since they were teenagers, he was also the unlikely composer of the disco classic 'Rock the Boat' performed by the band he managed, the Hues Corporation. I would imagine that his royalties from that song funded the festival for many years – I was very sorry to see it go, but cherish the memory of performing with many jazz greats including the then 99-year-old Herb Jeffries, at the time the last surviving member of the classic 1940s Ellington band.

Another gig involved playing outdoors in the afternoon on a well-known movie producer's terrace for his birthday, way out in the Valley. It was a very hot summer's day, and we were all wearing T-shirts and shorts, ready to change into tuxedos just before our set. I rode with the guitarist, with a stop to collect his tux from the cleaner's. Unfortunately, and unnoticed, his trousers slipped off the hanger on his way back to the car and off we drove. When it came time to change for the gig, he discovered to his horror that he only had the top half of his apparel. The producer's wife found a pair of her husband's dress trousers and our guitarist put them on. The only problem was that the producer was a foot taller than our man! Not only did the trousers drag over his shoes and across the floor, but they also resisted all attempts to turn them up – he looked as if he was a day tripper about to plunge into the sea with a knotted handkerchief on his head. Our only solution was to place him on a chair at the back of the band for the duration, which sadly didn't prevent us from cracking up every time we looked round at him.

I was reminded of the time I flew to LA arriving in the early afternoon and that same evening attended an awards event I'd been eagerly anticipating. As I put on my tuxedo I realized to my "horror" that I'd forgotten my black tie in London. "Ah well, it is California – no one will notice," I thought. As I arrived at the Beverly Hilton, with TV cameras rolling and the lobby thronging with the Hollywood aristocracy, Vic Mizzy, composer (and finger snapper) of the classic *Addams Family* theme, yelled out across the foyer, "Hello John – no tie?"

I also established my big band as a regular Los Angeles entity. Highlights were performing to huge appreciative crowds at the Hollywood and Highland summer festival, the Jazz Bakery and the Los Angeles County Museum of Arts, and regular appearances at the Los Angeles Jazz Institute Big Band festivals alongside all my peers. A very enjoyable concert was with James (son of Mel) Tormé and David (son of Marty) Paich of Toto performing Mel's *California Suite* live. I conducted the New West Symphony in Delius' 'On Hearing the First Cuckoo in Spring', then with James and the orchestra we performed some of his father's biggest hits, and finally I played a saxophone solo on 'It Don't Mean a Thing If It Ain't Got That Swing'. Bizarrely I've worked with James's father Mel and James's grandmother Dame Thora Hird (who was a huge fan of my uncle Sid Phillips, whose son Simon played in Toto with David and recorded with James, with whom I now appear regularly). Complicated or what?

I was having lunch in Studio City with Freddie Ravel, the superb keyboard player and composer who has played with Earth, Wind & Fire, and Santana, as well as helming his own band. I asked him if he knew any of the members of Toto. He replied he'd never met any of them and as he said this, David Paich and Steve Lukather of Toto walked into the restaurant!

My then-agent also looked after the wonderful composer Michel Colombier. I was a huge fan of his hard-to-get eponymous 1979 album that featured Herbie, Jaco Pastorius and Michael Brecker among other luminaries. I asked Michel if it was obtainable on CD, and he snorted derisively. "You'll be lucky! I will make you a DAT copy of the album." Which he did and I treasure it to this day. Sadly, we lost him far too early.

An advantage of living in Los Angeles was spending a lot of time with my mother's brother, Woolf Phillips. He and my aunt had retired to a Leisure Village (his son Nicky called it a Seizure Village!) and I either visited him there or met him halfway at our favourite deli. Often his other nephew, Simon Phillips, would join us. I remember Woolf once pointing out an incongruous little old lady hobbling down the street in the retirement complex. "She owns the Beverly Centre!" Before he was struck down with congestive heart failure and consequent senile dementia (awful to observe at close quarters) we were driving in his car and a Dorsey Brothers track came on the radio. He sang the entire arrangement, including the solos, from a recording he hadn't heard for sixty-five years! Recently the talented Nick Dellow has digitized a pile of radio transcription discs from my collection by Woolf's Concert Orchestra that haven't been heard since the 1940s – it seems incredible that Woolf and the wonderful Robert Farnon and Angela Morley were all staff arrangers at the same time for the Geraldo Concert Orchestra. When Woolf passed away the day after Benny Carter, my weekly LA routine – Benny on Thursdays, Woolf on Fridays – was sorely missed. Hopefully his son Nicky has Woolf's amazing scrapbook with signed photos of all the incredible performers he conducted for during the heyday of the London Palladium, and the reel-to-reel tape of Peter Sellers' complete variety act.

Possibly my strangest jazz assignment in Los Angeles was conducting the funeral for my friend, the great saxophonist Red Holloway. Red always encouraged me to "sit in" with his band whenever and wherever they performed and we socialized quite often when he was in Los Angeles and in Florida before and on the jazz cruises. The family requested that I take the humanist service (he had asked for me, apparently) although I have no qualifications – if indeed any are needed. A packed chapel endured my "sermon" and a raft of memories and music from his colleagues. Disconcertingly, it was an open-casket ceremony so every time I looked to the right I was staring at his face!

A regular patron of my jazz nights was a Scottish actress I had befriended named Louise Linton. She was always keen to hear live music. We lost touch until she emerged as the wife of Steven Mnuchin, the Secretary of the US Treasury in the Trump administration. I have to say, I never saw that coming!

One tradition that continued until my last visit to Los Angeles was a musicians' lunch at the now closed Jerry's Deli in Studio City. Organized by the President of the local Musicians' Union, Stephanie O'Keefe, and myself, it proved to be a wonderful chance to catch up with old friends. A rotating guest list has included the legendary vibes player Terry Gibbs, many of LA's leading studio and jazz musicians and vocalists (and composers) including the great multi-reed player Gene Cipriano, and other visitors from London such as composer John Scott. Three friends with strong Harry Nilsson connections were the late Perry Botkin, who discovered Harry (and unwittingly inspired the rise of hip hop with the sampling of his Incredible Bongo Band album by New York based DJs and rappers in the early 1990s), the unique Van Dyke Parks who wrote for and produced Nilsson as well as co-writing the legendary *Smile* album with Brian Wilson, and Stanley Dorfman, who put Harry on British television in two magnificent specials as well as starting *Top of the Pops* and the *In Concert* series, and directing many classic music movies and videos for the likes of George Benson, Linda Ronstadt, David Bowie and Ringo Starr (he was the first person to put Joni Mitchell, James Taylor, Neil Young and Jimi Hendrix amongst others on British television in the late 1960s).

A bizarre experience with Stanley Dorfman comes to mind. I had lunch with him in West Hollywood, drove back to my house (about 40 minutes away), went to my local supermarket and there was Stanley! At the moment I spotted him, the tannoy blasted out Blondie's 'Heart of Glass', the video of which was directed by Stanley!

My only similar experience was taking my Wurlitzer keyboard to a repair man in Islington, North London at 11am where I bumped into a guy I didn't know leaving the premises with a similar keyboard and the same missing note, now repaired. I then performed some errands around London and as the time was getting on, I decided to grab a meal at the Pizza Express on Finchley Road. The time was now 7.30pm and Finchley Road is around an hour from Islington across London. The only other customer in the restaurant was the man I'd seen that morning with the repaired piano!

Figure 58: Van Dyke Parks and the late Perry Botkin Jr. Author's collection.

A favourite long-term gig was with trombonist Conrad Janis's band. Conrad played Mindy's dad in *Mork and Mindy* and the regular audience was a wonderful cross section of "old Hollywood." Among those who performed or just came to listen were Tony Bennett, Bea Arthur, Linda Hopkins, Billy Crystal, Richard Benjamin, George Segal (a founder member of the band and still a sitter-in when he had the opportunity) and Mel Brooks. Our guitarist was Sheldon Keller, one of the writers of *The Sid Caesar Show* and the group included many jazz luminaries – drummer Paul Humphrey and saxophonist Plas Johnson (both of whom can be heard on Marvin Gaye's 'Let's Get It On') and, on clarinet and alto saxophone, the *Tonight Show*'s John Bambridge.

A regular at our gigs was the great songwriter Ray Evans (who wrote, with Jay Livingstone, the Oscar winning songs 'Buttons and Bows', 'Mona Lisa' and 'Que Sera Sera' as well as the much-loved TV themes for *Bonanza* and *Mr. Ed*). One of the great stories he told concerns a terrific song he and Livingstone wrote entitled 'Never Let Me Go'. It's a very sophisticated piece, often recorded by great jazz players. At the original Nat King Cole recording session, the great arranger Nelson Riddle walked over to Ray and Jay and said,

"Come on guys, you can tell me. Who wrote this song?"

"We did."

"Nah, you write simple crap like 'Silver Bells' – I won't tell anyone, I promise. Who really wrote it?"

Ray told me, "I'm pretty sure Riddle wasn't kidding!"

The band played a benefit/awards ceremony for the Actors' Studio. Conrad and our great trumpeter Jack Sheldon had their feet in both camps and the evening possibly was most memorable for a comment by our pianist Brian O'Rourke. Surveying the room, he turned to me and said, "Nice to see so many familiar facelifts!"

We also had a lovely shout out from James Coburn. Accepting an award from Rod Steiger, he made a point of mentioning the quality of the band, and also told how he based his whole acting technique on hearing the Count Basie Band at Birdland – long periods of calmness punctuated by a sudden explosion and then back to peacefulness again. He then came over to us and chatted to everyone stating how much he admired what we did. I later discovered from his daughter Lisa that he was a huge jazz fan and for her birthdays would take her to Tower Records on Sunset Boulevard and as a birthday treat, buy her a stack of the newest jazz albums.

20 Amy

Apart from during a short stint as a substitute teacher in the early 1970s, and the insincere fawnings of various shop assistants and waiters over the years, only three people have called me "Sir" to my face during my professional career. One was the legendary performer Eartha Kitt, who was brought to London to replicate one of her 1950s hits for an advertising campaign in the mid-1990s. She was charm personified and insisted on calling me sir throughout the recording session, as I produced her vocals and told her how to sing her own song! A second was Cyndi Lauper, who was convinced we knew each other from somewhere (we didn't)! The other was Amy Winehouse.

I first met Amy when she was sixteen years old. I had started my 10 Room Monday night jamming sessions with Patrick Alan. Patrick was at the time the lead singer of The Drifters, having been brought in by the legendary Johnny Moore, and he had previously started jamming nights in Los Angeles and New York where artists like Tupac Shakur had cut their performing teeth in front of appreciative and knowledgeable audiences. As I mentioned earlier, I had been a veteran of jam sessions in the jazz, rock, blues and folk scenes since the late 1960s and rued the fact that the opportunities for young performers to appear on stage with well-established artists no longer existed. In my youth I found it relatively easy to get on stage with the likes of Jimi Hendrix, Fleetwood Mac, Kevin Ayers and just jam along. If you knew what you were doing you would be invited back or told of other, similar sessions. It was not uncommon to find yourself trading licks with the likes of Hendrix, Elton John and Van Morrison, and many future relationships were born out of these spontaneous sessions.

Thus in 1999, as I discussed in the previous chapter, we began our Monday nights at the 10 Room, which ran for seven glorious years and hosted many legendary events. One of our earliest "patrons" was this extraordinary young North London girl, who insisted on calling me "sir." She was never shy of getting up on stage after the likes of Chaka Khan and Lionel Richie, although most weeks she would be happy to hang out with her friends and listen to the music. And many of these friends and musicians would be alongside her for her entire career, as members of her band and backing singers. She was extraordinarily loyal to those she grew up with. They in turn saw her through her darkest days with unvarying love and support.

It had all been so different when we first met. When she got up to sing with us, we must have presented a formidable challenge to a performer of that age. There was a mixture of widely experienced session players and singers onstage, mixed in with a precocious selection of "new kids on the block." But Amy often eschewed the cover versions of soul classics backed by four or five back-up singers, favoured by other guests. It would be her and me up front, interacting on a jazz standard from the catalogue of Dinah Washington, Etta James or Billie Holiday. Even when her first album came out she would never perform any of her own songs, although the 10 Room band provided some of the accompaniment on the albums *Frank* and *Back to Black*. And she would always deliver a performance to remember. (Two of my all-time favourite performers and people, Amy and Joss Stone, performed on the same night on one very memorable evening.) Occasionally we'd go and sit down and talk about music and writing. I'd recommend records and artists for her to listen to. (I put Jo Stafford, Lee Wiley, Helen Merrill, Julie London and Jeri Southern on her radar and suggested some obscure Dinah Washington.) We'd even discussed a jazz project for one day in the future. Sometimes I would suggest she went home, when she was the worse for wear.

Then, suddenly, she was a megastar, and almost as suddenly she was gone. I followed her meteoric rise to success and worldwide acclamation, delighted to have been a small cog in the wheel of her ascendancy, while hearing harrowing tales from her family, friends and bandmates about the company she was keeping.

On that fateful Saturday I was at Lord's cricket ground in conversation with the brilliant actor Benedict Cumberbatch, who has become a good friend over the years, Steven Moffat the frequent executive producer, writer and showrunner of *Dracula*, *Sherlock* and *Doctor Who*, his producer wife Sue and my old boss Michael Parkinson, when I received a text from Patrick: "Amy's gone!" The news hadn't yet broken in the media so after we were able to confirm the sad tidings, we talked about the vicissitudes of fame and how it had affected Amy. I recalled the last time we played together at the Berkeley Square Ball in front of Kate and Pippa Middleton. The audience had gasped in amazement when an emaciated Amy staggered on stage and was willed through a Motown classic with the help of her dear friend Zalon Thompson and the loyal guys in the band who would have done anything for her. I didn't recognize her backstage before the gig, at first, I'm ashamed to say, but after the truncated set we hugged and she said, "I didn't want any of this. I just wanted to make music with my friends."

"But we're your friends and you're making music with us!" I replied. It felt like a homecoming for her, and we were so glad when she went off into rehab and got healthy again and seemed ready to make a new start, but sadly it was a false dawn.

I'm always astonished when a record, movie, TV programme or live concert I've been involved with is remembered today, in some cases many years after the event. I've been lucky in this respect, as a huge proportion of the artists and movies I've worked with/on are still in the public eye. One is always conscious of, and at the mercy of, the passage of time in this business. I've met performers who have proudly told me about their number one record in 1991; I nod knowingly having never heard of it or them, then or now. I became very conscious of this phenomenon over the years. Attending two concerts in Brighton on successive Tuesdays by Bill Wyman's Rhythm Kings and the fabulous John Wilson Orchestra playing music from the 1940s I noticed that the demographic was far younger for the John Wilson concert than for Bill. When I showed my showreel to a group of 14- and 15-year-olds for a masterclass in Shanghai, I realized that all my clips from the 1980s and 90s would be totally meaningless to them.

"Any questions," I asked tremulously as the film finished.

"What was Jimi Hendrix like?" and "Did you know The Beatles?" were the first two things I was asked to my amazement. Nowhere was this brought home to me more than when I played a guest spot at a charity polo lunch in 2019. When I returned to my seat next to the 19-year-old daughter of one of the sponsors, she said to me, "I see from the brochure that you played with Amy Winehouse."

"Yes, I was lucky enough to mentor and play with her frequently," I replied. What she said next, floored me: "I've never actually heard her but my parents listened to her quite a lot." Of course she would have been four years old when Amy's first album broke through and barely eleven when Amy passed away.

So, what made Amy so special? How did we know she was something else? It may sound trite, but we just did! I think everyone knew it from the earliest days, even when she was clearly off her game. She had something then, something that the whole world recognized and responded to – and it's very rare that you can stand alongside and be a part of that. I have been lucky, it has happened to me over and over again during my career – and Amy stands up there, alongside Bob Marley, Hendrix, Muddy Waters and Van Morrison, among others. I have a couple of photos of us making music together, captured by Harrison Funk. When people see them, they inevitably say, "It must have been such a thrill and an honour for you to play music with her." It's difficult for me to respond without sounding egotistical but at the time it was a thrill for her to sing with us! It's not just my perception, it's something she actually said to me one evening. Watching clips of her in full flow is a bittersweet experience these days. I contributed to the Oscar-winning documentary on her life stressing her uniqueness and brilliance, not dwelling on her troubles and tribulations. When she was besieged by paparazzi and journalists outside her flat day and night, she would make them trays of hot drinks, sandwiches and biscuits. This is the Amy I want to remember – together with her deep friendship, her love of making music and her extraordinary once-in-a-lifetime talent.

Figure 59: With Amy Winehouse at the 10 Room. Photo by Harrison Funk.

21 More Legends (4)

(Michael Jackson, Quincy Jones, Prince, Mark Ronson, Sacha Baron Cohen, Mike Stoller)

I've already mentioned Don Black a number of times in this memoir. He was a great mentor to me, pushing me forward to write for many people, at a time when I had no idea that I wouldn't make a total idiot of myself. Don had written the song 'Ben' with another wonderful man, composer Walter Scharf, for Michael Jackson. Now they had written a musical based on *Peter Pan* (of course) commissioned by MJ, and I arranged and supervised the demo sessions. The tour of Michael Jackson's album *Bad* was happening around this time and I was sent tickets for the sold-out Wembley stadium concerts.

During his season at Wembley stadium, he commandeered CTS Studio 3 to record and rehearse some tracks. I was in the large Studio 1 recording a commercial with a 60-piece orchestra (those were the days). My music contractor who booked the orchestra popped out for a bathroom break and, when he returned, excitedly told us he'd found himself standing next to Michael Jackson.

"What did you say?"

"Hello!"

"What did he say?"

"Oh, hello!"

Fifteen minutes later the orchestra took their mandatory 10-minute break while I repaired to the control room to hear a couple of preferred takes. Minutes later a deputation of angry musicians materialized in the control room. It seemed that Michael Jackson had returned to Studio 3 and informed his entourage that someone had spoken to him in the rest room! Immediately, three huge security guards were dispatched to block entry to the bathroom presumably for the duration of his time in the studio. This of course did not sit well with the cream of London's orchestral musicians who justifiably argued with the bouncers that MJ couldn't possibly require exclusive access to the only restrooms on the premises for the entire day. I had to step in to defuse a very volatile situation.

On the day of the show, I received a phone call from CBS records: "Can we have your tickets back, please?" The assistant explained apologetically that the entire roster from CBS New York had decided at the last minute to fly over for the show and they needed the complimentary box where all the guests were located.

Reluctantly, I agreed and a messenger showed up with the biggest bouquet of flowers I'd ever seen, plus two tickets for a rearranged concert at the Milton Keynes Bowl. The VIP area there was a roped-off area at the top of the hill (the bowl is literally a bowl with no seating) and an entertaining diversion from the vain attempts to make out the speck on the distant stage (which apparently was Michael Jackson) proved to be watching a uniformed policeman nearby on duty dancing to the music, his helmet bobbing up and down. I later told director Peter Chelsom the scenario and he incorporated it into the finale of *Hear My Song*. The concert lasted two hours; it then took three hours to get out of the car park down the one track that was allowing traffic through.

Thirteen years later I won my Emmy award. At the afterparty, I ran into my friend Louise, who was there with Conan O'Brien. The next day she went up to Neverland, where she drove, babysat for, and hung out with Michael. He asked what she'd done on the previous evening and she said, "I went to the Emmys with Conan, but he didn't win anything."

"Oh, you must have had a depressing evening?"

"Not really because my friend John Altman won for best music."

"I know John, he did some arrangements for me!" said MJ.

"I know John too," said his other visitor, animator Don Bluth.

Louise excitedly rang me. That was my last direct contact with the controversial King of Pop until I was at a cricket dinner at Mansion House, the official residence of the Lord Mayor of London. I was sitting with the much-missed Ruth Strauss, wife of the then England captain Sir Andrew Strauss, as the auction took place. Up for grabs were two tickets to Michael Jackson's run at the O2 and the bidding was pretty intense. My phone suddenly showed an email – it was from Stevie Wonder's office, saying that Michael had passed away. This was hours before it was even announced that he was unwell. I ran up to the auctioneer and told him to stop the bidding, and the rest of the evening was spent trying to convince the diners that this wasn't a hoax. Ruth and I always talked about that evening in the years to come.

A major figure in the global impact of Michael Jackson was my hero, Quincy Jones. I first met him at a party given by Benny Carter. Benny kept asking me if I knew Quincy, and I assumed he was having senior moments. Then he had a formal dinner party, and I was seated next to Q (we talked the night away, mostly about his jazz career with Lionel Hampton in the early 1950s and his contemporaries like Clifford Brown and Lucky Thompson). He was also very upfront and amusing (but never sexist) about some of the female vocalists he worked with. His contribution to popular music since then has been immeasurable – as an arranger, composer, entrepreneur and facilitator of brilliant collaborations. His admiration for Benny Carter was and still is patently obvious. I had been a fan forever and subsequently I ran into him at many events and concerts over the ensuing years. The Michael Caine gala at the Albert Hall was the first time we'd worked together (as I mentioned in an earlier chapter, we even sang on an arrangement of Q's song written with Don Black, 'Get a Bloomin' Move On' from *The Italian Job*) and he wrote a wonderful dedication to me which I have framed in my office – "to my beloved and talented Brother John. U R da s**t!" His impact on modern music is immeasurable, I appreciate his support and friendship and admire his championing of the brilliant Jacob Collier. In addition, I treasure his dedication to me on the programme for the Michael Caine tribute and his testimonial for this book.

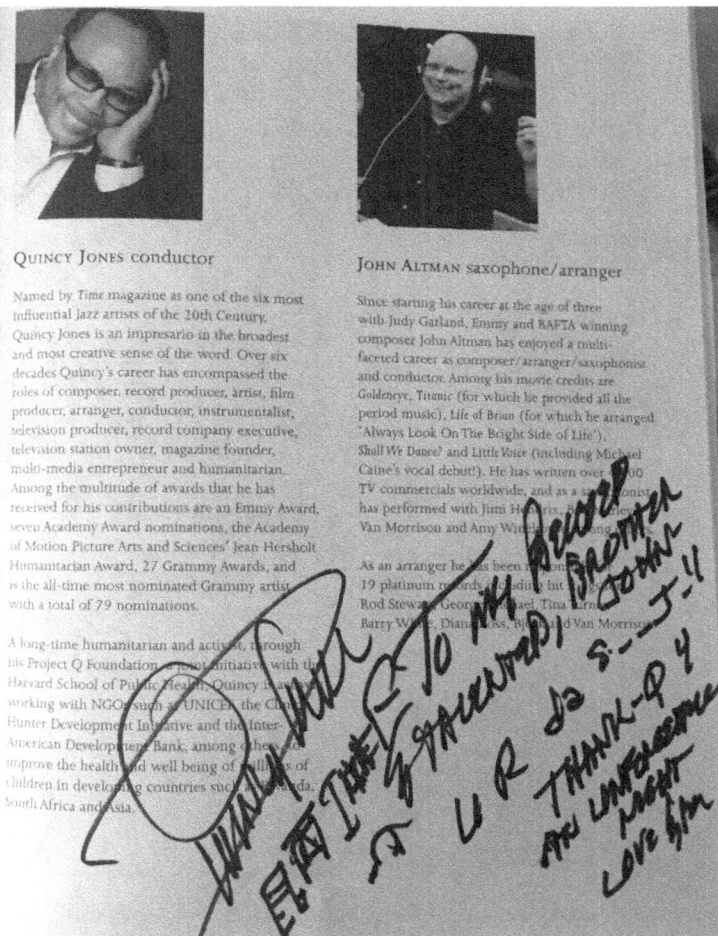

Figure 60: Quincy Jones's dedication to me. Author's collection.

Two modern, interconnected legends are Stevie Wonder and Prince. Our paths have crossed in so many unforeseen ways, in so many different places in the US and UK. I've been in Stevie's company frequently over the years as well as attending many of his seminal concerts and have become firm friends with many former and current members of his band – especially Victoria Theodore, his long-time keyboard player, saxophonists Ryan Kilgore and Mike Phillips, and backing vocalist Keith (son of Little Willie) John – in fact whenever he tours the UK, we set up a session where his musicians happily jam with the best of British. I particularly recall sitting with him at an after-party in Los Angeles following an all-star tribute show for Dionne Warwick where his enthusiasm shone through for every artist who performed at the party. At one point he requested a reasonably obscure hit song and the artist responded, "only if you'll accompany me!" Needless to say, he couldn't get on stage quickly enough and played the song perfectly. I've also watched him sit in effortlessly with jazz giants like the late Chick Corea and Toots Thielemans and warm up for a tribute to Barbra Streisand by jamming 'Giant Steps' with the band. He once came to a restaurant gig in Beverly Hills I played with the terrific Barbara Morrison and kept us busy answering his requests. Not only is he a genius, but he also genuinely loves music and musicians and supports and encourages them as much as he can.

Figure 61: With Stevie Wonder, Ryan Kilgore and Victoria Theodore. Author's collection.

The same applied to Prince, a musician and composer who straddled all genres. If he had just composed brilliant songs, or led first-rate bands, played guitar or piano, or been a sensational vocalist he would still have been counted among the all-time greats. I have many happy memories of attending his Oscar night parties at the Avalon in LA where he played till 5am, spending a lot of time with his musicians over the years and playing in Shanghai with his musical director Morris Hayes. I also got to jam with Prince at the Green Door in Los Angeles (he sat in on jazz piano) and was privileged to appear in two tribute concerts in London and Birmingham with his band the New Power Generation, soloing on 'Nothing Compares 2 U' – with Beverley Knight and then Mica Paris joining Mackenzie and the NPG. I first played with the NPG at the Pigalle and then at the afterparty hosted by Prince at Indigo2 (the same night as Amy Winehouse sang), along with many of my colleagues from the Pigalle jam sessions whom Prince had selected to perform with him during his 21-night residency. Our brilliant bass player, whom he chose to play at the afterparties, is named Rick James. He was warned by someone in Prince's entourage, "Don't tell him your name – he supported Rick James at the start of his career and Rick was mean to him – he can't stand to hear any mention of Rick James!" Prince showed up for the first four weeks of our Monday night successor to the 10 Room and sat in the balcony cherry-picking the talent. He was incredibly shy offstage – at one of the Oscar parties, I was in the VIP area with some friends while Esperanza Spalding and her band played to a very small inner circle and one of my pals said, "Why don't you go up and say hello to him?"

"What would be the point? He probably won't acknowledge me; I'll have to explain who I am and how I know him, and it would all probably be profoundly embarrassing."

This is how my appearance at the afterparties came about. One evening towards the end of his run I'd driven up to the West End of London to attend a reception given by a record label for an emerging artist. I didn't know anyone connected with the new album, but the "networking" seemed like a good idea. I drove to Golden Square at 8pm and there in front of the venue was a parking space. As I reversed into this bay, marvelling at my good fortune, my cellphone rang. Glancing at the unrecognized number I continued parking, reasoning that whoever it was would leave a message. However, for some reason it kept ringing and ringing. Eventually I gave in and answered – it was Prince's trombonist Greg Boyer, who said, "Do you fancy playing with us tonight at the afterparty?"

I'd already attended the main concert at the O2 and afterparty at the Indigo2 a week earlier and the thought had crossed my mind – I'd love to be up there playing.

I replied, "I'd love to, but I don't have my saxophone with me – let me see if I can catch my son at home." He was due to rehearse with his band in town that evening, and a quick call ascertained that he hadn't left the house yet.

Forty minutes later he arrived with my horn, an exchange was made, and I shot off to the O2 to catch Prince's memorable concert. A couple of hours later I was onstage with the NPG playing 'So What' by Miles Davis. While I was soloing, my mobile phone kept vibrating with messages from friends among members of the audience, "It's you!" and "What are you doing up there?" It was so "last minute" that I hadn't told anyone – in addition I never discovered what had happened to the emerging artist whose party I'd missed.

Prince's long-time musical director Morris Hayes and his last great arranger Phil Lassiter have also become good friends of mine, as are many of his band who toured with him – needless to say, we've all been enriched by the experience. At the end of the day his legacy is that of one of the great modern geniuses of music.

One early evening I got a panicked phone call from esteemed producer Mark Ronson. He had to record a jazz track overnight for the end titles of a movie he was working on, and a mutual friend had recommended me as the arranger. I'd been a fan of his work with Amy and others for a long time. I have unbounded admiration for Mark as a producer and artist, and our collaboration reinforced that impression. Not only does he understand the importance of arrangements and real musical instruments, but he is also not afraid to listen to other people's ideas and accept them if they are better than his own – which is a rare quality in this ego-driven business. Halfway through our collaboration, an email arrived from his co-writer in New York, with ideas for the arrangement. We trooped into his office to listen, while I saw my work about to be consigned to the trash after several hours of toil. A minute into playback Mark stopped the recording and said, "What we're doing here is much better than this." And back to work we went! By midnight we had written and recorded the whole arrangement – a brass section came to the studio at 10pm and polished off the chart in under two hours – quite an evening's work. People are always amazed that I never demoed any of my arrangements – and Mark showed the same trust in my work.

I first met Sacha Baron Cohen twenty-odd years ago at our 10 Room club night in London. His brother Erran, who writes all the music for his movies, was a regular on trumpet and Sacha proved to be a big fan of live gigs. I would then see him at various private concerts around London, such as a Herbie Hancock showcase, always 100 per cent into the music. Sacha, Isla Fisher and I sat together at the Emmys' dinner party in 2003 (neither he nor I won anything) and we used to see each other regularly both in London and Los Angeles. I was there the night he accepted his Britannia award, accompanied by a wheelchair-bound actress, supposedly the last surviving star of an early Chaplin film, that I predicted was a stunt. Sure enough, he accidentally nudged the chair and its occupant into the audience, eliciting gasps all round. When I greeted his father, he told me he had no idea what was coming – I make no claims for my realization other than that I knew exactly who had appeared in that movie thanks to my stint as a film researcher. It was easy to see how the likes of Giuliani, Trump and other prominent figures had been fooled by Sacha in his various Borat and Ali G incarnations. I once attended a concert in LA given by Erran's band and ran into Sacha (with director Jay Roach) backstage. My companion was overawed at meeting him and lost for words, gushing, "My friend thinks you're really funny."

I followed up with the logical next sentence, "I of course don't get the joke."

I'm honoured to call Mike Stoller a good friend. The man responsible with Jerry Leiber for writing some of the greatest songs of the last seventy years has regularly attended my gigs in Los Angeles, and we maintain contact via email and telephone. His catalogue is astonishing and his songs seminal – too many to list here but a Google search will reveal all. What isn't so widely acknowledged is his importance as an arranger and producer. On a gig of mine he pointed to my curved soprano sax and said, "we used a curved soprano on 'Spanish Harlem' as it was exactly the sound I was looking for." Amazing attention to detail that probably would pass most people by, but they heard it even if they didn't know or care how it was achieved. As an arranger/producer myself I'm very aware that it's those subtle touches that you apply that make the record stand out. Mike is, at the time of writing, in his late eighties but maintains his youthful enthusiasm for all things musical. He and his talented wife Corky Hale – a brilliant harpist and at one time Billie Holiday's pianist – were frequent attendees at my Los Angeles jazz gigs. My favourite Mike Stoller story is that he was returning from a European vacation and was rescued from the ship, the *Andrea Doria* which sank off Massachusetts in 1956. He was greeted at the dockside by his writing partner Jerry Leiber, who told him that their four-year-old song 'Hound Dog', performed by Elvis Presley, was number one all over the world.

"Elvis who?" replied Mike, still woozy from his ordeal. He'd never heard of him.

22 What Was That All About?

Over the years I've been thankfully blessed with good health apart from some strange blips. In the early part of 1999 I was doing what I'd been doing for many years, writing and playing music all over the world. I was working on the HBO movie *RKO 281* (for which I subsequently won the Emmy award for "Most Outstanding Music Score"). November '98 to spring '99 saw me in Los Angeles, London, Australia, London, the West Indies and Los Angeles again! Somewhere in the middle of all this I developed an eye infection and noticed my eyelashes had fallen out.

I went to the doctor, and she said, "It's the other way round. Your eyelashes fell out and you then got an infection. You have alopecia."

I replied, "If I've got alopecia, surely my hair would be falling out?"

She said, "It is," and pointed out a patch at the back of my head. "Keep an eye on it and we'll go from there."

As I was approaching fifty, I wasn't overly concerned. I'd had friends with alopecia, either after a shock or from stress and they'd seen their hair grow back. However, over the next couple of weeks my hair rapidly disappeared and I was left with patches all over.

I took to wearing a cap all the time, until a friend said, "Don't let it take charge of you, you take charge of it!" I went to the local hairdresser, had it cropped short, came home, looked in the mirror, got out a razor and took the lot off!

That evening I had an art opening to attend: the paintings of Cynthia Lennon, hosted by my old friend Pauline Sutcliffe, whose brother Stuart had been the fifth Beatle. I arrived at the gallery to see Cynthia and Julian Lennon being photographed for the *Evening Standard*. As I self-consciously removed my cap, the photographer motioned to me to get in the picture. As someone who'd been shoved out of the way on red carpets because a soap star was behind me (even when carrying my British Film award in my hand) this was a new experience and I thought, "Maybe it's not going to be so bad after all."

The introduction to my new look for most of my friends came via that photo in the *Standard*. My hair never did grow back. Within a few months I didn't need to shave my head (or my face) and I can proudly say I haven't shaved this millennium! Within the next year I had won my Emmy and appeared on TV as a "talking (bald) head" in several programmes. Somehow the new look gave me far more personal confidence than my old pre-alopecia look. My hair was becoming thin and grey and seeing "before" photos now, I realize that I have more confidence in myself today. I look younger and my "hairstyle" was even admired by our former Prime Minister Sir John Major. (A note about our former Prime Minister. I have played in his wife's charity cricket match for over twenty years and we are good friends. One day I was walking down the corridor in the hospitality area at Lord's cricket ground when someone crept up behind me, covered my eyes with his hands and said, "Guess who?" I can't imagine Margaret Thatcher or Boris Johnson doing that, although I used to sit with Denis Thatcher at charity lunches – he was very good company!) I also appeared on Sir Ken Clarke's jazz radio show, courtesy of Alyn Shipton. I used to see Tory Ken and Labour minister John Prescott together at jazz venues around London, burying their party differences by wallowing in some great music.

To even out the political bias, my car once broke down near Tony Blair's house, after a Living Room concert in the same square. It was soon surrounded by plain clothes and uniformed police, obviously convinced that a terrorist act was about to ensue. They were very helpful once they ascertained that I couldn't actually move the car. One even recognized my tenor sax case and didn't call it a trumpet or a banjo! I slept on a friend's sofa and the car was towed away the next morning.

From time to time I would meet some joker (usually drunk!) at a function who would come out with original lines such as "I like your barber's sense of humour." I would always explain about alopecia – I'm still amazed at how many people haven't heard of it (or profess ignorance as a cover for their insensitivity). I'm proud to be an ambassador for Alopecia UK and to do my little bit to raise awareness of this blip on the immune system.

It has been twenty-two years since my diagnosis (as of 2021). I can safely say I've never missed the hair although I wouldn't mind my eyebrows and eyelashes back. But at least there's no more smoking in clubs to irritate my eyes, although candlelight doesn't work too well for me.

In 2009, I developed some painful, irritating outbreaks all over my skin. It was if I'd been bitten by hundreds of mosquitos. I was in Los Angeles and saw an "expert" in Beverly Hills who apparently was more used to botox, collagen and surgical enhancements. He professed to have no idea what was wrong but was certain it wasn't mosquito bites. When I returned to the UK I saw a skin specialist who immediately diagnosed *erythema multiforme*. "It's very rare, you know – you'll probably never meet anyone else with this condition!" Within weeks I'd met three other sufferers. I went on a course of steroids and antiviral tablets. For the next three months I couldn't sleep under covers, wear trousers, socks or shoes or leave the house. And then one day it felt different – I got dressed and went for a walk – what was that all about?

It recurred during a Sussex University 50-year reunion in 2011, at which my all-star band performed. I had put together a terrific ensemble, including my old university pal, keyboard player and producer Pete Wingfield, Manfred Mann's charismatic vocalist and harmonica player Paul Jones (a university alumnus in her seventies nearly swooned as we passed her on the stairs, gasping, "It's you!" – obviously transported momentarily back to her youth), guitarist Ray Russell, bassist (and another Sussex graduate) Mo Foster and drummer Gary Husband. The list of their credits is impressively endless, and I got my friend and namesake John Altman (star of *EastEnders*) to come on in my place when my name was announced. It should have been a highlight of the year – however, not only did I struggle to get through the concert, I bitterly regret shrugging off several old friends who loomed out of the crowd to say hello, in my haste to get back to my apartment and lie down. Many of them I hadn't seen for fifty years and sadly have never seen again. Once again the antivirals eventually worked and thankfully I haven't had a major outbreak since. What was that all about?

Figure 62: Alopecia ambassador. Author's collection.

Figure 63: With Paul Jones during my all-star Sussex University gig – suffering with my erythema. Author's collection.

On 30th July 2016, I produced a vocal session for a commercial in London. On 1st August I flew to Cape Cod for a film festival and gig, after which I headed to Los Angeles. On 31st July I went to pick up some medication. As it was a hot day, I put on shorts and loafers and set off. On the way I started banging into lampposts and walls, decided it was the shoes and threw them away! In Cape Cod and LA I seemed to get more and more clumsy, unable to walk more than a few paces, falling over with some regularity, and then having to sit down while I played the saxophone on a fabulous gig arranged for me by David Gross, with Peter Gabriel's former drummer Jerry Marotta and Jonny Rosch, the vocalist from the Blues Brothers, among others. When I got back to London, I went straight to get some tests and was diagnosed, incorrectly, as having labyrinthitis. In the ensuing weeks I basically lost the ability to walk, balance, write in a legible and straight line, improvise music, co-ordinate left and right hands while playing the piano, climb up one small step without assistance, speak without slurring words, and generally show any enthusiasm for any activity. After seven MRIs, several CAT scans and blood tests, it was determined that I had an undiagnosed, probably viral, ataxia (everything came up negative!)

Over the next thirteen months I saw many specialists. During this time, I went on two cruises with difficulty. One was a jazz cruise, where I was barely able to play constructively and had to be helped up one step to the stage. I got a walking stick, used a wheelchair at airports, kept a disability badge and resigned myself to the new norm. I also developed type two diabetes. And I conquered it in a few months, by changing my diet and losing weight – certainly not via exercise! In the same way I defeated high cholesterol – it can be done! Those who saw me at the time will certainly remember the mess I presented. At the same time, I appeared in a video podcast hosted by the wonderful Scott Bradlee of Postmodern Jukebox. He streamed from his iPhone and blithely informed me that we had 17,000 live viewers. I managed (just about) to perform two tunes with him to the best of my ability. I just about got away with it, but I wince when I see and hear it now, knowing how restricted I was then.

To cut a very long story short, on 13th August 2017, while in Los Angeles I woke up one morning, disposed of some recycling at the front of my accommodation – and everything was back to normal. I consciously thought, "Hang on a minute, this is walking in a straight line!" It was as if someone had pressed a reset button overnight. So here we are at the time of writing, cane in the cupboard, disabled badge discarded, walking 5km a day completely normally, playing and writing as if those thirteen months had never happened and wondering once again – what was that all about?

23 Shanghai, Honeymoons and Chat Shows, Paris and Vladivostok

In the 2010s I became a regular visitor to Shanghai. This came about in a very odd way. I played saxophone on an album for a Polish singer based in London named Pola. Her songwriting partner was a keyboard player, Anne. Although Anne was from Bristol, her parents were Hong Kong Chinese, although she'd never been to China herself. When Anne's French husband's job sent him to Shanghai and the family relocated, she became bored in her new surroundings. So, she applied for, and got a job as Head of Music at the Western International School of Shanghai. Her star student was an American girl named Asha, whose father Michael Luevano ran the Formula 1 Chinese Grand Prix and the Shanghai Rolex Masters tennis tournament. Every year Michael sponsored an inter-school Battle of the Bands and this particular year he asked Anne if she could suggest some judges for the competition. Anne immediately thought of Pola and me. Arrangements were made and we flew off to China.

We judged the competition and instantly hit it off with Michael. We discovered that, apart from being a fine tennis player himself in his youth, he sang in a terrific R&B covers band, complete with brass section and great arrangements. Michael suggested we come back and be his guests for the tennis. In the meantime, he went to visit his family in Mexico and in the transit airport in Los Angeles spotted a familiar face. It was Andy Summers, the guitarist with The Police and one of my closest friends. Michael introduced himself as a friend of mine and then they discovered they were heading to the same place in Mexico. By the time they arrived Michael had suggested that Andy join us for the tennis, and this became the pattern for the next few years.

Figure 64: With Andy Summers. Author's collection.

Shanghai was always great fun over the years. I taught masterclasses at the Western International School (eventually they named a recital room after me!), brought in Andy, and Prince's musical director Morris Hayes, to play music with the kids, and even secured a 20-minute interview in Paris for one talented lad with his hero, Roger Daltrey of The Who (thanks Roger!). We had players' passes for the ATP Shanghai Masters Tennis and hung out in the players' lounge, where there were drums, keyboards, guitars and basses set up, primarily for the very musical Bryan brothers, the greatest doubles team in the history of tennis, and Kevin Anderson who enjoyed playing guitar. Andy and I were very welcome additions to the impromptu jams and Pola too when she was in town. One evening I watched the Bryan brothers in the doubles final – they'd never won the tournament among their 100-plus career Grand Slams. In ATP doubles there's a sudden death point if the scores are tied in the final set. The brothers lost the point, and I made my way round the backstage area thinking, "The last people I really want to see now are Mike and Bob." Of course, I bumped into them as they came off court and Mike said, "Hi John, fancy playing some music?" While we were jamming, I plucked up the courage to commiserate with the brothers: "Well you know it's just a game – some you win and some you lose. No big deal." Maybe a cliché but it never rang truer. And of course, they have since won the tournament and are now happily retired.

Figure 65: With Andy Summers jamming Police songs with the greatest tennis doubles team ever – the Bryan brothers. Author's collection.

One morning I left the hotel to meet my driver outside, missed my footing on the last step and fell into the side of the car. I was pretty shaken up, hit my head on the door and twisted my back, which is how I wound up on a massage table at the tournament next to Rafa Nadal. We stayed in the same hotel and became friendly with a lot of the players, in much the same way as I'd befriended the international cricketers. It was then always a pleasure to catch up with them during Wimbledon fortnight and experience the thrill of that iconic competition.

Talking of Wimbledon, one visit with my friend Carl entailed a panic as we got halfway there when he realized he'd left the tickets for the day on his kitchen table. Luckily he drives a Bentley, which happens to be the same model as the Royal Family's so we were waved into the Royal car park and strolled into the ground unchallenged.

The Bentley could also cause unforeseen problems. When Carl was on his honeymoon journey through Scotland, he arrived with his bride, Sunny, at their hotel. The car was taken away to be parked, they checked into their room and went down at one-thirty to the deserted hotel restaurant. A waiter wandered over and said,

"Can I help you?"

"Yes, we'd like some lunch."

"Oh, one moment sir, I'll fetch the *maître d'*."

"Yes, can I help you?"

"We'd like some lunch!"

"Er – one moment, sir, I'll fetch the manager."

The manager came over to the bewildered couple.

"Would you please follow me into my office?"

Completely nonplussed at these reactions, they went to his office where he sat them down and explained, "The hotel has been cleared for a lunch party given by the Queen for the royals staying at Balmoral. When you drove up, it was assumed because of your car, that you were in their party. Once they'd booked, all the existing reservations were cancelled. We wrote to you, but obviously because you've been driving round Scotland for a week you never got the letter. Our problem now is the security. If you are found here, you may be arrested or even shot as they comb the hotel thoroughly before you arrived. So, this is what we'll do. You go to your suite for the duration of your stay, and order anything you like from room service. Everything will be on the house. You cannot leave the room or even pull back the curtain to look at the arrivals. Any movement in the room and the security will act swiftly with hideous consequences! My apologies but have a nice stay!"

Carl later confessed to me they had a wonderful weekend – and they peeked!

Back in Shanghai I was quite amazed by the rapid exit of players once they'd lost. Virtually as soon as their match was over, they and their support staff were checking out of the hotel, en route to the airport and the next tournament.

This of course meant that the players' canteen, where we ate every day, went from being jam packed at the start of the week to empty, apart from probably Djokovic, Nadal, Federer, Murray and their entourages, by the weekend. Apparently the higher-ranked players were given a few extra days' grace if they should lose before the finals, but the life of a musician on the road seemed quite comfortable compared to most of those on the tennis circuit.

Immediately after one tournament final, Michael said to me, "Shall we go and visit Roger Federer?" I protested that as he'd just come off court victorious, he would want a shower and a rub down and certainly no visitors, but Michael said it would be fine. Roger came out of his dressing room and posed for a photo with me. I immediately realized he wasn't sweating at all! Quite remarkable after an ATP final.

Mid-tournament, one of the world's top players (no names!) challenged me to a game of pool. I protested I hadn't played the game for about thirty years and proceeded, much to the astonishment of the assembled tennis stars and myself, to pot virtually every shot. Accusations that I was a pool shark or hustler flew around the room. I redeemed my reputation slightly by being unable to pot the remaining 8 ball while my opponent caught up with me, but I did emerge victorious and thereafter everyone was wary of asking me to do anything competitive. The same player did invite me for a tennis knock-up, where I proved how useless I was, so that validated my protestations of hopelessness.

Figure 66: The John Altman recital room at the Western International School Shanghai. Author's collection.

Andy Summers is a world-class photographer and went off into the heart of China to explore. I'm afraid I was far truer to character, sitting in at various jazz and blues clubs and meeting some terrific musicians. Anne then moved to Hong Kong, and I had a wonderful trip there, teaching masterclasses and meeting more great instrumentalists and singers. Writing this in the heart of the pandemic, I hope those days come back soon!

I started to work frequently in Paris in the early 1990s. It began with heart-throb/singer/composer/one-time jazz guitar star Sacha Distel. His uncle Ray Ventura, who led France's top swing band before the war, and my mother had been good pals in earlier days. Sacha told me how he went to give Brigitte Bardot guitar lessons in the 1950s and emerged a week later a fully-fledged pop star. A wonderful musician who played with Lester Young, Miles Davis and the Modern Jazz Quartet in the 1950s, and wrote the magnificent standard 'The Good Life', Sacha was a joy to arrange, produce and conduct a single for. Sadly, the album we were going to make never happened. I do recall him calling me from Paris while I was in an advertising briefing. I had said, "Oh hi, Sacha," and explained I'd call him back after my meeting. I had to confess to the assembled agency, "Yes it *was* Sacha Distel!"

The last time I saw him we were guests, separately, on Ned Sherrin's radio show, *Loose Ends*. He was discussing his role in the West End show *Chicago*, and I was playing a number accompanying vocalist Joan Viskant, to promote our recently released album. As Sacha and I parted company after the show he called to me over his shoulder, "Don't go modal on me now!" (a style of jazz popularized by John Coltrane and by Miles Davis's *Kind of Blue*).

Spending a good deal of my time in Paris, I had an opportunity to utilize my long dormant O-level French and found to my amazement that not only could I understand what people were saying, I could also get them to understand me. I found this extremely useful in the Parisian recording studios – if you attempted to communicate, no matter how badly, in French, you had the musicians on your side. I also frequented many of the jazz venues around Paris and got to jam with many of Paris' finest jazz players. One evening I met the great Italian jazz pianist Enrico Pieranunzi. We later discovered that not only were we born on the same day of the same month of the same year, but the time difference between Europe and the UK meant we were born at the same time! The day we worked this out, we were wearing identically coloured outfits. Go figure! (Actually, I was overdue – had I been born when expected, my birthdate would have coincided with one of my favourite comedians, the late Garry Shandling. I told Garry this and his response was, "If I'd have known I'd have waited for you!")

I then accompanied music supervisor Ray Williams, who had put Elton John and Bernie Taupin together as a team, to arrange a classic Charles Trenet song 'Que reste-t-il de nos amours' for the wonderful Patricia Kaas, produced by Sade's producer Robin Millar, to be featured in an Anglo/French movie *Innocent Lies*. On the way to the studio one afternoon Ray said to me,

"We have to collect some music from the young composer of the score for this movie. Trust me, he's going to be the next big thing in film music." We stopped at the apartment of Alexandre Desplat. Ray was 100 per cent correct. I was delighted that Alexandre remembers this encounter and he told me he still enjoys the recording we did for the film.

My next visit was to meet with Luc Besson and Eric Serra, first on the movie *Atlantis* and then for *Léon (The Professional)*. Although we did all our recordings in London, the Paris meet-ups were very useful, and above all, fun. I recall after one dinner with Eric, Luc and Jean Reno we sat in Eric's Mercedes at about 2am, racing Luc's motorbike through the various Paris tunnels at very high speed. Not that we passengers were enjoying this experience. In fact, we were petrified – with good reason considering what had happened in Paris a few years later. There was also a very prickly meeting at Eric's studio when we had just started work on *Goldeneye* – and I realized that the producers' and editors' vision of the musical score was at variance with Eric's intentions.

Figure 67: The Godfathers of Groove featuring Bernard "Pretty" Purdie, Reuben Wilson and Grant Green Jr. Author's collection.

In 2009 I went to Paris for the Miles Davis exhibition with my good friends, Miles's son Erin, daughter Cheryl and nephew Vince. It was a wonderful exhibition, full of incredible memorabilia of Miles – one of his trumpets and several scores and parts for his classic collaborations with Gil Evans – and a fun-filled few days with my wonderful Parisian pals. A couple of months later, I went back to celebrate my birthday, and got stranded there when Eurostar was stopped because of heavy snow. There are worse places to be stranded, especially when Eurostar paid all my expenses for the extra time I had to stay. I called Vincent, the Miles Davis exhibition curator, to tell him I was still around but never heard back. Months later when I got to Los Angeles, I found a message on my US cell phone with a carefully planned exciting agenda for the remainder of my stay in Paris, dinner with Marcus Miller, ringside seats at his Paris show and so on. Too bad I never checked that phone except when I was in California!

A little later I returned with a wonderful band, the Godfathers of Groove – Bernard Purdie, Reuben Wilson and Grant Green Jr – to play at a top Parisian jazz venue, Sunset/Sunside, having also played with them in the UK several times. This was definitely a performing highlight, although I've never experienced such intense heat onstage – I thought I was going to pass out if I held a long note. And this was the middle of January!

I was subsequently cast in a stage version of *The Beggar's Holiday* (by Duke Ellington) to be staged at the Espace Pierre Cardin and starring the French baritone David Serero, who had obtained the rights to perform this neglected show. Having a month in Paris was a treat. I caught up with old friends, visited the jazz clubs (and occasionally sat in), hung out with pals such as saxophonists Scott Hamilton, Eric Alexander, legendary pianist Harold Mabern and my university contemporary Ben Sidran, from the American (and European) jazz scene, who were passing through Paris. And nightly performing the wonderful, hitherto neglected, Ellington score.

Figure 68: Jamming in Paris – Duc des Lombards. Author's collection.

My jazz quintet was also hired for some private parties. At one of them, the cabaret was the girls from the Crazy Horse. It certainly made the backstage hospitality room a lot more interesting and livelier.

On Saturday 14th November 2015, I was supposed to meet up with Andy Summers in Paris for his photo exhibition and for the opening night of a friend's restaurant. Then the unthinkable happened – the Paris terror attacks. I was on the telephone to Andy as the horror unfolded and he watched from the floor of his hotel room where he had been advised to shelter. I had played at the Bataclan a few years earlier and was deeply affected by the senseless events of Friday 13th. The great city (like London, New York, Mumbai and Manchester) survived and grew stronger and more unified in the face of terrible adversity.

And then there was Russia. I went back to Moscow, after many years, at the invitation of the Minister of Culture to take charge of a Russian musical production of *Crime and Punishment*. It was to be directed by the terrific Andre Konchalovsky with whom I'd done several commercials back in the 1980s and had music by the late Andrei Tarkovsky's favourite composer Eduard Artemyev. We all got on really well, but I could see that the producers and creatives had widely divergent ideas, and I didn't want to be caught in the middle. Moscow had changed a lot since my last visit, but some things never change. I accepted an invitation from my host to attend the Bolshoi that night with two local friends. We had the centre three seats in the front row of a packed theatre, and I couldn't help wondering who had been turfed out to make room for us! *Crime and Punishment* was a big success without me, I believe, so all's well that ends well and other clichés!

A few years earlier I received an invitation from the Mayor of Vladivostok (don't ask!) to bring a group to the Pacific Economic Congress (again, don't ask). I organized two brilliant Los Angeles musicians, guitarist Greg Poree and bassist Ryan Cross, to meet me in Vladivostok and prepared for my journey. My Russian friends all seemed to agree that the connecting flight from Moscow to Vladivostok would be uncomfortable, to put it mildly, and I set about obtaining a last-minute visa. My contact spoke to me on the phone and said, "Ring the Russian ambassador on this number and it will all be sorted." I assumed he meant the Russian Embassy and telephoned – it was indeed the Russian ambassador who answered! He knew all about my trip and told me to pick up my visa at the Embassy. I emerged from the station near the Embassy to find an answerphone message from the ambassador: "Please go to this address in East London, say who you are, don't queue and pick up your visa." The nine-hour flight from Moscow to Vladivostok on Aeroflot (seven hours of which were over Siberia) was quite possibly the most comfortable flight I've ever taken in my life. Quite a change from my first Aeroflot flight to Moscow in the early 1990s when the plane dropped several thousand feet (it seemed) without any warning. I met up with my pals who had flown from LAX via

Seoul in South Korea. We did a well-received set of jazz standards, and spent three very pleasant days in Vladivostok, which was off limits to most Russians for years as it was a naval base. In fact, we were invited to an endless display of naval might the day after our concert – it was the Russian Navy Day, so these displays were everywhere – complete with piped martial music, unfortunate cultural stereotypes and pomp, which were surely a hangover from the days of the USSR. For this extremely long afternoon the keynote speaker, a top economic advisor to the US government, and I were seated right in the middle of a troop of boy scouts, which made proceedings even more bizarre.

At lunch with one of our hosts, we were distracted by the noise of someone outside the restaurant mowing the grass verge opposite. Our host excused himself, went outside and returned almost immediately – the mowing had stopped. Some things never change! As Michael Jackson had recently passed away and we had all written for, played or recorded with him, we were invited to perform some of his songs at a plush nightspot in town. What the local audience made of our feeble attempts to struggle through a couple of songs from *Thriller* is a matter of conjecture. A great memory for the mythical bucket list, though.

Figure 69: Onstage in Vladivostok. Author's collection.

24 Awards and Recognition

Figure 70: My past is showing! Author's collection.

Awards are often just as meaningful for the ones you are given but don't actually receive (if that makes sense). I'm still waiting for several Golden Globe and Oscar certificates, multiple advertising awards and many certified gold platinum and even diamond awards. Some date back over thirty years so I probably wouldn't even know how to begin to chase them. I remember an irate George Harrison complaining to me he'd never received a Grammy certificate for *The Rutles* (as a matter of fact, I got mine after forty-three years thanks to some clever detective work by a friend – better late than never). It always struck me as odd that a Beatle, who must have been showered with accolades throughout his career, would be so concerned about a nomination for a comedy film in which he had acted, but that was George. (Two platinum albums for Tina Turner and Rod Stewart arrangements did materialize some thirty years later after some intrepid digging, which included speaking to a current major label employee who asked me, in all seriousness, "what is a platinum disc?")

In a career of 50-plus years, it has been an occasional thrill to win an award – even it was for lasting the course. The first ceremony I was honoured at was the British Film Awards of 1992, where I won the Anthony Asquith award for film music for *Hear My Song*, which was presented to me by Princess Diana. Although they've now merged this with the BAFTA Awards, in those days they were separate ceremonies. The music award was the top award of the evening, and I was honoured and flattered to receive it, but reality kicked in as I left the venue and was elbowed out of the way by the assembled photographers scrambling to get a picture of a current member of the cast of *EastEnders*. I also received a BAFTA nomination for the same film and with my fellow nominees had to suffer the results of someone's bright idea to have a troupe dance to the nominated music – I shudder to think what they would have done with *Schindler's List*! Around the same time came Ryuichi Sakamoto's Golden Globe for the musical score of *The Sheltering Sky*. Once again, I was supposed to receive some sort of certificate acknowledging my arranging and conducting contribution to the movie's soundtrack. I'm still waiting.

Next up was the Television and Radio Industries award for the best TV theme, won by my composition for *Peak Practice*, at one point the most popular and longest running television drama series in the UK. The lunch with many old friends was delightful. I had a long chat with Dame Vera Lynn and her husband about my family (she fondly remembered my mother's cooked breakfasts at 4am as the Ambrose band returned from a gig), and I didn't even have to make a speech beyond "Thank you." I loved working on *Peak Practice*. Scarily, at one point during its almost ten-year run on television, I was the only person connected with the show who had worked on every episode from the pilot onwards. Eventually the studio sessions became a weekly thing, as the next episode would arrive ready for scoring while we were recording the previous one – not an uncommon turnaround on a successful television series, but it kept me on my toes.

Soon afterwards, a Gold award from the Irish Advertising Festival arrived via a messenger one day. It's very handsome, but to this day I have no idea what I won it for! I guess it makes up for multiple advertising awards that not only I have never seen but have also never been notified about winning. To compound the unpredictability, I would quite often get certificates for editing and/or direction of commercials (for which admittedly I had written the music). I could never quite understand the logic at work. One I did receive around that time was my Golden Reel nomination for my score on *Little Voice*. Although it is theoretically an award primarily for editors, at least this one is for music.

The day I won my Emmy award was pretty entertaining. It started with a barbecue at Andy Summers' house, where Andy and Jack Bruce gave me a thumbs-up send-off in my tuxedo in extremely hot September weather. I drove to Pasadena in my bottom-of-the-range hired Nissan to be waved on by the parking valets as I arrived amid the limos.

A few weeks earlier I had gone for a meal at an upmarket Los Angeles restaurant. The parking valet took the Nissan away and, when it was returned at the end of the evening, the trunk was minus its carpet! The valet immediately lost all comprehension and command of the English language and I decided that someone was probably carpeting their home with fragments stolen from various cars. The whole thing seemed too ridiculous to report, but the car hire employee to whom I spoke had a good laugh about this the following morning – he had certainly never heard of a similar incident.

Back at the Pasadena Civic Auditorium I said to my friend, "They must know where I need to park," and she replied, "No, they're sending you back out onto the road." Sure enough, I had to drive along the freeway for around ten miles and then turn back to arrive at the same place, where the valets once again started waving me out to the street. By now my casual saunter to the Emmys had become a race against time. My pal wound down the window and screamed, "He's a nominee!" And this time we got lucky. After making our way along the red carpet I realized I had left my mobile phone in the car, so I ran back to the valet with my ticket, and they eventually reunited me with the phone after about 20 minutes. By now it was 4pm and the outside temperature was over 100 degrees Fahrenheit. We went into the theatre where no refreshments were allowed and settled down to the seemingly endless seven-hour ceremony.

For the very first category the fellow in the seat next to me was nominated and lost. I felt sorry that he'd have to sit through the next 70-odd awards. In fact, I managed to fall asleep at around number 54 and was nudged awake just before the music nominees were announced. Debbie Reynolds and Cheri Oteri read the nominations and, before I knew it, I was racing up to the stage to make my acceptance speech. Of course, I had nothing prepared and blanked after thanking the producers and director, trying to remember the network contact who had greenlighted the whole project. Fortunately, my mental block only lasted a few seconds and I managed to thank cast and crew, family and friends and the wonderful orchestra. The next few hours are a blur, although someone did take the award away from me as I left the stage. When I protested, he said, "It's a prop we use for all the awards," and gave me the real statue. I do remember lining up for the official portrait of me holding the award in front of the Emmy backdrop. The photo consisted of one snap by the cameraman. "What happens if the camera fails?" I asked Halle Berry who had just been photographed. Guess what – the camera failed!

The dinner was fun but the big HBO party was the following week. My Australian friend Carl (see the Balmoral story in Chapter 23), who had organized my nomination party in Los Angeles in July, had promised to fly in to celebrate if I won the award, which he did. We headed to Spago – for some reason HBO didn't do too well that year so I was definitely the centre of attraction. I was delighted that my pals James Gandolfini and Peter Boyle and my sometimes bandmate Bruce Willis were there to share the moment as well as the casts of *Sex and the City* and *Friends*.

Figure 71: With James Gandolfini. Author's collection.

Everyone remembers the late James Gandolfini as the star of *The Sopranos*, a charismatic actor taken before his time. As he was also a one-time saxophonist and jazz fanatic, who had worked back in the day as a bouncer at one of New York's premier jazz venues, we bonded over music and he was always very supportive of my writing and playing. Last time we met was in the car park at Soho House in West Hollywood – our conversation was cut short by the arrival of our respective cars, and shockingly a few weeks later he was gone and an incandescent light and talent was extinguished.

Martin Lewis, producer of *The Secret Policeman's Ball*, asked, "Did you do the red-carpet interviews on the way in?" When I said, no, I'd just sneaked in unnoticed, he dragged me out and made me walk the line. That's why, to my friends' astonishment if they were watching, I suddenly appeared on the UK and Australian *Entertainment Tonight* shows. I must admit I did feel a bit of fraud as I had won my "craft" award a week before the glitzy main ceremony that evening, but my award was one of the very few on view at the after-party, so my guilt was assuaged somewhat. (Both *RKO 281* and, later, *Shall We Dance* have also gained me prestigious ASCAP awards.)

Figure 72: ASCAP award winners – including Phil Collins, Mark Isham, Trevor Jones and Craig Armstrong. Author's collection.

Three years later I was nominated again for the TV remake of *The Roman Spring of Mrs. Stone* starring Helen Mirren and Anne Bancroft. I thought I had a good chance of winning this time, but it wasn't to be. My transport on this occasion was a limousine provided by Showtime. When we decided to leave the nominees' dinner and "do the town," our driver informed us that he was only able to take us to one destination before clocking off. The upshot was a fun night out with the Baron Cohens at my LA "home from home," the Whiskey Bar. My colleague George Fenton told me that when he received his Academy Award nomination he had a suite at the Beverly Hills hotel, fresh flowers daily, and a stretch limo to the ceremony. When he left the Oscars empty-handed his limo had vanished and he had to hail a taxi back to the hotel!

In 2006 I was awarded a Gold Badge by the British Academy of Songwriters and Composers. It's a Lifetime Achievement award, a bit worrying when you feel your career is by no means over yet. Everyone else honoured over the years has been a major figure in the UK music scene, so I was thrilled and humbled to be included in the ranks. The much-loved comedian and actor Sir Lenny Henry wrote a terrific encomium for the souvenir book that made me feel I was someone special. Once again Carl flew over from Australia, and my family and friends had a great afternoon. The acceptance speeches dragged on for hours and I was very happy to make my speech short and sweet and even get some laughs. It was, and is, an honour to have this recognition from one's peers and to keep such august company – even if fifteen years later, at the time of writing, I'm still standing.

I received two more Lifetime Achievement awards: from the Monaco International Film Festival, where I had the honour of chairing the judging panel and played a short set with my old friend Donovan, and in the UK at the Romford Film Festival. I was also gratified to be offered an honorary doctorate in music by my alma mater Sussex University. What was especially moving was that I was awarded my degree on the stage of the Brighton Dome almost exactly forty years after Noël Coward had stood in the same spot receiving his honorary doctorate, while I sat awaiting the presentation of my Bachelor of Arts degree. Subsequently I was invited every year to the dinner at the Brighton Pavilion for the new honorees. One year I sat between two men, one roughly my age and one slightly younger, and started telling them about my musical career. It turned out that the older man had been social secretary at Birmingham at the same time as I'd been at Sussex and we reminisced about groups I'd played with or been friends with. Eventually I turned to the younger fellow on my left and said, "So what brings you here?" "Oh, I discovered graphene and was knighted and won the Nobel Prize." Chastened, I turned to my social secretary friend on the right and said "… and what brings you here?"

"Oh, I discovered protein molecules that control the division of cells. I was knighted, and won the Nobel Prize!" replied the chairman of the Royal Society, Sir Paul Nurse. Me and my big mouth! I was reminded of a garden party at the home of Jason (son of Sean) Connery in Los Angeles when I was telling three other guests a convoluted story about something that happened on an outside court at Wimbledon. "Of course, if you'd ever been to

Wimbledon you would know the outside courts are intimate and they have the feel of a local park." One of my listeners pointed to the man in the middle and said, "He won the Australian Open!" Foot firmly planted in mouth. Brad Gilbert was very charming, but I still felt like a prize idiot.

Figure 73: Receiving my honorary Doctor of Music at the University of Sussex. Author's collection.

I was also delighted to have been awarded a star on the Brighton Music Walk of Fame on the Palace Pier. My association with Brighton dates back to my university days in the late 1960s at Sussex University and has continued through to this day. The Walk was the brainchild of songwriter David Courtney and it honours musicians who have a strong Brighton connection. The plaque is on the right as you enter the pier from the main road and I'm always thrilled to receive photos from friends who have made the trek down to see it. Along with the John Altman recital room that I mentioned in the Shanghai chapter, it's something that hopefully will perpetuate my achievements and memory long after I'm gone.

Figure 74: My plaque on the Brighton Music Walk of Fame. Author's collection.

25 The Ones That Got Away

Many people I met in Hollywood seemed to define themselves by what they didn't do. "Hi, I'm Chet. I should have had the lead role in *21 Jump Street*." If a project doesn't happen, or someone else is chosen as composer, I tend never to give it another thought. However, I did think it might be an interesting exercise to try to recollect the "nearlys" and what might have been.

As a working saxophonist there were opportunities I turned down (The Rumour; Van's American tour). I was in the mix, but somehow it never happened. This may have been because the whole concept was rather ludicrous, such as a tour with a trio consisting of me, Allan Zavod (who had been Frank Zappa's keyboard player) and George Benson. I'm not sure George even ever heard about this idea of Allan's! Others are things that nearly happened, but something stymied them at the last minute (these include Hot Chocolate's US tour; an abortive attempt to purchase the then derelict Elstree Film Studios in North London when no money materialized; playing in Paris with the Miles Davis Electric Band; a four-saxophone tour of Europe with three giants of the instrument, and me lagging far behind; not to mention taking the big band out with Björk).

As I was becoming reasonably well-known at the various UK TV channels in my early days of television work I was called by David (Daisy) Bell, one of the top music programme producers at London Weekend Television. He wanted to know my availability to act as the musical director for a new show featuring the likes of James Brown, Ray Charles and Aretha Franklin. The only problem was that he spoke to my mother who told him, correctly, that I was in central London and probably wouldn't phone in all day. In those pre-cell phone and internet days, out meant out! She had no idea where I was or when I'd be back. Indeed, when I got home at around 8pm and rang Daisy, he told me they'd hired someone else. My disappointment was alleviated by the fact that this was the last I ever heard of this project – I don't think the pilot show even got made.

Not a movie project as such, but while I was working with director Russ Karel on a Channel Four documentary about the cartoonist David Low in the mid-1980s, Russ asked if I wanted to join him in the purchase of the top two floors of Butler's Wharf, then suffering decay and neglect by the River Thames. "You can convert one floor into an apartment!" My negative response seemed like common sense at the time: "Why on earth would I want to build there? No roads, no public transport, no shops, no restaurants, no street lights – no chance!"

An apartment there today would probably sell for tens of millions.

As an arranger there are many projects I either narrowly missed, or they went the way of many good ideas. I mentioned earlier the ballet to be composed by Jule Styne featuring Gerry Mulligan. I'd have loved to have arranged that! Then there was a collaboration between Michel Legrand and Stephane Grappelli (too busy); a duet between the late Maria Callas (using her isolated vocals) and Placido Domingo, inspired by the Nat Cole/Natalie Cole duets (never happened); Seal's debut album (out of the country); Dusty Springfield standards album (she was too sick to follow it through); Amy Winehouse jazz album (talked about but went no further); an album of songs from the classic American songbook with the great salsa star Ruben Blades (after playing a show where he sat in and effortlessly sang a couple of standards); a big band event and recording with Diana Ross (they used my suggestions for the New York based big band led and arranged by my pal Gil Askey); orchestral renditions of Björk's compositions (budget too expensive); and the music of Bob Marley (still waiting for the next step twenty-five years later). And I can think of quite a few more.

In the early 1980s my old producer/record company boss came back from MIDEM in Cannes having acquired another label and its catalogue and roster of artists. He rang me and said, "You're into jazz aren't you, fancy doing an album with Johnny Hartman?" And how! The *Standards* album with John Coltrane has always been one of my all-time favourites. I made contact with Johnny, and he promised to send me some demos of songs he'd picked. My mind was racing – an intimate small group session, or a big band blockbuster, or a "with strings" epic? The tape duly arrived, and I slotted it expectantly into the cassette player. On came six or seven of the saddest disco-style "songs" I've ever heard – songs that made Boney M sound like The Hi-Lo's. I rang my pal – "are you *sure* we can't do an album of standards?" He informed me that Johnny was coming to London to perform at the jazz club The Canteen, so we met there for lunch. Johnny had a terrible sore throat (he could barely speak) and was going to see a specialist that afternoon. I couldn't see how he could open with his voice shot like that, and sadly he was immediately diagnosed with cancer and flew home the next morning. The world lost a great voice and I'd like to think I could have persuaded him to make one more classic standards album. Posthumously his reputation grew when a huge fan, Clint

Eastwood, featured his recordings extensively in the hugely popular movie *The Bridges of Madison County*.

As a composer I regret ignoring Sting's offer to collaborate on some songs. I assumed it was just idle chit-chat and of course later found out he collaborated more than anyone I've ever known in the business. Likewise, when both Amy Winehouse and Joss Stone suggested co-writing – what is the matter with me? Then there's a host of movies and TV series where I either reached the last two or they simply evaporated: *The Last Horror Movie* directed by David Winters which my friend Caroline Munro had recommended me for (I was too squeamish!); a nature series for David Attenborough where I was to compose and record the music first and then they would shoot appropriate footage (whatever happened to that?); *Austin Powers*, where I had a great four-hour meeting with Mike Myers and Jay Roach. I suspect I was backup insurance for another composer who had a date conflict that he was able to work out. (My agent felt so guilty about having me fly to LA on 24th December that she invited me to an "old Hollywood" Christmas lunch with Dick Van Dyke, Norman Lloyd and others.) I know it was nothing personal as Jay later introduced me to his wife Susannah Hoffs of The Bangles as one of the finest movie composers around! I also had several meetings with the producers for *Band of Brothers*, and I read the book I'd been given, on which the series was based, from cover to cover – then my friend Michael Kamen got the gig. I'd signed a contract to compose the music for *Life on Mars* (best TV script I'd ever read), but the producer had an attack of nerves about me being in Los Angeles so often. On *Everybody Wins*, I lost out to my old friend Mark Isham but director Karel Reisz asked me aboard anyway, as orchestrator and conductor. Again, I lost out to Michael Kamen on *The Krays*, and on *Unstrung Heroes* I lost out to Thomas Newman. (I eventually scored a television movie produced by and starring Diane Keaton, *On Thin Ice*.) Then there was an odd piece about a love affair between a lawyer and a traveller that I ceded to Joe Strummer of The Clash; a couple of Michael Winner movies that I watched in disbelief at his house and passed on; *The Whole Nine Yards*; *East Is East*; *V for Vendetta*; and *Town and Country* for which I was hired, hung around on the roster for a couple of years, became the victim of studio and producer politics and was fired and paid in full without writing a note!

During the time that *Town and Country* was dragging on, there were many script changes and revised endings. Diane Keaton had to leave the film to work on another project but one new scene they were shooting required her to be in shot with Warren Beatty. Her double, who had worked with her for years and handled any non-speaking assignments for Diane, was on set but couldn't be cast because if she spoke, even if the lines were to be dubbed later by Miss Keaton, she would have to be moved up a performance category and retrospectively paid thousands of dollars for being on the film for over a year – union rules. Therefore, they hired a third Diane Keaton, on a day rate, seen only with her back to camera, standing on a lower step to hide the height difference, and speaking lines that would later be replaced by Diane number one. While this shot was being filmed I was seated off camera, next to Diane Keaton number two, who nudged me in the ribs and whispered, "This is all wrong, *I'm* Diane Keaton!" Ah, Hollywood!

When *Town and Country* was shooting in New York I happened to be staying there with the parents of two of my closest friends and I was able to visit the filming. My friends' mother and father were celebrating a significant wedding anniversary and the dad – let's call him Woody – had been Warren Beatty's best friend and roommate when they were in their early twenties. They had fallen out and not spoken for around thirty years. I suggested to Woody's youngest daughter that she bury the family hatchet with Warren, as I saw him regularly on set and had become more than a nodding acquaintance. She came along to the shoot and we waited outside the make-up trailer until he emerged. "Hi Warren, I'm Woody's daughter," said my friend. Neither of us expected the response we got – Warren flung his arms around her and rocked her from side to side with tears streaming down his cheeks. "Oh, I really miss Woody, I'm overwhelmed to meet you! How is he – I'd love to see him again."

Excitedly my pal rang her older sister and said, "You have to come down to meet Warren, his reaction is unbelievable." Her older sister came to the location, walked up to Warren and said, "Hi Warren, I'm Woody's older daughter."

"Nice to meet you," replied Warren, shaking her hand, and off he went. Ah, Hollywood!

I've been lucky (or unlucky) to be blessed with the same surname as one of the greatest directors in the history of movies – Robert Altman. I was a big fan of his work but my first encounter with him was through our mutual friend Annie Ross, who sang and acted in several of his best movies. She gave me the phone number of the people she was staying with in LA and when I rang, a man answered the phone. "Who's calling please?" When I said "John Altman," all he said was *"Hah"*. How odd, I thought. I later discovered she was staying with the Altmans and he had answered my call. Some years later I was recommended to compose the score for his movie *Gosford Park*. "I've got four Altmans on the movie already, one more and they'll crucify me," was his response. My offers to change my name went unheeded and I never got to work with him. After he passed away, the British Film Institute in London organized a tribute evening to him and I was invited. When they telephoned me the day before to make sure I was attending, I started panicking. "They're going to present me with something or get me to make a speech – I bet they think he was my father!" I attended the event and thankfully wasn't called upon to do anything. Hopefully that was the only time my name prevented me from getting a job!

TV commercials have always seemed to be a lottery. I remember being at a party with another composer, who excused himself as he had an important piece to write for a commercial where he'd been told he was the only man for the job. This sounded very familiar to me, and I asked the name of the product. It turned out that I was writing for the same client and brief, and also recording the next day. In addition, I had been given an identical build-up by the advertising agency! We were of a mind to submit the same track and see whether anyone noticed.

Another time I was summoned to the West End of London at 5.30pm on a Friday in mid-summer. My producer had informed me I was the only man for the job. Therefore, I shouldn't have been surprised to find a colleague/rival leaving the building as I arrived. I went home and wrote down the first piece of garbage that came into my head – the client loved it, but the commercial went the way of many ideas and was never made. My friend and synth player Nick Glennie-Smith (now one of Hans Zimmer's main arrangers and conductors) told me he would often demo for the same product for two different composers in two different studios in the morning and afternoon. The same clients would troop through the door and Nick would do nothing to spare their embarrassment, greeting them with a hearty "Great to see you again!" One commercial I did turn down as I was too busy was the UK ad for Go Compare – that is one I really don't regret at all!

All movie composers, however great and famous, seem to get fired sometimes. It appears to go with the territory. I was called once to meet the producers on a movie (I won't name it to save any blushes). The first thing they said to me was, "We had a score written by Jerry Goldsmith and it's crap!" I'm afraid they lost me there and then as it was impossible for any Jerry Goldsmith score to be rubbish. Most composers I know just shrug their shoulders and move on – although I know Elmer Bernstein was particularly hurt by this kind of callous rejection when he suffered it. I have been removed from a couple of projects – the aforementioned *Town and Country* where I was the victim of a power struggle, and a TV two-parter in the UK where the director was returning after a lengthy break and wanted his usual team around him. It worked in my favour as the theme written by his regular composer didn't sound any different to my music and I was immediately able to use what I'd written in a US TV movie with a full orchestra as opposed to the synthesized score (possibly with one extra live musician) which is all I would have been able to afford for the British miniseries. I even had one movie replete with bankable stars and director collapse after the first day of shooting as the financing had fallen through.

Gergely Hubal has written a fascinating book about rejected film scores (*Torn Music*). Together with replacement castings and changes of director mid-movie, they provide an alternative history of the cinema – what might have been. But it doesn't pay to dwell on them too much except as a fascinating diversion – the ones that got away!

26 Today and Beyond

I'm writing this final chapter as we come out of another lockdown. Apart from a weekend in Brighton and two lunches in North and Central London I hadn't been anywhere since February 2020, and as I write it's now a year and a half later. A very surreal state of affairs, but at least it has enabled me to write this memoir, something I've been threatening to do for the last few years. I've conducted a few online masterclasses and hooked up with some amazing people I probably would never have had the chance to talk to in the "real world." We have had a couple of Monty Python reunions on Zoom, with much laughter and some wonderful transatlantic hook-ups with great contemporaries from iconic bands like Santana, the Mothers of Invention and the Headhunters. Of course, I miss playing and hearing live music and long for the day when my big band and quartet can perform again, and when we can discover the new Amy Winehouse at one of our jamming sessions.

If I never get to play or write another note of music, something I gave a lot of thought to during my 13-month "indisposition," I am very aware that I've been luckier than most people. My passion became my profession, so I could literally dedicate seven days a week and every waking hour to fulfilling my musical aspirations.

One year I was prevented from attending the tennis in Shanghai by my mystery ataxia. At around the same time I was offered a monthly residency by the PizzaExpress, Holborn, a top jazz venue in the UK. I responded that I didn't really feel capable of sustaining a whole evening of music making, but how about my playing a few tunes and then interviewing an esteemed colleague and friend in the business? The club was very receptive to this idea and thus was born my "evenings with" — a very successful formula. Guitarists Mitch Dalton, John Etheridge or Rob Luft and I would play a few tunes, then I would interview a star guest who was welcome to sing a few numbers with us if they felt like it. Before the programme was interrupted by the ongoing pandemic, we had hosted the comedian and actor Sanjeev Bhaskar, my old friend Sir Michael Palin, the mercurially talented Goldie, actor/comedian Rob Brydon, my university chum from *Downton Abbey* Jim Carter and his brilliant wife Imelda Staunton, comedian/actor Sir Lenny Henry (I met him on his first day in London when he was 16 years old), all-round personality Bradley Walsh and *Line of Duty* star Adrian Dunbar who had written and starred in *Hear My Song* all those years ago. (We jointly composed a song, 'We're Moving', sung in the movie by Adrian and James Nesbitt.) I had a list of wonderful future guests lined up including Sir Tim Rice, Joss Stone, Alexander Armstrong and James Nesbitt – hopefully we can resume the series (or will already have done so by the time you read this book).

Figure 75: With Sir Michael Palin at the PizzaExpress Holborn. Photo by Danny Clifford.

It's amazing for me to think that I've interacted with Charlie Chaplin on the one hand and John Legend on the other – quite a journey through the history of modern entertainment. Along the way I've played with and written for the best of the best and virtually everyone I've worked with has retained their popularity to this day. Many of my movies and records are still being bought, listened to, or watched, years after I was lucky enough to be involved in their creation. It's heart-warming to see the huge interest in Nick Drake, Bob Marley, David Bowie, George Michael and Amy Winehouse and to realize that I am a part of their story – and to be contacted by people who love *Titanic*, *Funnybones*, *Little Voice*, *Life of Brian* or *Goldeneye* or even be reminded of an obscure movie, record, commercial or TV show that I contributed to. I thoroughly enjoyed my four-year term on the Council of the British Academy of Film and Television Arts (BAFTA) and helping in a very small way to integrate BAFTA Los Angeles into the BAFTA fold. Although I have left the ASMAC Board, I participate in their weekly inspirational Zoom webinars, reaching out to composers and arrangers worldwide.

Figure 76: With Jim Carter and Imelda Staunton. Photo by Danny Clifford.

Figure 77: With Adrian Dunbar. Photo by Sanne Gault.

Figure 78: Conducting my big band album session. Photo by Danny Clifford.

I am thankful that I'm still in demand, with exciting movie offers, composing assignments and arranging gigs still being offered for the immediate future – watch this space!

Figure 79: Conducting a big band recording in Abbey Road Studio 2 (the Beatles' studio). Author's collection.

Index

10 Room, The 200–3, *201*, *204*, 229–30, *232*

'Abednego' 50–1
Act of Vengeance 130–1, 215
Adams, Bryan 96
Adler, Larry 147
Alan, Patrick 202–3, *204*, 229–30
Ali, Muhammad 67–8
Almond, Johnny 220
Almonds and Raisins 134, 149
Altman, Harold 3–10, *4*, 14
Altman, Johnny 197, 220, 242
Altman, Robert 266
Altman, Rose 3–10, *6*, 14
'Always Look on the Bright Side of Life' 57–8, 151, 163, 188
Ambrose, Bert 7, 13
Anderson, Al 51, 66
Armstrong, Craig *259*
Armstrong, Louis 13, *14*
Artemyev, Eduard 253
Askey, Gil 194, 264
Aspery, Ron 120
Assassin of the Tsar 137–9
Astaire, Fred 149
Atkinson, Rowan *93*
Ayers, Kevin 28, 30, 38, 51, 66, 202, 209, 229

Bacharach, Burt 154
Bad Behaviour 165–6
Bailey, David 176, 182
Baker, Chet 36, 155, 224
Bakke, Brenda 215
Balfe, Lorne 143
Bancroft, Anne 168–9
Bardens, Peter 34, 86
Barkin, Ellen 130
Baron Cohen, Sacha 214, 239–40, 260
Batiste, Jon ix, 199, 210
Beatty, Ned 135–6, *136*
Beatty, Warren 266
Beautiful Joe 213
Beautiful Thing 165–6
Beck, Jeff 59–61, *61*
Bedford, David 150, 209
Beggar's Holiday 252
Benedetti, Nicola 129, *129*
Bennett, Richard Rodney 142
Bennett, Duster 30, 33, *35*
Bennett, Tony 103, 147, 228
Benny, Jack 11–12
Berens, Harold 135
Bergman, Ingrid 77–8
Berle, Milton 31–2, *32*
Bernal, Gael García 170
Bernstein, Elmer 35, 132–3, *133*, 267
Bertolucci, Bernardo 140
Besson, Luc 139–40, 251
Best, George 72
Bhaji on the Beach 165
Bhaskar, Sanjeev 62–3, *62*, 268
Björk 115–17

Black, Don vii, 80, 122, 132, 205, 233
Black Mikado, The 81
Blake, Howard 74, 106, 207
Blank, Minna 137–9
Blethyn, Brenda 166–7, *167*
Botkin, Perry, Jr. 226–7, *227*
Boulting, Roy 121, 123–4
Bowie, David 79–80
Bradbury, Stan 151–2
Bradlee, Scott 77, 244
Brando, Marlon 197
Bronson, Charles 130
Broad, Chris 100
Brooks, Elkie 102
Brooks, Mel 169, 228
Brosnan, Pierce 113, 131–2, *131*
Brown, Errol 69–70
Bruce, Jack 208, 257
Bryan, Bob & Mike 247, *247*
Buckley, Tim 39–41
Burdon, Eric 64
Burstyn, Ellen 130
Butcher, Mark 204
By the Sword Divided 121

Cadogan, Susan 66
Caine, Michael 166, 205, *206*
Callery, Sean 223, *223*
Cameron, James 161, 163–4
Candrix, Fud 8
Carl, George 159
Caron, Leslie 160–1
Carrack, Paul 72, 204, 213
Carter, Benny 152–3, *154*
Carter, Jim x, 26, 269–70, *270*
Castles in the Air 171
Chambers, Jimmy *50*, 51
Chaplin, Charlie 47
Chapman, Graham 57, 62
Chelsom, Peter x, 134–6, 158–61, 170, 173
Cipriano, Gene 152, 226
Clapton, Eric 15, 59–61, *61*, 85
Cleese, John 55, 58, *61*, 62, *93*
Cleveland, Carole 62, *62*
Clough, Brian 65–6
Clyne, Jeff 108
Coburn, James 228
Cohn, Al 156

Cole, Xhosa 210
Coleman, Cy 145–6
Coleman, Ornette 151
Collier, Jacob 209–10, *210*
Collins, Phil 59–60, *259*
Colman, Stuart 124
Colombier, Michel 225
Connolly, Billy 36, 59, 213
Cook, Paul 144
Cook, Peter 58, 92–3, *93*, 127, 214
Cooper, Ray 56, 64, 204
Coslow, Sam 152
Courtney, David 262
Cowan, Dennis *50*, 51
Cramer, Ross 123
Cronkite, Walter 195
Crosby, Bing 149
Cross, Ryan 253–4
Cumberbatch, Benedict 230

Dalton, Mitch *20*, 35, 46, 66, 68, 105–6, 109, 117, 190, 193, 268
Daltrey, Roger *101*, 247
Daniels, Eddie 180
Davis, Erin 203, 251
Day, Doris 192–3
Davis, Kristen *169*
Dennis, Matt 148
Desplat, Alexandre 251
DeVito, Frank 223
Diana, Princess 105–6, *105*, 135
Dietrich, Marlene 79–80
Distel, Sacha 250
Donovan, Terence 176, 182
Doohan, James 161
Dorfman, Stanley 38, 226
'Downtown Train' 111–12
Drake, Nick 24–5, 28, 36–7
Driver, Minnie 123, 167–8
Dudley, Anne 111,
Dunbar, Adrian 135–6, 269–70, *270*
Dupree, Champion Jack 28–9
Dury, Ian 19, 66, 213
Duvall, Robert 44

Eager, Vince 54, 193
Echols, Johnny 27, 200
Ellington, Lance 205

Ellis, Pee Wee 89
Emanuel, Elizabeth 97–8
Enchanted April 142
Erivo, Cynthia 204
Etheridge, John 42–4, *50*, 51, 268
Evans, Ray 227–8

Fairweather, Digby 83
Federer, Roger 249
Felder, Wilton 200
Fenby, Eric 53
Fenton, George 79, 121, 260
Ferguson, Craig 93, 217
Fernbach, Andy 29, 36
Fidel 170
Fitzgerald, Tara 135–6
Fleetwood Mac 27, 33, 51, 229
Formby, George 96–7, 124
Foster, Mo 60, 242
Franciosa, Tony 85–6
Freeman, Bud 21, 198
Frishberg, Dave 156–7
Fulson, Lowell 28, 189
Funnybones 158–61

Gaillard, Slim 194–7
Gandolfini, James 258–9, *258*
Gardner, Ava 147
Garrett, Betty 144–5
Gaye, Marvin 102, 196
Gere, Richard 170
Germain, Nora 210
Gibbs, Richard 114
Gillespie, Dizzy 156, 195
Gilliam, Terry ix, *62*, 63
God on the Rocks 123–4
'Godfathers of Groove' 252
Goldblum, Jeff ix, 99, 199–200
Goldeneye 113, 141–3, 251
Goldie 118, 269
Grant, Eddy 51, 92
Green, Grant, Jr. *251*, 252
Green, Peter 28, 30–1, 33–5, *35*, 42, 202
Grusin, Dave 154
Gussak, Billy 32

Halsall, Ollie 55, 67

Hancock, Herbie 84, 199, 203, 211–12, *212*
Hardin, Tim 38–9, 67
Hardy, Chips 176
Harrison, George 38, 84, 96–8, *97*, 256
Hart, John 234
Hartley, Dave 151, 160
Hartman, Johnny 264–5
Hayes, Morris 237–8, 247
Hazelhurst, Ronnie 76
Head, Murray 64
Hear My Song 48, 134–6, 256, 269
Hefti, Neal 154
Hendrix, Jimi 36, 42, 202, 209, 229
Hendry, Ian 52–3
Henry, Lenny 39, 53, 121, *122*, 260, 269
Henry, Thierry 181, *182*
Herman, Mark 166–7
'Hey Manhattan' 110
Hill, Bernard 127, 165
Hirschhorn, Clive 144
Hitchcock, Nigel 100, 134
Hoffman, Dustin 65, 98
Holloway, Red 200, 225–6
Holmes, Wally 224
Hope Springs 166–7
Horn, Trevor 78, 111–12
Horner, James 165, *165*
Horrocks, Jane 166–7, *167*
Hoskins, Bob 180
'Hot Chocolate' 68–75, *71*
House, Son 28–9, 39, 41
Howard, Ken 121–3
Hylton, Jack 8, 13

'I Wish You Would' 27
'I'd Have You Anytime' 98
Idle, Eric 55–8, 63
Innes, Neil 55–7, 59–60, 62, *62*, *93*, 96, 121, 126–7
Innes Book of Records 57–8, 121, 126–7
'I Salonisti' 161–4
Isham, Mark 59, 89, *259*, 265
'It's Oh So Quiet' 115–17, *116*, 190
Italian Job, The 205–7

Jackson, Michael 150, 233–4

Jagger, Mick 95–6
James, Steve 57
Janis, Conrad 227–8
Jankel, Chas *20*, 19, 39, 59, 66–7
Jemmott, Jerry 114, 200
Jewell, Derek 193
Jimmy Riordan 132
John, Doctor 82, *82*, 189
John, Elton 36, 66, 229
Johnson, Plas 124, 150, 200, 227
Jones, Aled 106–7
Jones, Chuck 177, *177*
Jones, Davy 180
Jones, Philly Joe 23
Jones, Paul 127, 242, *243*
Jones, Quincy ix, 205, *207*, 210, 234–5, *235*
Jones, Terry 57, 62, *62*, *93*, 127, 174
Jones, Trevor *259*
Just a Gigolo 79–80

Kamen, Michael 265
Karel, Russ 134, 264
Kastner, Elliott 132
Kaye, Danny 3, 11–12
Keaton, Diane 265–6
Kelly, Dave 28–9
Kelly, Gene 144
Kelly, Jo Ann 28–9
Kerr, Jim 111
Khan, Chaka 126, 199, 200, *201*, 229
Kilgore, Ryan 236, *236*
King, Ben E. 124
Kisses on a Postcard 81
'Kissing a Fool' 108–10
Kissoon, Katie 85
Kitt, Eartha 150, 180, 195, 229
Konchalovsky, Andre 176, 253
Korner, Alexis 42, 180–1
Kossoff, Paul 18, 91–2

La La Land 174
Laine, Denny 27
Laine, Frankie 120
Lang, Mike 223
Lara, Brian 215–16
Larnyoh, George 81
Lawrence, Elliott 180

Leat, Allan 198
Lee, Albert 200, 208
Lee, Spike 201, 203
Legend, John 203
Legionnaire 166
Leitch, Donovan 59–60, 64, 260
Lennon 127
Léon (The Professional) 139–40
Lerner, Alan Jay 178
Lewis, Jerry 148, 158–9, 161
Lewis, Martin 59–60, 98, 258
Life of Brian 57–8, 62–3, 96
Linton, Louise 226
Little Voice 166–7, 205, 257
Locke, Josef 134–5
Lopez, Jennifer 170
Lownes, Victor 145
Luevano, Michael 245, 249
Lynn, Vera 5, 13, 256
Lynott, Phil 83–4

MacKenzie, John 130–2, 215
Major, John *100*, 241
Malkovich, John 216, 222
Mancini, Henry 150, 190
Mandel, Johnny 154
Mankowitz, Wolf 134
Marley, Bob 1, 35, 51, 66, 92
Martin, Steve 56, 136
Martin, Tony 12–13
Martyn, John 24–5, 29
'Matching Tie and Handkerchief' 55
Matchmaker, The 166
Maxwell, Robert 193–4
McAloon, Paddy 110–11
McCallum, David 135–6, *136*
McCartney, Paul 108, 110
McClaren, Malcolm 114
McDowell, Fred 30, 39
McDowell, Malcolm 137
McGhee, Brownie 87
McGregor, Ewen 166
McKenna, Dave 151
Melina, Alan 26, 41
Mercer, Chris 68, 75
Mercer, Mabel 145
Mercury, Freddie 73–4
Michael, George 19, 108–10

Midgley, Vernon 135
Miller, Marcus 252
Milligan, Spike 16, 95
Minnelli, Liza 147
Mirren, Helen 168–9
Miss Marple 121
Money, Zoot 55, 209
Moon, Keith 31, 38, 51, 57, 202
Moore, Dudley 94
Moore, Roger 222
Morricone, Ennio 150
Morrison, Barbara 200
Morrison, Van 19, *40*, 66, 81–2, *82*, 83–90, *85*, *87*, *88*, 189, 197, 229
Moss, Stirling 193, 212
Most, Mickey 69, 72
'Mother' 118
Moyet, Alison 104–6, 190
Muldaur, Maria 24, 53, 189
Mulligan, Gerry 155–6

Neame, Ronald 46
'Nearer My God to Thee' 163–4
Nesbitt, James 135, 269
'New Power Generation' 203, 237–8
Nicholas, Fayard 148–9
Nicholas, Harold 147–9, 158–9
Nightingale, Annie 49
'Nights in White Satin' 127–8
Niles, Richard 111
Nilsson, Harry 31, 38, 98, 226
No Time to Die 143
Norman, Monty 143
Norris, Noel 66, 69–70

O'Connor, Donald 144–5
Ogdon, John 95–6
Oldfield, Mike 26, 30, 209
Oldman, Gary 141
Orbison, Roy 127
Original Comets 200
Ottman, John 220
Owen, Mark 181

Page, Jimmy 193
Paich, David 225
Paige, Elaine 65
Palin, Michael x, 58, 62–3, *62*, *93*, 269, *269*

Palmer, Earl 23–4
Park, Nick 113
Parker, Alan 132, 135
Parker, Graham 102
Parkinson, Michael 76, 107, 230
Parks, Van Dyke 226–7, *227*
Parnell, Ric 19, *20*, 41
Peak Practice 121, 128, 256
'Pearls II' 102
Pearson, Tommy 205
Penniman, Richard 36, 124–5, *125*
Phillips, Harry 5, *5*
Phillips, Ralph 5, *5*
Phillips, Sid 4–5, *5*, 11, 13–15, *14*
Phillips, Simon 15, 59–60, 225
Phillips, Woolf 3, *7*, 7–8, 11–13, 15–16, 31–2, 53, 76, 120, 144–5, 153, 189, 225
Phoenix, River 132
Piernunzi, Enrico 250
Pinter, Harold 14
Polanski, Roman 97
Poree, Greg 253–4
Powell, Nik 26, 164–5, 215
Prince 99, 202–3, 237–8
Pruess, Craig 107
Purdie, Bernard *251*, 252
Pyne, Mick 104, 108, 147, 190

'Queen' 73–5

Radford, Michael 84, 174
Raksin, David 153
Ravel, Freddie 225
Reagans, The 170
Reed, Oliver 159–60, 183
Reeves, Keanu 130
Reiner, Carl 136
Rice, Tim 193, 269
Richards, Andy 110
Richie, Lionel 200, 203, *204*, 229
Riddle, Nelson 150–1, 227
Rivers, Joan 168
RKO 281 168, 240, 259
Rock Around the Dock 121, 125–6
Roman Spring of Mrs. Stone, The 168–9, 259
Ronson, Mark 238
Ronson, Mick 82, *82*

Ross, Annie 136, 145, 266
Ross, Ben 168
Ross, Diana 118, 264
Ross, Ronnie 80
Rushdie, Salman 176
Rutles, The 55–7, 63, 96, 188, 256

Sakamoto, Ryuichi 139–40
Saunders, Theo 223
Savalas, Ariana 77
Savalas, Telly 76–8
Sayer, Leo 28
Schwartz, Arthur 152
Scott, Ridley 19, 149, 168, 176, 184–6, *186*
Scott, Ronnie 53
Scott, Tony 198
Secret Policeman's Ball 58
Secret Policeman's Other Ball 58–61, 213
Seeger, Pete 98
Sellers, Peter 11, *15*, 15–16, 47
Serero, David 252
Serra, Eric 139–41, 251
Sex Pistols 60, 144
Shall We Dance 170–1, 259
Shandling, Garry 250
Shannon, Del 192
Shatner, William 220
Sheilas' Wheels 177
Sheltering Sky, The 139–40, 216, 256
Shenton, Joan 51–2, *52*
Shooting Stars 172–4
Short, Bobby 147
Sidwell, Steve 108
Siffre, Labi 74–5
'Simple Minds' 111
Sinatra, Frank 3–4, 11, 13
Sinatra, Frank Jnr. 13
Sinclair, Jill 46, 78
Sloman, Tony 130, 134, 137
Smith, Derek 222
Smith, Jimmy 197–8
Smith, Putter 223
Snell, Richard 100
'Spiteri' 51–2, *52*
Springfield, Tom 78
Springfield, Dusty 78, 264
St. John, Bridget 24–5, 29, 209
Stanshall, Vivian 31, 38, 51

Starr, Ringo 31, 98, 226
Staunton, Imelda 269–70, *270*
Stevens, Mark Z. 224
Stewart, Ian 95, 127
Stewart, Patrick 220
Stewart, Rod 111–12
Sting 36, 60–1, *61*, 179, 208, *208*, 265
Stoller, Mike 240
Stone, Joss x, 129, 201, 205, *210*, 230, 265, 269
'Street Fighting Years' 111
Stritch, Billy 147
Styne, Jule 35, 80–1
Summers, Andy 245–7, *246*, *247*, 250, 253, 257
Swanson, Gloria 144

Taylor, Derek 38
'That Ole Devil Called Love' 94–6, 190
Theodore, Victoria 236, *236*
Thomas, Ian 108
Thomas, Terry *15*, 15–16
Thompson, Zalon 230
Thornton, Billy Bob 214–15
Tippett, Michael 178
Titanic 161–5
Torme, James 35, 225
Town and Country 265–6
Townshend, Pete 59–60, 111
Troup, Bobby 148
Turner, Tina 112–14

Ulyate, Lloyd 120

Vallee, Rudy 145, *146*
van Hooke, Peter 19, *20*, 40, 64, 66, 72, 82–3, 92, 107
Vandross, Luther 217–18
Vangelis 97
Vanian, Dave 125
Vas, Olaf 103
'Very Special Season, A' 118
Villiers, James 52–3
Viskant, Joan 107, 192, 220

'Walking in the Air' 106–7
Waller, Fats 6
Walsh, Bradley 269

Walters, Julie 180
Warleigh, Ray 36
Warren, Harry 151
Washington, Kamasi 210
Waterman, Peter 66
Waters, Muddy 18, 39, 41–2, *43*, 73
Watts, Charlie 42, 90, 95
Wayne, Jeff 78, 121
Welles, Orson 134, 149
White, Barry 54, 113
Wilburn, Vince, Jr. 199, 203, 251
Wilde, Marty 120, 193
'Wildest Dreams' 112–14
Williams, John 136–7
Williams, Ray 150, 250–1
Williams, Robin 56, 161
Wilson, John 231
Wilson, Reuben *251*, 252

Winehouse, Amy 1, 36, 201, 203, 229–32, *232*, 265
Wingfield, Pete 29, 40–2, 86, 88, 104, 192, 242
Wonder, Stevie 111, 236, *236*
Wood, Evan Rachel 98
'Wrecking Crew, The' 200
Wyman, Bill 95, 100, 204, 231
Wyper, Olav 164

Yankovsky, Oleg 139
Yates, Paula 183
Young, Terence 147–8

Zappa, Frank 32
Zavod, Allan 194, 263
Zimmer, Hans ix, 143, 174

www.ingramcontent.com/pod-product-compliance
Lightning Source LLC
Chambersburg PA
CBHW050340230426
43663CB00010B/1936